I hope this book gives you some new and exciting ideas.

RITES
⊙OF
PLEASURE

An exploration and celebration of sacred human sexuality, its diversity, and its connection to Pagan spirituality, myth, magic, community, and culture. Provocative, frank, and insightful, this wonderful book is a must-read for all Pagans, regardless of their gender, sexual preference, or lifestyle.
— Gerina Dunwich, author of *Wicca Spellbook, Gemstone Sorcery, Exploring Spellcraft*, among others

Imagine that you were given the power to move with a thought from campfire to campfire at a dozen pagan gatherings where the young ones and the old hands were sharing the deepest parts of their hearts. *Rites of Pleasure* gives you that power and perhaps the encouragement to explore the heart of your sexuality as a spiritual being.
— Ivo Dominguez, Jr., Wiccan Elder, Gay/Poly/Kinky person, and author of *Beneath the Skins: The New Spirit and Politics of the Kink Community* and *Castings: The Creation of Sacred Space*

Hunter has written an engaging, insightful book that will both inform and enlighten everyone, from the faithful monogamist heterosexual to the fetishist omnisexual and all shades of in-between. An honest look at the Pagan sexual climate and an entertaining read.
— Dianne Sylvan, author of *The Circle Within: Creating a Wiccan Spiritual Tradition*

A joyfully juicy romp through the various flavors of NeoPagan sexuality— from all-natural vanilla to double-chocolate chunk with cherries on top— and a large scoop of magic as well. Jennifer covers all the bases (and home plate too) with thoughtful interviews and insights on every aspect of those rites we find so pleasurable. Love it with someone you read.
— Venecia Rauls, author of *The Second Circle: Tools for the Advancing Pagan*

This is a fascinating book! Jennifer Hunter is one part historian, one part sex therapist, one part anthropologist, one part minx, and one part tour guide to the hidden ins and outs of NeoPagan sexuality. She mixes playfulness and common sense into a book I wish had been published twenty years ago.
— Isaac Bonewits, author of *Real Magic, Rites of Worship, and Witchcraft: A Concise Guide*

OTHER BOOKS BY JENNIFER HUNTER

21st Century Wicca
Wicca for Lovers

RITES
OF
PLEASURE

*Sexuality in Wicca
and NeoPaganism*

JENNIFER HUNTER

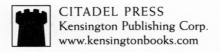

CITADEL PRESS
Kensington Publishing Corp.
www.kensingtonbooks.com

CITADEL PRESS BOOKS are published by

Kensington Publishing Corp.
850 Third Avenue
New York, NY 10022

All Kensington titles, imprints, and distributed lines are available at
special quantity discounts for bulk purchases for sales promotions,
premiums, fund-raising, educational, or institutional use. Special
book excerpts or customized printings can also be created to fit
specific needs. For details, write or phone the office of the Kensington
special sales manager: Kensington Publishing Corp., 850 Third
Avenue, New York, NY 10022, attn: Special Sales Department;
phone 1-800-221-2647.

First printing: October 2004

10   9   8   7   6   5   4   3   2   1

Printed in the United States of America

Library of Congress Control Number: 2004109741

ISBN 0-8065-2584-3

To all the people who are having their very first orgasms right now.

Contents ❧

Preface ❧

I'M AWARE THAT many may have picked up this book hoping for a glimpse into the lurid and unfettered orgiastic world that is Pagan sexuality.

> JACQUI OMI: *I think a lot of people come into Paganism . . . [because] they think it's free love, and everybody's gonna lay down and spread.*

True, NeoPaganism is much more accepting than most other religious paths of sexual diversity and expression. True, many NeoPagans are nonmonogamous, comfortable with nudity, and all that stuff. But our sexuality is more than just about getting off. It's about connecting with each other and the divine; it's about transformation, healing, magic, worship, play, and, of course, pleasure.

Rites of Pleasure provides an in-depth look at different practices of sacred sexuality in NeoPaganism (with some historical and mythological background). Unlike my first two books, this is not mainly a "how-to" text. I'll assume you either know how to, or can pick up another book that will tell you how to. *Rites of Pleasure* is a distillation of interesting information on Paganism and sexuality from many sources, spiced up with real-life thoughts, feelings, and stories from Witches, Wiccans, and NeoPagans. Although it may not give you step-by-step instructions, it will give you something more vital: creative and erotic inspiration. And, as

I think we lovers can all agree, although technique is always useful, passion is much more important.

NEOPAGANISM is a diverse religious movement that has seen tremendous growth in the past two decades. Because it is so decentralized, it is extremely hard to calculate how many Neo-Pagans there are, but latest estimates put the American number between 200,000 (very conservative) and 768,000 (optimistic).* In 1998, the *Chicago Tribune* reported that (with the standard disclaimers), NeoPaganism appeared to be the fastest growing religion in North America.† The same thing has since been asserted in the United Kingdom in 2001‡ and Australia in 2002.§

Although the term *NeoPaganism* encompasses a wide array of paths, certain generalizations apply to most NeoPagans:

1. We are either polytheistic, duotheistic (God and Goddess), or worship only a mother earth/moon Goddess—but regardless, we believe that deity exists within in the physical world (not necessarily limited to it, however). This leads to a strong connection with and reverence for nature, and a respect for all individuals as embodiments of the divine.

2. We practice magic, through ritual, spellcraft, and less formally, through movement of energy. Most of us believe that

---

*Shelley Rabinovich and James Lewis, *The Encyclopedia of Modern Witchcraft and Neo-Paganism*, 303.

†Jefferson 21st Century Institute <www.j21c.org/challeng.htm> accessed Dec. 25, 2003.

‡*Pentacle Magazine* (Jan. 2003) <www.pentaclemagazine.org> accessed Dec. 23, 2003.

§*UK Psychics* (July 2002) <www.ukpsychics.com/witchcraft_oz.html> accessed Dec. 25, 2003.

what you put out eventually returns to you; we take great pains to be ethical in our magic.

3. Through both magical and mundane means, we have a general inclination to try to create positive change in ourselves, our communities, and the world.

4. We travel between worlds, connecting with the divine, with spirits (human, animal, and nature), and practicing divination.

5. We believe that pleasure is a divinely bestowed gift that is perfectly okay to enjoy (within sane limits). We do not believe in sin or any code of behavior beyond the Wiccan rede: "An' it harm none, do as ye will."*

6. We tend to believe in reincarnation, or, at the very least, some kind of soul recycling. We see time as a circle, rather than a straight line. However, our emphasis is on the here and now.

7. We do not proselytize. Most people come to Paganism after reading a book or meeting a Pagan, saying, "This is what I believed all along; I didn't know it had a name." We do not believe that there is one right path, just what is right for each individual.

You may be opening this book with a lot of guilt and shame attached to your sexuality. Even if you're a self-described sacred harlot with a cadre of lovers, chances are you've got some hang-ups about your body and/or your sexual desires. Maybe you hate

---

*Rabinovich and Lewis, *The Encyclopedia of Modern Witchcraft and Neo-Paganism*, 289. This is taken from Doreen Valiente's poem "The Witches' Creed," which states, "Eight words this witches' rede fulfil, / 'An harm ye none, do what ye will." This, in turn, was inspired by Crowley's "Do As Thou Wilt Shall Be the Whole of the Law; Love Is the Law, Love Under Will."

your flabby arms. Maybe you worry about whether you'll be able to cum, or whether you'll cum too fast. Maybe you feel guilty about your desire to give or receive erotic pain. Virtually no one on earth is totally at home in his body or with his sexuality, and you won't be, even after you read this book, sorry. Just accept your issues, examine them, but don't get too hung up about them. Nothing good can come of guilt over guilt, or shame over shame. Accept yourself as imperfect.

When I tell people that my two main interests are sexuality and religion, they almost always laugh and say, "Wow, that's an odd combination!" Yet, why should it be?

> PHIL BRUCATO: *Sex has become such a commodity in our society that its sacred dimensions have been lost. To most folks, sex can be a sin, a joke, a gimmick, a titillation, an assault, a lure, a confrontation. But worship? Hardly!*

Sex and religion have more in common, and are more compatible, than one might think. They share a common element: the desire for union with the "other." The most common religious traditions in America today have divorced sex from spirit, at least in mainstream practice, but it need not be that way.

> DOSSIE EASTON: *The historical division between sex and spirituality is a fallacy, and, as far as I'm concerned, if your sex is not spiritual, you're missing something.*

Notes About Style

I prefer to spell "magic" without the k at the end. When I quote someone who uses the k, I change the text to conform to the rest of the book. The exception is when mentioning titles of texts. I also capitalize the words *God* and *Goddess*.

Unlike most books that refer to ancient Gods and Goddesses in the past tense, I have chosen to refer to them in the present tense. The exception is when I refer to specific events that have specifically taken place in the deities' past.

Not all Witches capitalize the initial *w*, but I prefer to.

When speaking in generalities, I use male and female pronouns interchangeably, to avoid both awkwardness and sexism. Although many of the people interviewed used "they" as a third-person singular pronoun, the publisher's style didn't allow for that, so it was changed to "he or she."

Some Netspeak is used in this book. If you see some strange "punctuation," or an acronym you don't recognize, just ignore it—and buy a computer at your earliest opportunity.

The People in This Book ❧

INTERVIEWS WERE either conducted by phone or through e-mail. In a couple of places, I have included quotes that have previously been printed in other books; I have referenced those with notes. Some of my interviewees are quite famous, and some are not. The interviewees wrote their own bios.

Anahita-Gula, in her mid-40s, of Canada, is a Gardnerian Witch and Elder living in Canada. She is an academic by trade, and a single middle-aged woman by the luck of the draw. She lives with cats and has numerous hobbies from calligraphy and dance to reading fiction and nonfiction. She has been a Witch since the early 1970s and identifies herself as culturally Jewish and religiously Wiccan.

Jezebel Dawn Blessing, 30, of San Francisco, says, "I get different responses when I tell people my name is Jezebel. Why would I choose to carry the name Jezebel, which comes with about 1,500 years of baggage, and make it my own? Jezebel is immortal, Jezebel is powerful, and Jezebel is who I truly am. I am a Priestess of Ishtar and a sex worker. I share as much of my knowledge and experience as I can to help as many people as I can reach in their search for a happy, healthy sexuality. I have hosted discussion groups, volunteered with local organizations, and read as many books as I can get my hands on to further my education, and I intend to keep doing this for the rest of my days. My hopes and intentions are to help human beings find the sacred within the sexual and to help them to bring the sexual into the sacred."

Phil Brucato, 39, of San Francisco, a professional author and artist since the 1980s, has followed an eclectic Pagan path for nearly two decades. Currently, Phil maintains a massage practice while working on various multimedia projects. Though polyamorous, Phil prefers heart-connections over casual sex. His award-winning books—including *Mage: The Ascension* and *Deliria: Faerie Tales for a New Millennium*—have been translated into half a dozen languages. His current projects include two novels and a self-help series based on his "Roleplay for Lovers" personal workshops. (www.roleplayforlovers.com)

Daniel del Vecchio, 52, of Ann Arbor, Michigan, was born at a very young age in Hackensack, New Jersey. He was two when his family chose to move to North Carolina, and he went with them. He was educated first by his brothers, then by his sisters and a series of public school experiences. He earned a B.A. (high honors) and a B.S. (very high honors) from the University of North Carolina. He married while still a student and stayed married for thirty years. He and his wife moved to Ann Arbor, Michigan, in 1974, where his two very wonderful kids were born. At the age of forty-six, he met Pagans and heard the word *polyamory*. He took up with them, eventually divorced, and later started polyamory networking groups in Detroit and Ann Arbor. At the moment, he is hard at work on a workshop titled "Conversations for Extraordinary Relationships from a Pagan Perspective."

Dossie Easton, a.k.a. "Scarlet Woman," 58, of San Francisco, is a therapist who has been a Pagan and an active sex radical since 1961. She is coauthor of *The Bottoming Book, The Topping Book, When Someone You Love Is Kinky,* and *The Ethical Slut,** all of which document, in one way or another, her spiritual ideals and practices. Poet, feminist, mother, survivor of the politically correct era, leatherdyke, whipmaker, and killer femme slut, she lives in rural West Marin, wandering about declaiming poetry to the vultures and hosting seriously outrageous pajama parties.

LaSara Firefox, 31, of northern California, is a renaissance woman who likes to keep herself busy with growth and the encouraging of growth. She designs and performs ritual theater, creates and facilitates workshops, and writes in just about every existing genre. Educator, radical, neofeminist, workshop presenter, mom, wife, lover, magician, exhibitionist, and writer, her life revolves around her family, her creativity, her sense of adventure, and her wild mood swings. She lives in the hills of noCal with her two smart and beautiful young daughters and her handsome, bright, and talented husband. For more information on LaSara, please visit www.lasara.us.

Rhomylly Forbes, 40, of Missouri, is bisexual, kinky, and has been a practicing Pagan for eighteen years. In her youth, she tried to sleep her way through the East Coast Pagan community, but has, in her old age, found happiness in monogamy. She is sure her old friends will be surprised by this change.

---

*Terms like *slut, witch, dyke,* and *fag* are all in various stages of being reclaimed from the hatemongers.

Francesca Gentille, 45, of the San Francisco Bay Area and Reno, Nevada, was raised in a conservative Midwestern family, lost her sense of authentic self, and became addicted to food and infatuation to relieve the pain. For the past twenty years she has explored theater, dance, health, communication, psychology, spirituality, addiction recovery, and sacred sexuality as an integrative path to wholeness, holiness, and wellness. She is in her third career as a life coach and workshop leader (her first two were television host/producer and health educator). In the past five years, she has received her second-degree Wiccan initiation, published two poetry books, and taught sacred sensual dance, conscious flirting, and "Sacred Sex 101" to hundreds of people across the country. She is the co-creator of two personal growth centers: the LifeDance Center (www.lifedancecenter.com) and the Nevada Center of Cultural and Martial Arts (www.nvcama.org). She is also the High Priestess for the Temple of Ishtar—Integrating Sexuality, Transformation, Health and Relationship (www. ishtartemple.org). She lives with her soulmate and codirector John Mariotti and her ten-year-old son, Dylan.

Judy Harrow, 58, of the metropolitan New York area, is the High Priestess of Proteus Coven, a twenty-plus-year-old group. She serves as chair of the Pastoral Counseling Department of Cherry Hill Seminary and is president-elect of the New Jersey Association for Spiritual, Ethical and Religious Values in Counseling. Judy has written two books, *Wicca Covens* and *Spiritual Mentoring*, and edited the anthology *Devoted to You*, in addition to writing many magazine articles. Judy invites you to visit her coven's Website at www.draknet.com/proteus.

Honeyblossom, 25, of Somerville, Massachusetts, is a member of the "altsex" community. She has been exploring sacred sexuality for nine years. She feels that it is a powerful tool for helping heal sexual wounds inflicted on survivors of nonconsensual sex and those who have been taught that sex is sinful. She hopes it could also play an important role in healing the spirit-body split in our culture in the future. She was recently handfasted to her primary partner of two years.

Raven Kaldera, 37, of Massachusetts, is a polyamorous, pansexual, perverted, FTM transgendered intersexual. He's also a farmer, homesteader, writer, pornographer, astrologer, shaman, activist, and king of a very small Pagan kingdom. He's the author of *Hermaphrodeities: The Transgender Spirituality Workbook*, coeditor of *Best Transgender Erotica*, and coauthor of *Urban Primitive and Hera's Blessing: Pagan Handfastings*.

Kitty, 22, of San Francisco, is a bisexual, polyamorous, perverted Pagan who was born and raised in the Bay Area. She earned her bachelor's degree from the Johnston Center at the University of Redlands, graduating with a self-made degree titled, "In Search of Her Spirit: Culture, Religion, and Women." She currently lives with a lover, a friend, and two of the best damned cats in the world. —=^..^=—

Don Kraig, 51, of Venice Beach, Califoria, began teaching occult subjects after many years of study. He has lectured all over the United States, and his books *Modern Magick, Modern Sex Magick*, and *Tarot and Magic* are highly respected. Donald has been initiated into and studied with many groups, including ones that are Hermetic, NeoPagan, and Tantric. He has worked as a musician, a sleight-of-hand magician, a courier for a bank, an instructor on computers at the University of Southern California, and in the quality assurance department of some major computer software firms. He received a bachelor's in philosophy from the University of California, Los Angeles, and is certified as a clinical hypnotherapist by the American Board of Hypnotherapy and the National Guild of Hypnotists. Don is currently working toward a doctorate in hypnotherapy through American Pacific University.

Leon, 32, was born in the Sierra foothills just north of Sacramento, California, where he lives to this day. Though soulfully artistic and skilled in many crafts, he has yet to attract an audience for his artistic endeavors. He "urns" his income selling coffee for a major retail outlet, while harboring dreams of homeownership, financial independence, and a coffee shop of his own. Leon claims the purpose of his life is "to create the space for my Tribe, whoever they turn out to be."

Magenta, "50+," of Minneapolis, has been involved with the NeoPagan and Craft communities since the 1970s. She is very eclectic and a cofounder of Prodea, which is a nonhierarchical coven that has been together since 1980. She has helped start a lot of groups and organizations in the Twin Cities, including her latest involvement, the New Alexandria Library and Resource Center, a center for the study and teaching of Pagan and magical paths (www.magusbooks.com/newalexandria).

Magdalene Meretrix, 36, of Idaho, was raised in a family that shared an intense interest in various expressions of spirituality and has continued to place great importance on mysticism, meditation, and magic. One vital component of her spiritual path has been her work of over a decade and a half as a professional sex worker. She has poured her spiritual focus and study of sexuality in modern and ancient traditions into her path of service. Magdalene is the author of the career manual for sex workers, *Turning*

Pro: A Guide to Sex Work for the Ambitious and the Intrigued, and many columns, articles, essays, and works of fiction dealing with sexuality, spirituality, and the blending of the two.

Jacqui Omi, 56, of Douglas, Arizona, was born in Roswell, New Mexico. She graduated from Florida Tech in 1989 with a master's in systems management. She has a bachelor's of divinity, is finishing up her master's of divinity, and has been accepted into the doctoral program. She was the second female Teamster in the United States, and the first in the city of Chicago. She was in the first group of women to pass the Illinois State Troopers Exam and is also a licensed flight instructor and ground instructor in flying planes.

Carol Queen, Ph.D., 46, of San Francisco, is a noted author of erotic fiction and memoir, sex information, and cultural commentary (see www.carolqueen.com for a bibliography of her work). She's also appeared in several sex education videos, most recently *G Marks the Spot*, for which she wrote the script. She is staff sexologist at Good Vibrations, the women-owned, worker-owned sex shop, and is also director of the new nonprofit Center for Sex and Culture (www.centerforsexandculture.com). She lives with her partner Robert, with whom she frequently teaches, and Teacup and Bracelet, the two cats who manage their schedule.

Shai Shahar, 49, of Amsterdam (originally Philadelphia and then Israel), is an entertainer, author, webmaster, and famous ex-gigolo. He is regarded as Europe's best-known professional ladies' man (the "Real American Gigolo"). He has been featured on TV and in publications far and wide, with interviews appearing in *Penthouse* (United States) and most recently in *HEEB Magazine* (New York), *The Jerusalem Post*, and *Yediot Ahranot*, not to mention the award-winning and highly controversial "white socks" photo (in *Esquire*, *The Face*, and *GQ* magazines) for the Accu.2 "Secs-Machine" chronometer. He is also the subject of Yaron Ben-Nun's acclaimed documentary *Hell's Angel*. He is the webmaster and coordinator of the Sex Academy (www.thesexacademy.com). Shai retired from the "paid life" in September 2000 and, after a two-year hiatus from all public appearances, came back in his new incarnation . . . as "The Brown Eyes," performing in cabaret venues and continental nightclubs.

Annie Sprinkle, Ph.D., 48, of San Francisco, is the prostitute/porn star turned performance artist/sex educator. She has passionately researched and explored sexuality in all of its glorious and inglorious forms for thirty years, then shared her findings through producing and starring in her own unique brand of feminist sex films, publishing her erotic photography, and teaching workshops and classes. In addition to her transmedia work promoting nonjudgmental approaches to sexuality, she has championed sex worker rights and health care. Her most recent book, *Hardcore from the Heart: The Pleasures, Profits and Politics of Sex in Performance*, won the Firecracker Book Award. She was the first porn star to get a doctorate. She presently lives in San Francisco with her domestic partner, Beth, and together they continually practice the arts of making love and sex magic. See www.anniesprinkle.org (as in orgasm) for lots more.

Dave Sylvia, 38, of the Boston, Massachusetts, suburbs, has an M.Ed. in counseling and is currently practicing in the suburbs of Boston. He lives in a big, beautiful, cooperatively run house with five adults and three kids. When not at work, he spends much of his time pursuing shamanic studies such as breathwork and meditation, and practicing/playing/performing various art forms like dancing, firespinning, drumming, winemaking, and sculpting.

Wyrdotter, 41, of Columbus, Ohio, has been a solitary, eclectic Kitchen Witch for about twelve years, and is a self-educated herbalist. She has been life-mated to Wyrdseal, female, 48, for sixteen years (so far!). She is a proud and doting mama to three dogs, four cats, one hamster, and two parakeets. She loves pugs in particular and is an active member of Ohio Pug Rescue. Her basic life philosophy is that we are all here to learn and teach, help, and to learn to accept help, and that no one has the wisdom to dictate another's path. "There are no free rides—everyone should contribute something to earn their keep on the planet."

Oberon Zell-Ravenheart, 60, of "NorCalifia," inspired by Robert A. Heinlein's polyamorous science-fiction novel *Stranger in a Strange Land,* founded the NeoPagan Church of All Worlds in 1962. Committed to a polyamorous lifestyle from that time forward, Oberon has never had a monogamous relationship. First to apply the terms *Pagan* and *Neo-Pagan* to the newly emerging nature religions of the 1960s, and through his publication of *Green Egg* magazine (1968–75; 1988–96), Oberon was instrumental in the coalescence of the NeoPagan movement and has been featured in numerous books on the subject. In 1970, he first formulated and published the thealogy of deep ecology, which has since become known scientifically as the Gaia hypothesis. He currently lives with his "senior wife," Morning Glory Zell-Ravenheart, and three other members of the Ravenheart family. His Web sites can be found at www.mythicimages.com and www.caw.org.

INTRODUCTION ❧

WHAT DOES IT MEAN when we say "sexuality is sacred" in a NeoPagan context? On one level, because we believe that all existence is infused with the divine, we believe that all things are sacred.

> MAGDALENE MERETRIX: *Sacred means consecrated, and my entire life is consecrated. I can't take a breath or have sex or skin my knee or eat an apple without it being a major incident in some way. In one sense, it seems redundant to label anything as sacred when my personal belief on the sacred is more in line with the Sufi notion that the entire earth is a sacred space and if anything appears nonsacred to us that is because we are viewing the world through the veil of our humanity rather than seeing the world as Allah sees it.*

On the other hand, there are plenty of aspects of existence that we don't want to celebrate or promote. One might say, "Sexuality is sacred because it involves the movement and/or exchange of energy." But so does a knock-down, drag-out fight. One reason sexuality is sacred, and needs to be acknowledged, celebrated, and enjoyed, is that it allows us to give and receive pleasure, something that is a gift from the Gods.

> JUDY HARROW: *In my belief, our Pagan path is the path of pleasure, which means that it's the path of gratitude. The essential practice of our spirituality is to appreciate all the good and beautiful things. Spirituality grows from basic theology, and our theological orientation is immanence. That means that we seek and find the sacred here and*

1

now, within the manifest world. From that perspective, sex is absolutely sacred; no more and no less sacred than a sunrise, or a glorious piece of music, or any other beautiful experience. The idea is to be open to the beauty that surrounds us at all times, to be grateful, and to let that process gradually and gently bring us closer to the sacred.

JACQUI OMI: *I frequently thank [the Mother] in the sex act, for being a part of it, for entering my partner, be my partner male or female, and allowing me to have this enormous amount of pleasure in her name.*

The experience of pleasure helps us to be grateful, not only for that good feeling, but also for all other aspects of our experience. It is a way to bring us closer to the divine. The Charge of the Goddess reads: "Let My worship be in the heart that rejoices, for behold, all acts of love and pleasure are My rituals."* It can also bring us closer to each other, functioning as a way for people to express love, desire, caring, and affection toward one another.

Sexuality is a manifestation of the creative life force. Even if conception is not intended or achieved through a sex act, our sexual drive exists biologically in large part for the purpose of creating a new person: something quite significant in a nature religion. Every person you see today is the result of an ejaculation: every person is here as a result of pleasure. Every person you see in your life grew within a woman's body and, barring surgical necessity, came into the world through the vagina, and the vulva, and just past the clitoris. And how significant is it, that in sex, when a hand or a tongue or a penis penetrates the vagina, the lover is entering into that same passageway that carries new life into the world! It don't get more sacred than that, folks.

---

*The "Charge of the Goddess" is one of the few common pieces of Wiccan liturgy. Its origin was in *Aradia: Or, the Gospel of the Witches* by Charles G. Leland (1899), a book about a family tradition of Witchcraft in Italy, the legitimacy of which remains unconfirmed. It was adapted into verse and then prose form by Doreen Valiente.

2

Of course, although sexuality naturally has sacred elements, the type of consciousness and intention surrounding it, in practice, makes a big difference in terms of its effect.

FRANCESCA GENTILLE: *I found, as a teacher, that there are two schools of sacred sexuality. One viewpoint is "All sex is inherently sacred, whether it was good sex, whether it was bad sex, whether you don't have it for a while—it's just all sacred. It just is." And then there's a school of sacred sexuality that says that sex is sacred when we bring . . . our intention . . . to it; that, like any magic, it's an issue of bringing in our will and our consciousness. This room that I'm standing in is just a room, until I . . . cast my circle. Then, this is no longer just a room; it is a sacred space. . . . So I belong to the school of sacred sexuality that says it's our intention, it's our consciousness, our declaration, that actually makes it sacred. I sometimes say sex is like Jell-O . . . where it will sort of take on the flavor of anything you put in it. If your intention is to hurt someone, it'll be hurtful. If your intention is union, it can have union. If your intention is transcendence, or invoking the deities, it can be that.*

Several years ago, I went to see the movie *Starship Troopers.* Behind me sat two parents and their young son. The movie was incredibly violent, and I was horrified that people would bring a child to a movie like this. Then there was a very tender sex scene, in which an actress appeared topless. The parents instructed their son to cover his eyes until the scene was over. My boyfriend and I were utterly stunned and furious. How is the human body so evil that it is even worse to view than bloody carnage?

Sexuality is, in our culture, often synonymous with "dirty." Where did this come from? It goes back to the Zoroastrians (starting in 1500 to 1000 BCE), who first imagined the duality of good versus evil, which got picked up by the ancient Greeks, who took it further to imply that the physical was somehow lesser than the spiritual. Of course, it was Christianity that most effectively promoted that belief system.

SHAI SHAHAR: *I think the Catholic Church is a great example of what happens when you try to square a circle by doing something like suppressing sex and making it sinful. Is it any wonder that it is falling under the weight of the sex scandals heaped upon it, . . . having its own internal perversions being brought to light?*

But as we all know, thinking sex is nasty doesn't stop us from wanting it.

LASARA FIREFOX: *John Whiteside Parsons, in* Freedom Is a Two-Edged Sword, *observed that sex is both pedestal-ized and denigrated at the same time in our culture. I think that's totally accurate.*[1]

WYRDOTTER: *Our society is so saturated with the idea that sex is nasty, disgusting, evil, and immoral, and something you should only share with the person you love the most (I just love that little irony. If it's that evil, why inflict it on a loved one? If it's good enough for the person you love the most, how can it be evil everywhere else?), that it makes it difficult to get anyone to even think along the lines of sex as spiritual or sacred.*

My mother, in her vegetarian phase, told me that eating meat was to be avoided because it has a "lower vibratory level." My response as a Pagan was, "What's wrong with that?" Her position was that higher was intrinsically superior to lower, and that one's goal should be to move energy up from your lower chakras* into the higher ones. This is supposed to help you move toward enlightenment. But the Pagan viewpoint emphasizes balance between earth and sky. In an earth-centered religion, dirt is holy. If being lusty means having a dirty mind, then hallelujah! The Goddess is one dirty mama. Incidentally, my mother went back to eating meat, realizing that she actually felt more grounded that way.

---

*Chakras are energy centers in the body, according to the Tantric tradition.

DOSSIE EASTON: *[My friend said], "Look, I know my fantasies have dirty roots." That stopped me in my tracks, and I realized, "How else can you grow flowers?"*[2]

Modern Western culture has severed the body from the sense of self. People view spirit (if religious) or mind (if not) as separate from, and superior to, the body. The body has urges we can't control; it develops diseases; it has power over the way we perceive ourselves and others perceive us. We objectify the body, trying to mold it, shape it, and subdue it, as if the body were separate from the true self, some *thing* to schlep around from place to place. We hold in our stomachs and butts, trying to shape ourselves into a more acceptable form. This is not only uncomfortable, but can actually cause health problems like irritable bowel syndrome and compressed nerves. Chronic stress also inhibits breathing. Human lungs can hold seven pints of air, but we usually only take in one pint at a time.[3] Often, we are not even aware of our bodies until something goes wrong, and then it's an annoyance, something to have repaired. Seeing a doctor becomes like taking your car to a mechanic.

This separation of body from spirit/mind is both born from and perpetuates a fear of the body and the desire for control over it. Sexuality is a powerful force, which can be frightening and threatening, in ourselves and in other people.

PHIL BRUCATO: *For its own survival, a society craves an illusion of control. And given the horrific possibilities of rape, molestation, AIDS, unwanted pregnancies, and other violations, that craving is perfectly legitimate. Problem is, fear of all those things and more stifles the sexual soul—or leads it down careless paths where disaster is more likely to strike. Fear of sex locks away life's very essence; giving in to that fear destroys life's integrity.*

This fear of the loss of control is, in my opinion, the basis of the conservative right's "slippery slope" argument: that first you accept homosexuality, and then ultimately you're going to have people fucking animals and children. Christianity, the religion of the conservative right, teaches that humans are tainted with original sin and that we will naturally do evil things, unless kept in line by rules and the threat of eternal punishment. The philosophy of NeoPaganism is that people are basically good and ethical, and, when given free rein and *respect*, will generally choose to do things that are beneficial to their fellow humans and themselves (junk food and cigarettes notwithstanding).

CAROL QUEEN: *A lot of people need to stay really fucking shut down, not to fully experience their bodies, and not to fully be who they are sexually, and not to step away from a rather restrictive and punitive notion of spirituality.* [Jen: It's the fear of a loss of control, and the lack of trust in yourself—] *Or the lack of trust in your flock. This comes down from on high, pretty much. I agree, I think there are a certain kind of people who really want others to tell them what to do, and need to have that kind of structure, but which came first: the desire for structure, or the structure? I'm not really sure. But the grain of truth to the "slippery slope" argument is that if you step outside a cage, you find you're outside the cage.*

What they absolutely refuse to acknowledge, that is a really important thing along with this, is that everybody who has learned to respect themselves and realize that they do have the power to step off the narrow path, also retains the knowledge that they can have boundaries . . . that boundaries are good for them on all kinds of levels, boundaries are good for this society and the groups that we form with one another. The difference is that we get to . . . decide in our own hearts what they're going to be.

The people who slide down a slippery slope in the way that the right wing says is going to happen are sociopaths. . . . They're the people who almost certainly would have slipped anyway. . . . It's not the same thing to decide, "The restrictive mores that I've grown up with are not ones that are meaningful to me now that I'm a young adult or an adult; I'm going to find my new tribe; I'm going to find my new ways, and the people who should be with me, and my family, and all of that." . . . Everybody who comes to Paganism, or comes out as queer, has some version of that story to tell, and almost none of those people are running around causing mayhem. Those people are just like everybody else; they just made some different choices, and that's a secret that the right wing doesn't want to get out.

One of the central ideas in NeoPaganism is "Thou art God," an affirmation taken from Robert A. Heinlein's book *Stranger in a Strange Land* and made popular by the Zell-Ravenhearts' Church of All Worlds. If we envision each other and ourselves as divine, it's going to affect the way we practice our sexuality. It seems to me much more likely that the spirit-body split is itself to blame for many of the destructive manifestations of human sexuality. Margo Anand writes in *The Art of Sexual Ecstasy: The Path of Sacred Sexuality for Western Lovers*, "Deprived of its sacred dimension, sexual energy is repressed and eventually directed against life itself. This, in turn, results in disrespect, disease, abuse, rape, and other forms of sexual violence."[4]

> KITTY: *If another human being is not seen as divine in his own right, it is much easier to treat him as if he were an object and disregard his boundaries and desires.*

Georg Feuerstein, in *Sacred Sexuality: Living the Vision of the Erotic Spirit*, makes the point that when we objectify the body and separate our consciousness from it, magically and spiritually speaking, we're actually *losing* control over it.[5] For example, if you are unhappy with something your spouse is doing, you might be tempted to withdraw emotionally, but that will not solve the problem and may actually make it worse. You would instead need to accept your spouse as he is and work to get closer to him and improve your relationship and communication before hoping to have any effect. Likewise, if you want to change something about your body—improve its health, change its shape, or enhance its capacity for sexual pleasure—it's critical to bring your consciousness more deeply into your body first, to accept it as it is right now and to *own* it, before you attempt to change it.

Historically, it has specifically been women's sexuality that has been the most strictly controlled. According to Dossie Easton and Catherine A. Liszt in *The Ethical Slut: A Guide to Infinite Sexual Possibilities*, "In this worldview, men are hopelessly sexually voracious and predatory, and women are supposed to control and civilize them by being pure, asexual and withholding. The openly sexual woman destroys civilization."[6] The diagnosis of "nymphomania," common in the Victorian era, is an example of how female desire was pathologized. Clitoridectomy, also known as "female circumcision" but more accurately as "female genital mutilation," is currently practiced in some Third World countries and was done in the name of medical science to young American girls as recently as the nineteenth century, as a cure for masturbation. But both women *and* men have been damaged by our culture's sexual hangups.

Getting Body-Positive

In a religion where we are all clergy and the entire universe is part of the body of the Goddess, the human body can serve as a place of worship. After all, the Charge of the Goddess encourages us to enjoy our bodies: "Sing, feast, dance, make music and love, all in My Presence, for Mine is the ecstasy of the spirit and Mine also is joy on earth." But of course, many of us—even those who are considered conventionally attractive—have big issues with our bodies.

FRANCESCA GENTILLE: *I had my parents tell me when I was fifteen or sixteen, "If you lost weight, we'd get you liposuction." And I don't have an overweight, icky body. . . . But my culture was reflecting back to me that unless I was airbrushed and perfect, there was something wrong with my body.*

The time to enjoy your body is *now*—not when you lose weight, firm up, or have a partner who gives you ego strokes. No matter what we do, the vast majority of us will never look like supermodels. And as we know, *even the supermodels* don't look like supermodels, as their images have been altered with makeup, photographic techniques, and computers.

PHIL BRUCATO: *In today's marketplace, physically impossible icons set standards that cannot be attained by human beings—but which seem possible if you buy this pill, purchase this magazine, attend this gym, follow this diet, do this workout, drink this beer, and so on. I was a model myself, and thanks to that experience I can see the wires holding that curtain aloft. Many people, however, calibrate their self-image machines to match this eternal stream of Photoshopped falsity, not really recognizing that it's all an illusion to make people buy shit. And that, to someone who values sex as communion, is a real problem.*

Riane Eisler, in her book *Sacred Pleasure: Sex, Myth, and the Politics of the Body—New Paths to Power and Love*, points out that the fairy tale of "Cinderella" conveys the message that "for a girl to be saved from a life of misery, her body must fit certain specifications." Left out of the Disney version is the part where the evil stepsisters cut off parts of their feet in an attempt to fit into the glass slipper.[7] Foot binding and genital mutilation are extreme examples of this kind of body-hatred in the real world. Less horrific, but still damaging, is the culture, pretty much universal at this point, which glorifies dieting, uncomfortable clothing and shoes, and stick-thin models. This trend leads to eating disorders and a general feeling among most women that their bodies aren't good enough. Even more distressing is that all this is geared toward one end: being attractive to men (or, to be more precise, to measure up to the advertisers' ideas about what men want).

FRANCESCA GENTILLE: *The reason I chose Paganism initially was to be able to claim my body, and my sexuality . . . and to be able to claim myself as divine. Before, I . . . was so ashamed of my body that I needed to get dressed and undressed in the dark. . . . It was shameful to me; it was ugly to me. I have a Marilyn Monroe kind of figure. I'm five-four and around 140, which is the U.S. average. And it's a perfectly fine figure, but I always felt that I was ugly, and there was something wrong with my curves; there was something wrong with my fleshiness. In* Some Like It Hot, *there's a point where Marilyn Monroe is running to the train, and Tony Curtis and Jack Lemmon are looking at her running, and they're going, "Wow. That's like Jell-O on springs." And they're so thrilled that every part of her is shaking. It's this soft, shaky body. And I saw that at one point, and I was thrilled and shocked, because we live in the time of the "hardbody." I think that I needed a way to reclaim the feminine principle, in all of its different manifestations, as beautiful.*

This prejudice is so pervasive that it even extends into the Pagan community. When I was in a coven that practiced skyclad, I recall that a generously sized woman in our group would not tell me her weight. I could see every inch of her buck-naked form in living color, yet she was still ashamed about the number of pounds she weighed. The covers of popular books on Neo-Paganism rarely show nonskinny models. The cover of Don Kraig's *Modern Sex Magick*, a book that is extremely sex- and body-positive—and that, incidentally, was authored by a nonskinny man—features a couple straight off the cover of a romance novel, both slim, with the woman sporting massive cleavage and long red fingernails.*

Many overweight people feel comfortable in the Pagan community, because there is a much more accepting mind-set about bodies and their shapes.

> ANAHITA-GULA: *I started out as a fat kid hating my body. As I have become more Pagan and more open to the different faces of the Goddess, I have also become more supportive of Fat Acceptance movements, and now love to see myself in lingerie.*

But unfortunately, many folks are so relieved to finally be accepted for who they are, that they stop there, never increasing body awareness or making healthy changes. We tend to oversimplify, thinking that if we make an effort to hone our diets and get some moderate exercise, that we have bought into the impossible media standards for appearance. My roommate in college, a feminist fat activist, criticized me when I took up jogging, certain that I had buckled under to the patriarchy.

> JACQUI OMI: *The large earth mother, with full-flowing breasts and enormous hips, represents fertility. She doesn't represent being a glutton, allowing your body to be in a state that's not healthy. There aren't enough Pagans anyway, so please, let's take care of ourselves. Do a little walking. Put the fork down a little more frequently. We need to breathe more. We don't exercise; we drive around in cars all the time. It's just not healthy, and it's not real good for your sexuality, either, because you don't have the stamina. When it says, "Do as thou wilt, an' it harm none," whether you accept that as the whole of the law or*

---

*Lest you accuse me of hypocrisy, I should make it clear that I did not choose the cover of *this* book!

not is irrelevant. The point is . . . something of the form of the golden rule has to apply to your own body. And if you have high blood pressure, high cholesterol, bad knees, bad back—I don't think I've ever met a Pagan who didn't tell me he or she had a bad back—then perhaps it would be prudent for the whole religion and yourself to exercise a little, eat a little more regular, natural food, as it comes from the ground, respect the earth by growing something that you can put in your mouth that's good for you . . . have more sex! Sex takes off 100 calories; let's go!

Of course, curvy chicks can be sexy. I'm a size sixteen, and I do fine. Even morbidly obese chicks can be sexy, but carrying 100 extra pounds is just plain bad for you. When we practice sacred sexuality, we are using our bodies as magical tools. They need to be in decent working order, and we need to stick around long enough to get as much pleasure out of them as we can.

Another critical aspect of becoming body-positive is getting comfortable with our genitals. No, more than that—falling in *love* with our genitals. The only way women can get a really good look at their genitals is with the help of a mirror. This may seem absurd if you have never done it, but think of this: You have a body part that, after twenty, thirty, forty years, you have never actually *seen*. *That's* what's absurd. Men would do well to employ a mirror, too, since it affords them a good 360-degree view of their penis, balls, and anus. How can you expect to use these parts, to really enjoy them, if you don't even know what they look like? Look when you're aroused and when you're not. Practice enjoying them for the pure aesthetic. Imagine you're someone masturbating to a picture of them in a porn magazine. See them as a wonderfully functional work of art that the Gods made just for you.

Mind-Body Connection and Pleasure

The sacred, in Paganism, is not up, but *in*, deeper than the level of everyday consciousness. Deeper awareness of the physical plane can lead to greater spiritual awareness, allowing us to transcend the personal, the limited, the ordinary. Feuerstein says, "To transcend does not mean to evaporate; rather, our body image is widened to include all other bodies. We become the magnificent body of the universe itself, the total field of existence."[8] Transcendence means dissolving the illusionary boundaries between things.

> MAGDALENE MERETRIX: *My . . . boundaries between what is me and what is not-me become very permeable in states of orgasm, intense sensation, rhythm, etc., and my awareness expands to a point where I no longer feel contained within my body, but part of everything. Everything physical is all just molecules, and when my consciousness is tuned to a particular frequency, my perception of those molecules is changed from a solid, discrete universe to a fluid, osmotic universe where molecules vibrate in sympathy with an overarching symphony, perhaps the Music of the Spheres itself.*

> LEON: *I try to be in the now, to open myself up to and be aware of the energy flow. It really enhances the physical sensations a lot.*

> HONEYBLOSSOM: *Spirituality has taught me ways of connecting with what I'm feeling, getting in touch with myself, and then reaching out to another person. I've learned through my years of meditation how to be truly* present. *These things make sex much more meaningful and intimate.*

The goal in becoming body-conscious is not to achieve some kind of constant state of ecstasy. Besides being exhausting, that would get tedious. No, it's natural for your body to hurt, get tired, get tense, feel sick sometimes. The trick is to stay aware and accept whatever is going on in your body. Can you feel your body right now? How are you breathing: in your chest or in your belly? Fast or slow? Cyclical or raggedly? Does anything hurt? Are there any parts of your body that you can't feel at all? Are you holding any muscles in tension? Are you slouching or otherwise curled up? Stretch and breathe, and notice the difference.

Our society is extremely ambivalent when it comes to pleasure. On one hand, we have the constant stimulation, entertainment and materialism of modern culture, which is designed to provide pleasure, albeit at a very shallow level. On the other hand, we are urged to diet, follow exercise regimes, work long hours, and eat food that's chosen for health over taste. And pleasure is definitely not perceived as a road to self-improvement or spirituality. Who would imagine that the road to spiritual enlightenment is paved with great sex, long naps, and delicious food? But why *can't* it be? How is denial any more holy than pleasure? Although masturbation is no longer considered "self-abuse" by the medical and mental health communities, and people (okay, *women*) are gradually getting over their hang-ups about it, you get many more brownie points for going to the gym than spending an evening with your vibrator.

Since we are so cut off from our bodies, we rarely feel full pleasure. Anand writes, "Making love through your thoughts is a bit like trying to do differential calculus with your genitals."[9] And given that most of us pass our days in a state of relative numbness with regard to our bodies, it's not surprising that we find our sex lives less than satisfying. We ignore our bodies all day long, using and abusing them, and then expect them to "perform" on command and make us feel good. If they fail, we are humiliated, crushed, frustrated, or even angry. If you treated a person that way, you would be not just a slaveowner, but a cruel one.

14

When pleasure is a foreign sensation, at best, we go through the motions and if we're lucky, we "get off" in a brief orgasm and then we're done. Easton and Liszt point out, "When sex becomes goal-oriented, we may focus on what gets us to orgasm to the exclusion of enjoying all of the nifty sensations that come before (and, for that matter, after). When we concentrate our attention on genital sex to the exclusion of the rest of our bodies, we are excluding most of ourselves from the transaction."[10] The entire body is capable of feeling pleasure, not just the genitals. This seems obvious, but are we really conscious of this fact while having sex, or in our everyday lives? First of all, if the only time we give ourselves pleasure, or allow someone else to give us pleasure, is during sexual activities, that means we are not feeling pleasure for the vast majority of our lives, and second, when we do have sex, it becomes that much harder to accept such an unfamiliar sensation. On the other hand, if our bodies are used to receiving pleasure, and we are aware of what we enjoy (something that can only be achieved through practice), then we will be that much more open to sexual pleasure.

FRANCESCA GENTILLE: *It's my perception that most people in the world—I'm not saying Pagans—but most people in the world . . . have sex to get off. They fuck, whether they're fucking each other or fucking themselves . . . they're doing what they're doing to their own body or someone else's to get off. And . . . then there's moving into pleasure. So if I'm actually concerned with this state of pleasure, now I'm going to take longer with my own body. I'm not going to just be masturbating; I'm going to be self-pleasuring. Or if I come to you, I'm going to be looking at, "How can we engage in maybe more extended pleasure with one another?" Maybe we'll get out the oil. There's going to be more body involved than just genitals. It's a little less goal-oriented, because there's more involved in pleasure than just in orgasm or ejaculation. My sense*

15

is that a lot of what's taught in this country around sacred sexuality or Tantra is in the realm of pleasure: How can we expand a genitally focused sexual encounter into a more body-oriented, pleasure-oriented encounter?

Then, if we keep moving further along that spectrum, we can achieve loving. Making love, or self-loving. If I'm truly distinguishing making love, creating love, generating love, with myself or with a partner, not only do I have the oils out, but I definitely have lit candles, there's music going on, and there's affirmation. Now, if that affirmation is from myself to myself, I am now taking the oil from the bottom of my feet to the top of my head, I am stroking and caressing my body, feeling the curves of my skin, and I am saying, "I love you. I love you, Francesca. You are beautiful, Francesca. You are precious. You are the Goddess. You are the Goddess giving life. You are the creative force." If I'm with my partner, I am—and this is whether it's out loud or just in my mind—I am thinking, "This person is the divine force; he is precious. His life is precious. His spirit is like a jewel. He is sacred." And when I'm really at that place of just "precious, precious, precious"—you know how we sometimes look at our children that way—when I'm in that place, my eyes will water, and I will just feel deeply, deeply moved, either by my own life, or that of my beloved. And to me, that's truly making love.

SHAI SHAHAR: *If you never get beyond seeing your partner as a body you use to masturbate with, no number of partners will ever be enough.*

Before you can learn how to give pleasure to another person, you need to be really good at giving it to yourself. That may mean eating food you love, taking a nap when you need it, dancing in your living room, and wearing clothes that fit well and feel nice. Many activities that feel good physically—massage, dance, wearing comfortable clothes, long hot baths, and swimming nude—also help to open us up emotionally and spiritually. Most of us are taught that pleasure is something we should give to other people and that people should give to us. Women feel that they need to learn how to have "vaginal orgasms" through intercourse alone; men feel guilty for jerking off, and/or angry with their partner for making them "need" to. But the magic and grandeur of sexuality is not something that can only be attained through a partnership. It may take the alchemy of God and Goddess to create the universe, but each of us carries that essential combination within ourselves.

As part of the messages we get from our culture, many of us have internalized the idea that we do not deserve to feel good, or that we have to justify it as a reward for something or as a means to get something else. Easton and Liszt astutely point out, "Even people who consider themselves sex-positive and sexually liberated often fall into . . . the trap of rationalizing sex. Releasing physical tension, relieving menstrual problems, maintaining mental health, preventing prostate problems, making babies, cementing relationships and so on are all admirable goals, and wonderful side benefits of sex. But they are not what sex is *for*. Sex is for pleasure, a complete and worthwhile goal in and of itself."[11]

Sexuality in NeoPaganism

Having said all that, now I'll make the point you were waiting for: The experience of healthy sexuality can provide the engine for powerful magic, it can transform you, and it can bring you closer to the divine.

> ANNIE SPRINKLE: *Sexuality is not only something that can be used for the enhancement of an intimate relationship, for physical pleasure or procreation. It can also be used for personal transformation, physical*

and emotional healing, self-realization, spiritual growth, and as a way to learn about all of life . . . and death.

To Pagans, the very fact that sex feels good is proof positive that the Gods want us to have sex. Pleasure is a divine gift. Why waste it?

OBERON ZELL-RAVENHEART: *As far as I'm concerned, all sexual encounters are holy communion with the Goddess through her avatars.*

Some may argue that the Pagan inclination toward sexual exploration—with multiple partners, new activities, and pushing boundaries with BDSM—indicates the pursuit of newness for its own sake, as a rush, or as a way to be intentionally "weird." It may also be argued that people who are drawn to Paganism are the very sort who tend to be unconventional anyway and who like to expand their horizons. Or one might just refuse to judge or analyze and just appreciate the fact that NeoPagans tend to be such sexually exuberant people.

HONEYBLOSSOM: *An unshakable belief that sex was holy, not sinful, propelled me from Christianity out into the wide unknown. That journey eventually led to Paganism.*

Many folks I interviewed credited their adoption of the Pagan path as something that allowed them to more fully accept themselves as sexual beings.

SHAI SHAHAR: *My ex-wife told me that when, immediately after I came on her face for the first time, I kissed her and told her I loved her, she felt clean about it for the first time.*

DAVE SYLVIA: *My knowledge of Goddess-based spirituality has helped me to free myself from the shame and guilt that our society teaches us to attach to sexual pleasure, allowing me to view it as the sacred gift it is.*

LEON: *It's amazing how much better life becomes once you get it through your head that desire for sex is healthy and natural. . . . I was raised to believe that sex was dirty and vile. . . . During most of my early teens I felt very depressed because I just knew I was somehow evil for having so many sexual thoughts and desires. I seriously thought I might be sent to Hell for excessive masturbation and wanton desire. I'm feeling much better now. Paganism provided a context where those desires were not only natural, but perhaps even sacred. Now some of my friends are trying to convince me that some women actually like sex. My wife can be very persuasive at times.*

LASARA FIREFOX: *My sexuality is a powerful force that I have at times felt out of control of. I love intensely, feel more than many are willing to, and sometimes that's been a hard "cross to bear." My spirituality has given my sexual expression a very positive place to call home, a place to ground and nourish.*

In our culture, sex is most often seen either as a wholesome expression of love and commitment between two people, or a filthy disgusting romp in the sack, devoid of meaning. To open oneself up to the expression of sacred sexuality, it's important to look beyond this dichotomy. Sexuality is, by its nature, extremely fluid and complex, not just between different people, but also within each individual's personal experience and in her preferences from moment to moment. In *Leatherfolk*, Carol Truscott writes, "[Sex] can be a way of affirming good feelings—of making love—between two [or more] people, a spiritual experience, a tension reliever, and it can be just fun. It doesn't *always* have to be any one of the above, and it can probably also be 'other.'"[12] Sexuality can also be a tool in and of itself, as a way to grow and change as a person.

SHAI SHAHAR: *Only after I had experienced all I felt I needed and wanted to experience, sexually, was I in any way fit to be a lover,*

*husband, and father in the real sense. . . . to be a "family man." That is
my truth.*

The simple fact is, as Easton and Liszt state, "Sex is nice and
pleasure is good for you." The Gods designed our bodies with
the capacity for ecstatic pleasure; all the trappings and baggage
were invented by humankind. Eisler points out that it is precisely
the separation of the clitoris from the vaginal opening that proves
women are designed not just for reproduction but also for pleasure in and of itself.[13] I think we should also include the prostate
in men, which is accessible only through the anus!

Sexuality in NeoPaganism is about both "mirth and reverence,"
to borrow from the Charge of the Goddess. Lovemaking,
whether in a formal ritual context or not, almost always has a
flavor of worship to most Pagans. It's holy work. It's divinely
inspired. On the other hand, it's meant to be fun. If the Gods
created reverence, they also created mirth, and anyone who's had
sex more than once or twice knows that there are no lack of silly
moments. To the mainstream, laughter and worship are just as
opposed as sex and worship. To NeoPagans, it's not necessary to
be solemn to be respectful.

Caveats

You didn't think I'd write a book about sex without including
some cautions, did you?

Just because we identify sexuality as "sacred" does not give
sanction to every possible expression of sexuality. And just
because we don't feel ourselves constrained by the rules of mainstream society does not mean that there need be no rules at all. It
just means that we need to redefine our own boundaries based
on what makes us comfortable and uncomfortable, and not what

"other people" might think or say. Nonconsensual sexual acts, which include any kind of attack or manipulation, as well as any act in which one party, such as a prepubescent child or someone overwhelmed by a mind-altering substance, is not able or ready to consent, are a negative and destructive expression of a God/dess-given gift. It is the individual's responsibility to act in whatever way he or she believes is the most ethical, striving always to treat others as they would wish to be treated.

Some taboos are healthy; these tend to be intuitive and natural. Take the taboo against incest, for instance. People are not generally attracted to their family members; they don't need to be taught that they are off-limits. On the other hand, taboos against masturbation must be taught and enforced—it is natural to masturbate and unnatural to suppress it. Anand makes a great point when she says, "I believe that the sexual urge as we experience it individually is not nearly as 'natural' as it seems. It is continuously being influenced by cultural conditioning."[14] No matter how much we may identify ourselves as countercultural, we are still going to be influenced by advertising, TV shows, movies, and the "mainstream" people with whom we interact. As people who consciously practice a "nature" religion, it is our responsibility to listen to a deeper voice inside.

It's tempting to get carried away with one's sexuality after discovering a religion and subculture where sex and physical pleasure are not just okay, but encouraged. Although NeoPaganism is a sex-positive religion, with lusty Gods, and lusty holidays, and an aura of acceptance of all forms of consensual pleasure, that is not its sum total. Gods can also be barren, solemn, ancient, childlike, and in other ways not too frisky. Sure, we frolic at our springtime holidays, but there are just as many holidays in the winter. Sexuality is only one aspect of life. So are work, learning, parenting, play, exercise, creating, and so on.

ANAHITA-GULA: *I think some folks take the "All acts of love are in my honor" statement as their focus for their entire Pagan identity and miss a great deal of the richness of other things Pagan by this.*

MAGDALENE MERETRIX: *I think that sometimes people—both NeoPagan and other—can get caught up in the sexuality of some forms of NeoPaganism, or the sexual openness that often permeates NeoPagan communities, and begin to conflate the path and the act, forgetting that there's more to NeoPaganism than copious "free love." Despite this occasional pitfall, I'd be very sad to see a fear of this conflation lead to any sort of suppression of the vibrant sexuality so often found in NeoPagans and NeoPagan paths.*

RHOMYLLY FORBES: *Most NeoPagans confuse sexuality with fornication. They then tend to use the fact that Paganism has relatively few sexual taboos as an excuse to make sexual activity their entire spiritual practice. This is not balanced, and so often, someone is hurt . . . I think we as a community need to put less emphasis on sex, and more on a wholly balanced person/practice.*

It is in no way mandatory to have sex (or any particular type of sex, or type of relationship) to be Pagan. If you are a virgin, you should have sex when and if you feel personally ready. Being a virgin does not make you any more or less sacred to the Gods, or any less a sexual being. If you are not involved with anyone, do not get involved with a particular partner solely to achieve a spiritual or magical end or because you feel incomplete. No one needs a partner in order to be complete. Boundaries are critical. Be able to say no, even if it's really "I'm not sure." Just because you *can* doesn't mean you *should*.

It is normal for people's libidos to wax and wane, like the moon, depending on stress level, amount of physical energy, hormones, health, emotional connection with others, self-image, a sense of spiritual connectedness, and so on. There's a great quote by Jack Lee Rosenberg in *The Art of Sexual Ecstasy*: "Many men and women mistakenly believe that if they experience their sexual energy, they must do something about it—they must perform, act it out, discharge it. Since having sexual energy is simply a function of being alive, all they need to do with it is experience it."[15]

> DAVE SYLVIA: *There's a difference between a healthy libido and sexual addiction. One good indicator of that is how the nonsexual areas of your life are going (professional, home, heart-connections with friends).*

> RHOMYLLY FORBES: *One of the ways I attune to the seasons is how high (or low) my libido is. Mid-April through early May is torture <grin>, and in late November and December my sex drive is really, really low.*

I would also like to note that it is by no means necessary for us Pagans to try and make every sexual encounter something meaningful and magical, with candles, ritual, and mood music. Quickies have their own unique power.

> KITTY: *As for just straight up "getting it on," well, even a Goddess simply needs a good fuck sometimes.*

Some people use alcohol, herbs, marijuana, psychedelics, and other substances to alter their consciousness as part of their sexual practice, believing that it enhances the experience. Far be it from me to deny anyone a few sips of wine, but don't numb yourself out—you'll only be reducing your capacity for pleasure. More important, there is a delicate balance in sex between keeping control and losing it; more so when altered states and magical techniques are brought in. Please play safe and use common sense.

> HONEYBLOSSOM: *It's a challenge to practice sacred sex in a culture that is so sex-negative. It is very difficult even to find people who are*

comfortable with and learned in sexuality in general. There's an old quote from Pat Califia that I'm very fond of: "How ironic it is that promiscuous women are called 'easy,' given the struggle that is necessary to make pleasure holy in a world that thinks it is a dirty joke." I think that exemplifies the difficulty.

We have our work cut out for us.

1. A Very Brief History of Pagan Sexuality 🐚

Wait! Don't let your eyes glaze over! I hated history class, too. But it's particularly important for us as NeoPagans to take a look at the history of Pagan sexuality, since it can determine what elements we want to keep and what we want to ditch.

Yes, there are bits worth ditching. Pagans are inclined to romanticize the past, especially with regard to free love. It's nice to think of it all as one long frolic under the maypole, but that's not the way it was—at least not all of it. Although we might like to blame Christianity for the ideas of body and nature being inferior to mind and spirit, and of women being inferior to men, Persian Zoroastrianism, Hinduism, and Buddhism all contain these value judgments. In classical Greece and Rome—pagan through and through—such beliefs were popular, and especially espoused by the Stoic philosophers.[1] Even within the pagan cultures that include an element of sacred sexuality, there was still plenty of room for misogyny, homophobia, and the acceptance of rape.

Sure, various cultures had the kind of practices we might call "alternative" today, like BDSM, homosexuality, ritual sex, and body modification. But get caught practicing one of those in the wrong culture, and you're in big trouble with the shamans/priests/head honchos. As NeoPagans, we have a lot more freedom than our ancestors did. So if you're a kinky feminist lesbian with tattoos, remember that older doesn't necessarily equal better.

It's also important to realize that many of the values that we take for granted—a personal two-way relationship with the divine, the importance of ethical conduct, and the idea of being somehow punished for your transgressions and rewarded for good deeds (either in this life or the next)—originated in early Judaism. To the early pagans, the Gods probably didn't give much of a hoot about what people did, as long as they sacrificed to them and performed the required rituals. The Gods themselves, personifications of human beings, had their own moral and ethical failings. NeoPagans tend to imbue the Great Goddess with the serenity, wisdom, and gentle parenthood of the Judeo-Christian God. There's nothing wrong with this—in fact, I consider it an improvement on both systems—but let's not fool ourselves into thinking that the ancients saw things this way.

I know there is no way I could possibly cover the world history of sacred sexuality in Paganism in one chapter. It would be challenging to cover it in a single *book*. So I'm not going to be able to go deeply into anything, but hopefully this will give you enough of an overview to put the rest of the book in context and inspire you to read further.

Early Religion and Sacred Sexuality

The nature of prehistoric religion is the focus of continual debate among scholars. Because there are no written records, all we have to go on are the bits and pieces of art that have been found. The predominant interpretations have changed throughout history. Most NeoPagans believe that prehistoric folks worshipped a single Great Goddess. As I've recently come to understand from the fabulous book *Triumph of the Moon: A History of Modern Pagan Witchcraft* by Ronald Hutton, there is absolutely no evidence that any such deity was ever even imagined before the nineteenth century. But there is absolutely no proof that she *wasn't*, either. This is where the line between history and myth begins to blur. There's no proof that Jesus actually rose from the dead, but that didn't stop Christianity from becoming a hugely popular religion. We may never know the true nature of prehistoric religion, so we might as well imagine it the way we want to. As Wolf Dean Stiles Ravenheart says in *Modern Pagans*, "Do you remember the time when women ran wild and free in the forest and were never afraid? Well, if you don't remember such a time, make it up!"[2]

Our conception of the earliest religions is that they were fertility religions, in which sexuality and the body were considered the most powerful, magical, and sacred things of all. As you can imagine, that would have influenced people's attitudes toward sexuality and their bodies in a positive way.

The beginnings of human civilization were toward the end of what is known as the "old Stone Age," or Paleolithic times: 30,000 to 13,000 BCE. This is the time period where we find, mainly in Europe, the "Venus" figures, small female statues of stone or clay, with exaggerated breasts, hips, bellies, and vulvas. Historians have made various guesses as to their purpose. Some think they were some kind of Paleolithic porn, designed to be ogled and fondled.[3] Others concede that they had an erotic meaning, but believe that they functioned primarily as symbols of the cycle of life, meant to be used in stories or rituals.[4] Because there was no understanding of the reproductive process, people at this time assumed that women reproduced on their own, through parthenogenesis;[5] this might have encouraged a vision of women as a sort of deity, or the idea that supernatural deities must be like women. Although there is huge debate on this point, Stone Age societies were probably polytheistic, honoring many Gods and Goddesses, and possibly also animal spirits. Although we like to think that they worshipped "The" Great Goddess, as Hutton says, it's probable that "the overwhelming majority of ancient pagans genuinely believed that the different goddesses were separate personalities."[6]

In trying to figure out the purpose of the Venus figures, we must realize that we are viewing them through our modern filters, which draw a distinction between "profane" and "sacred." In a religion where sexuality—specifically female sexuality—was revered as a life-giving force, it's likely that these boundaries wouldn't even exist. Why couldn't a Stone Age guy, rubbing the breasts of a stone figure, be at once aroused and also in a state of religious communion with a Goddess? In that framework, it would be the perfect way to worship—at least, if a real woman weren't available. Riane Eisler notes that historians have given little attention to the idea of sexual pleasure in their discussions of ancient sexual images, instead focusing on religious significance; she attributes this to our "antipleasure" religious and cultural heritage.[7]

Between the end of the Mesolithic period and the start of the Neolithic (13,000 to 8000 BCE), the retreat of the polar ice caps exposed fertile land and precipitated a shift from hunter-gatherer to agricultural society. From about 8000 BCE on, more permanent villages were developed. Another major change was that the male role in the reproduction process became understood. Over time, more male and masculine figures (bulls, buffalo, and human figures with horns) began to appear in cave paintings. Neolithic Goddess figures have phallic necks and head, and/or hold snakes (phallic symbols). Because intercourse was obviously the way to create life, sex became sacred as well. People were doing what the Gods did. The role of animals in the art suggests that, rather than defining themselves as separate from the animal world, humans at this time embraced animals as their cousins and strove to incorporate positive elements of animal nature (strength, transformation, etc.) into their own.

Unfortunately, the combination of agriculture and the new male role in reproduction and (consequently) religion didn't bode well for the rights and status of women. Restrictions on women's sexual partners became more important because it was the only way to know which man had fathered a child; this led to monogamy and polygyny (one husband with more than one wife). Small tribes and families worked well in a hunter-gatherer society, but agriculture required permanent settlements and lots of laborers to work the land. By Neolithic times (11,000 to 3000 BCE), women became valued mostly for their ability to produce workers and came to be treated as a commodity.[8]

It's important to note that sex and fertility, while important to our ancestors, were not isolated from the rest of life. They were an intrinsic part of a cycle. Obviously, if all we did was procreate and never die, the results would be catastrophic. Eisler says, "Our early mythical imagery reflected a world view in which death was neither an isolated event nor a final destination. . . . Rather, it was part of the same cycle: a cycle of sex, birth, death, and rebirth, in which the Goddess reclaimed what was hers to give, and in which sex played a mysterious but central part. As our ancestors realized that women only give birth after sexual intercourse, they apparently concluded that the rebirth of animal and vegetable life every spring . . . is also generated through some kind of sexual union."[9] Bodies were now buried in round tombs, to symbolize the earth mother's womb. There was an "importance not only of women but of sex in prehistoric burial customs and rites."[10] In the cycle of birth, death, and rebirth, human sexuality could play a key role in getting in good with the Goddess who recycles all. And the masculine deities in agricultural societies became dying-and-reborn vegetation Gods.

LaSara Firefox: *The doorway to birth is the same doorway as the one to death, and equally potent. It's one doorway, whether you're coming in or going out. And giving birth is the closest I have ever been to dying. It is an initiation, just as death is: to the person being born, and to the person giving birth.*

Between the fourth and second millennia BCE, there was a shift from agriculture to pastoralism in Europe. Archaeological finds show the Goddess figures gradually disappearing and an increase in warfare. Based on the evidence of a sudden shift in the dominant language, Eisler says it's apparent that this was not a "natural progression in social evolution."[11] Feminist scholars attribute it, instead, to a wave of invasions by pastoral Indo-Europeans. How did this happen? One possibility is introduced by the geographer James DeMeo, as cited in *Sacred Pleasure*. He suggests that due to severe climatic and environmental changes, some tribes' farmland grew scarce, and these groups had to travel and take over other areas. This meant they had to develop a dominator mentality and a thick skin; this (Eisler and others believe) led to not only subordination of women, but also to repression of sexual pleasure. In these societies, man was dominant. The perception of the reproductive process was now that male seed was the thing that grew life and the woman's womb only functioned as a holding place. Georg Feuerstein suggests that the fact that the penis can't be controlled by will led people to believe it was associated with some powerful outside force. Add the power of fertility, and it became associated with God(s).[12] The male deities became more important than the female.

Additionally, nomadic pastoralism tends to perpetuate itself, as grazing uses up resources and necessitates roaming into a wider area. Eisler also suggests a connection between the domestication of animals and the view of women as property kept for breeding purposes—ugh![13]

Polytheism and Sacred Prostitution

Now we come into the time period where we actually have written records, and we no longer have to rely on guesswork. Sacred sexuality is going to be, to one extent or another, an intrinsic part of any polytheistic religion. If you have multiple Gods and Goddesses, with gender, they will have sex with each other, and thus human sexuality has got to be a good thing. There isn't room in this chapter to even *list* all the world religions in history that included some form of sacred sexuality, much less to explore them in depth. Still existing currently we have the indigenous polytheistic traditions in developing countries (such as parts of Africa and South America), sects of Buddhism and Hinduism (including Tantra), and the surviving Native American traditions. Historical religions include those of the Near East (Sumerian, Babylonian, and Egyptian), Greco-Roman religion (including the Minoans), and the Aztecs.

One common aspect of polytheistic religion is "sacred prostitution." Prostitution was a thriving business in most of the city-states of the ancient world. Since ancient times, there have been two types of prostitute. One was the standard hooker, who gave sexual pleasure in exchange for money. Much the same way as today, many (not all) of these "profane" prostitutes were forced into that line of work through circumstance—in their cases, this usually meant poverty (i.e., the lack of other available ways for a single woman to make a living), having been sold as a slave or captured in war.

The other type of prostitute, and the one more relevant to this book, was the temple priest or (much more often) priestess, who gave sexual pleasure to worshippers as the representative of a deity, usually a Goddess. Money was exchanged, but as an offering, which went to the temple, which in turn supported the priestesses. This sort of service was often considered an honor.

31

These priestesses have been called temple prostitutes, sacred prostitutes, sacred harlots, sacred whores, and many other names that are specific to different cultures. (The somewhat negative term *temple prostitution* was invented by nineteenth-century scholars).[14] This practice could be found in the ancient Near East and Mediterranean civilizations, Meso-America, and much of Asia.[15]

Ideally, when such a priestess received a worshipper, they would both be participating in a transformative experience. The priestess would achieve a sense of spiritual communion with her Goddess. And although the priestess was the only one functioning officially as a channel for deity, the worshippers' role was that of heavenly spouse. This was not the place for "Wham, bam, thank you, ma'am." He was not there to get off; he was there to worship. So one would hope that he made an effort to be a considerate lover. In return, the worshipper would experience a sense of intimacy with the divine. Children born of the union were often considered offspring of the Gods[16] and were sometimes also dedicated to the temple.

Some sex-positive feminists believe that the sacred whore represents women's power (power from within), and the profane whore represents men's power over women. This is an oversimplification, which ignores the fact that many women, then and now, may choose prostitution as a career. But the sacred harlot usually did quite well and had more opportunities for education and prosperity than the average "respectable" married woman.

Although in NeoPaganism we say that "sex is sacred," there is certainly a difference between a back-alley fuck and lovemaking as ritualized sacrament. This distinction is something worth considering when thinking about sex work in the context of ancient paganism and NeoPaganism. Why would a prostitute choose the bordello over the temple? Did profane prostitutes make better money, in which case doing it through the temple was a labor of love? Why would "clients" choose either the bordello or the temple? Did they distinguish between just wanting to get their rocks off and wanting to have an ecstatic religious experience? Unfortunately, there aren't many details about these practices, and what details there are often came from antagonistic cultures.

In all the reading I have done on sacred prostitution, the vast majority of these folks are assumed to be women. Men serving in this capacity were often crossdressed, and/or were eunuchs, and also received male worshippers. This corresponds to the standard role of hooker and john in the modern world, where the prostitute is usually female and the client usually male. There are male sex workers today who cater to women, but they are very few. None of my sources suggested a reason for this largely one-sided worship. The cultures that historically employed temple prostitutes were polytheistic and worshipped male Gods as well as Goddesses. Why wouldn't a female worshipper have wanted to make love to her God through a temple priest? Additionally, did women ever come to the temple to make love with the female priestesses? These questions remain unanswered.

In looking at the history of sacred prostitution through a modern lens, I think the critical issue is that of personal freedom and choice. In cultures where time served in the temple was a requirement, I have to wonder who invented these customs—men or women? And why didn't any men have to serve in this way?

In *Whores and Other Feminists*, Cosi Fabian writes, "Sacred prostitute stories reveal an understanding of women as gateways to transformation. In them, women use combinations of sexual ecstasy, formal ritual, and informal teaching, and are seen to embody incarnations of their goddess. . . . How refreshing to discover guiding religious metaphors . . . in which female sexuality *saves* rather than *damns* humankind."[17] There will be more about sacred prostitution, as a modern practice, in chapter 8.

THE NEAR EAST

The very earliest form of written literature is the narrative of a sacred marriage rite between the Babylonian Goddess Inanna and her brother/lover Dumuzi (more on them in the next chapter), circa 3000 BCE. In a scene as explicit as any triple-X-rated movie today, Inanna exhorts Dumuzi to "plow her vulva." What I love about this text is that it can function as both porn and liturgy at the same time.

According to the Greek scholar Herodotus in the fifth century BCE, the custom in Babylon was that each woman, once in her life, had to go to the temple of their love Goddess, Mylitta, and offer herself to any man who wanted her. Among the Phoenicians, every woman had to be ritually deflowered by a stranger, such as a high priest or king, before she could be married. Sumerian texts circa 2000 BCE describe prostitutes as "wise women, able to educate, civilize, and tame men."[18] In the Sumerian *Epic of Gilgamesh*, a temple harlot is the only one who can tame the wild man Enkidu. She "helps him become wise, like a god."[19]

There were three categories of sacred prostitutes in Babylon: An *ishtaritu* was a virginal priestess who was lover only to Ishtar. A *qadishtu* was the more standard kind of temple prostitute. They would work as priestesses in the temple and make love to countless men, but they also were often landowners and businesswomen from wealthy, well-accepted families. As you might expect, they were trained to be excellent lovers. A *harimtu*, although officially a priestess, was in it for the money and would work in the taverns.

In Egypt, prostitutes were often also slaves. Temple prostitution was especially associated with the God Amon and the Goddess Bast (a cat Goddess associated with love). Queen Hatshepsut (1500 BCE) claimed that she was the offspring of the sacred union of her mother with the God Amon, quite likely during a visit of her mother to the temple—this suggests the existence of a male sacred harlot.

According to the prophet Ezekiel, the ancient Hebrews learned this practice from the Egyptians, and it was the symbol of everything that was wrong with the holy city. "In the Old Testament, the prophet Hosea's wife is reported to have dressed up in all her finery for her regular visits to the temple, where she made love to men other than her husband."[20] Oh horrors!

INDIA

Hinduism is an extremely complex polytheistic religion that is still thriving today. Sexuality is a major aspect of the theology, mythology, and general religious symbolism. The Gods and Goddesses are often portrayed mostly or partly nude and in flirtatious poses. They are lovers with each other and seem to beckon us to be their lovers as well. Hindu symbolism is extremely intense and powerful and equally balanced between light and dark.

Sacred prostitution in India dates back to the time of the Indus civilization (circa 2600 BCE). Their priestesses were called *deva-dasis*, which means "slaves of God" in Sanskrit. The deva-dasis, besides being sexual representatives of the divine, were trained in the art of classical music and dance from childhood. Sick baby girls would be given to the temple, and if they lived, they were officially married to the Temple God at puberty, as a sign of gratitude. In the dances, both public and private, the deva-dasi would symbolically make love to the God of the temple. She was allowed to take lovers and to initiate young men in the sexual arts. The temples in India were centers of not just dance and music, but also theater, poetry, crafts and fine art, philosophy, and culture. The deva-dasis had high social status. The Leela Dance Theater Web site tells us, "Historically the temple dancers

35

of India were influential women who were not only acclaimed for their artistry but also for their untold wealth and their influence in politics. So great was the power of their art that they conversed with royalty as equals."[21]

The Indian tradition of Tantra has been a major influence on NeoPagan sex magic. Its roots go back more than five thousand years. The basic principle of Tantra has to do with the union of the God Shiva and the Goddess Shakti. Shiva is the embodiment of pure consciousness in its most ecstatic state, and Shakti is the embodiment of pure energy. Shakti, through uniting sexually with Shiva, gave his spirit form, and thus created the universe. Shiva and Shakti are considered to be united in one body, providing a wonderful hermaphroditic deity for folks who identify as transgendered. Tantric practitioners can reenact the cosmic coupling either symbolically ("the right-hand path") or physically ("the left-hand path").[22] *Shakti* is also a term applied to female Tantra practitioners.[23]

According to Tantra, the body's primal sexual energy is symbolized as a serpent that begins at the base of the spine and uncoils to the head. Along the way, there are seven centers of concentrated energy, called chakras, each one corresponding to a different aspect of being (see the glossary). Through meditation and ritual, this serpent, called Kundalini, can be awakened and one's energy cleansed and magnified.

GREECE

Many of us are familiar with the escapades of the Greek Gods from our basic childhood education. Aphrodite, Zeus, Eros, Dionysus, Hermes, and Pan—it was like one big soap opera, full of drama, love, and lust. But by the time of ancient Greek civilization, things were pretty well "civilized," so sexuality had become very compartmentalized; aside from small mystery cults like those devoted to Dionysus, and some degree of sacred prostitution, there wasn't much sacred sexuality going on.

Although ancient Athens (fifth century BCE) was polytheistic and citizens worshipped many strong Goddesses, the culture was male-dominated. There was a whole lot of free love going on in Athens, but the right to practice it without repercussions extended only to men. The Greek love feasts, *symposia*, would include music and dance, gluttony and drunkenness, as well as "crude orgies" with participants "taking advantage of courtesans and young boys." Wives were not invited.[24] In fact, they were considered lesser human beings and the property of their husbands. Baby girls were often exposed to the elements and left to die. Maintenance of female chastity was of paramount importance; a father could sell his daughter into slavery if she lost her virginity before marriage. Women could not vote, hold office, or even obtain a secular education. Plato made a distinction between sacred and profane love and said that the former was only possible between men. And unfortunately, Athenians were also fascinated with rape, depicting it frequently in myth and art.[25]

Ancient Greek culture had room for harlots both sacred and profane, with many shades of gray in between. The *hetaera* were respected courtesans, who were romanticized and often taken as wives by their customers. Some were well educated and owned land. Temple prostitutes were called *hieroduli*. It's not clear-cut in which cases temple prostitutes were answering some kind of spiritual calling, and in which cases they were just hookers working out of a temple. The thousand Harlots of Corinth were sacred slaves, or hieroduli, in the sanctuary of Aphrodite. But they were sacred in name only; in practice, they were more likely forced into the lifestyle by economic necessity. The purer kind of temple prostitution in Greece was motivated by religion more than economics. The woman offered her body in service to the God-dess of the temple.[26]

Monotheism

If the earliest monotheists were to succeed, they would have to steer people away from their pagan practices. According to *The Hebrew Goddess* by Raphael Patai, most ancient Hebrews and Caananites were polytheists. Ishtar/Astarte was at least as popular as YHVH, and she enacted a *hieros gamos** with Tammuz/Ba'al. The Goddess Asherah was known as the wife of YHVH and was worshipped alongside him up until the destruction of the second temple in Jerusalem in 70 CE. Because YHVH was so remote, the ancient Hebrews likely stayed loyal to Ba'al (lord) and Ba'alat (lady, a.k.a. Astarte), originally Canaanite deities whom they had adopted. In the Pentateuch, the "Hebrew prophets are constantly exhorting their people against backsliding to the worship of the Queen of Heaven, railing against 'the whore of Babylon' and the sinful 'daughters of Zion.'"[27] Of course, Abraham's clan succeeded in its efforts, and monotheism was born.

The God of Judaism and Christianity has no sex. This can be taken in two ways: God is beyond gender, and God doesn't have sex (as in sexual congress). Since God is neither male nor female, and since *we* have gender, we are in some way "not-God." It also means that sex as an act is also "not-God."

Judaism has always been extremely patriarchal and controlling of sexuality, especially women's sexuality. Eve (Chava) was por-trayed as a temptress whose rebellion and curiosity led all human-ity to ruin, and Orthodox Jewish women are subject to many

---

*A Greek term meaning "sacred marriage."

special rules regarding modesty and menstruation. Yet, elements of sacred sexuality exist: Jewish men have a religious obligation to sexually satisfy their wives and it is considered a mitzvah* to make love on the Sabbath.

Eisler suggests that the advent of patriarchal monotheism was a sign of civilization turning to a "dominator" mentality. It did bring some pretty unfortunate changes to religious life in the Middle East. With this new paradigm, women became more sexually repressed and men started using sex workers—prostitutes, slaves, and concubines—for gratification. Religion moved away from the celebration of fertility and into the celebration of the intellect.

By the time of Yeshua ben Yosef (a.k.a. Jesus Christ), there were still remnants from the old ways in practice. *The Women's Encyclopedia of Myths and Secrets* tells us, "In the east, the God's lingam or the erect penis of his statue was anointed with holy oil—Greek *chrism*—for easier penetration of his bride, the Goddess, impersonated by one of the temple virgins. . . . Jesus became a Christos when he was *christ*-ened by Mary, the magdalene, or temple maiden."[28]

For what it's worth, the sermons of Jesus did not condemn women or sexuality. For that, we can credit "saints" Paul and Augustine, who cemented the idea of the body—especially the woman's body—as corrupt. Augustine, in his youth, followed the Persian religion of Manichaeanism, which was strongly dualistic: the world was divided into good and evil.[29] As a Christian, he invented the concept of original sin, stating that the acts of sex and childbirth were "the instruments of God's eternal punishment of every woman and man" for this sin.[30] He can also be credited with creating the celibate priesthood. And it was Paul who said,

---

*Mitzvah literally means "commandment," but in everyday use means "good deed."

"It is good for a man not to touch a woman, but . . . it is better to marry than burn."[31]

In Christianity, the mothering aspect of Goddess morphed into Mary (Miriam), a woman who was nothing more than a vessel for God. At least Eve had some spunk; by the time we got to Christianity, the female archetype had become totally passive and sexless. Church doctrine claimed that her hymen even remained intact during childbirth.[32] Both Eve and Mary are negative stereotypes of what should be sacred elements of femininity: sexuality and mothering.

> SHAI SHAHAR: *The Egyptians had Isis, and Osiris, and Horus to represent the original (and very human) "Holy Trinity:" Mother, Father, Child. The [Christians] took away our Mother and gave us the Holy Ghost . . . alter-ego of the Son. They left us without wives and lovers and left us to seek the divine through the intercession of virgin-madonnas and a whore who repented for her sex. Gee. Thanks.*

If all humans are corrupted by original sin, it would follow that they require strong social and political control. "If men have to be protected from being 'polluted' by woman's sexuality, sexual love is dangerous. And so is any relaxation of male control over women."[33] Condemning sexuality, Eisler suggests, was also a way for the church to gain control over people who still remembered and perhaps practiced earlier religious traditions that sacralized it.

Christianity created the image of the witch (small *w* intentional) as a rampantly sexual, evil woman in consort with the Devil, who seduces men and has sex with demons. There is a great deal of lore about these "witches" and their sexuality, but since that has much more to do with fear of sexuality than with Paganism, I'm choosing to skip it.

With Christianity, the passion that was once focused on sex, love, and regeneration became redirected toward punishment, sacrifice, and death. It was as if a vital, central part of life was erased—or, more accurately, swept under the rug. This focus on suffering was perpetuated by the threat of eternal torment as a punishment for disobeying the rules. This was a big change from the Goddess who recycled all.

The new focus on suffering and sacrifice also significantly altered the nature of the hieros gamos. First, rather than being a sacred marriage between a God and a Goddess, or man and woman, the marriage was to be a purely platonic one between the individual and God. Second, ecstatic suffering replaced sexual pleasure as a pathway to the divine. Mystics inflicted injury and pain on themselves to prove their love of God, draw closer to him, and/or to be like him. I make no negative judgments about the sacredness of pain and its use as a method of altering one's consciousness, but as a replacement of sacred pleasure, it was, in my opinion, a step backward.

. . . And then we pretty much have a thousand-plus years of sex-negative monotheism. The only major religion still surviving in which sexuality plays a large role is Hinduism, and Indian friends tell me that since the culture is very repressed these days, the sacred sex is strictly metaphorical. Along the way, there have been brief glimpses of an alternative in mystery "cults," intentional communities, and small liberal sects of the major religions. Nothing much more to report there. The dominant world culture still bears the marks of Paul and Augustine. It remains to be seen whether NeoPaganism will ever become large and influential enough to turn the tide.

A Very Brief History of Wicca and NeoPaganism

Wicca's roots, as explored by Ronald Hutton, appear to originate from a variety of sources. These include the Romantic literary

41

movement of the nineteenth century, secret societies such as the Masons, ceremonial magic traditions from the Golden Dawn and Aleister Crowley, writers on myth such as Sir James Frazier and Robert Graves, and old European folk traditions (real and imagined). Various "secret societies" flourished in England from the late nineteenth to early twentieth centuries, many with ritual elements that would seem extremely familiar to modern Pagans.

Dion Fortune, although she had some serious hang-ups about things like masturbation, homosexuality, and BDSM, can be credited with bringing sacred sexuality into the forefront of British mysticism. Sadly, however, she believed that the energy of passionate attraction could best be harnessed unfulfilled to accomplish magical ends.[34]

When England's antiwitchcraft law was repealed in 1951, a gentleman named Gerald Gardner began publishing his books about a tradition (then called Wica, which he also called Witchcraft) into which he said he had been initiated. There is no proof that his claim was true and quite a bit of evidence to indicate that it wasn't. (Since then, after much deliberation and in-fighting, the majority of the Wiccan community seems content to let the mystery of its origins lie, and instead focus on the present and the future.) A few other Craft traditions and covens popped up at that time, none with traceable origins. Gardner and the other big names of the time like Alex Sanders were often demonized by the media, which did damage, but also earned them more publicity. More books were written, and daughter covens hived off to form their own.

Wicca took off in the United States in the early 1960s, where it found a comfy home with the countercultural trends of that era. In the 1970s and 1980s, it joined forces with the women's movement, and feminist/Dianic Wicca was born—this friendship has given Paganism a big boost, but has also unfortunately built some anti-male sexism into it. Since the 1970s, the United States has been the center of the NeoPagan world.

The term *NeoPagan* was actually first coined in 1891 by critics of those poets who were romanticizing Paganism in a sentimental passion for the English countryside.[35] Oberon Zell-Ravenheart (then Tim/Otter Zell) began using the term for his own group, the Church of All Worlds, in the 1960s. Although Wicca is still by far the largest "denomination" of NeoPagan, many people choose to define themselves only as "Pagan" or "NeoPagan"—not realizing, perhaps, that many elements of their practice stem from Gardnerian Wicca.

2. SEX GODS AND SYMBOLS ❧

THIS CHAPTER is not meant to be an exhaustive compilation of all sexual symbolism and Gods associated with sexuality. It couldn't possibly be. It is meant to introduce you to these subjects, to inspire you to learn more about them, and to work with them. Perhaps reading will be the jumping-off point for meditation or ritual. Perhaps you can work some of the symbols and deities into your sacred sex or sex magic. Perhaps you can find aspects of these things inside yourself and bring them out to play.

You need not believe in the Gods as literal separate entities in order to experience and enjoy them. They can be aspects of the one God, metaphors, archetypes, aspects of human existence—whatever. In the end, what matters is what works.

Sexual Symbolism and Fertility

Sigmond Freud had the right idea about dream interpretation. The subconscious mind speaks in symbols and metaphor. And the part of our brains that we awaken through magic, ritual, and trance is the same part that composes our dreams. Sure, a cigar is sometimes just a cigar, but for our purposes as Pagans and magicians, a maypole is definitely a schlong.

Some male symbols are athame, line, maypole, pinecone, smudge stick, staff, stick, sun (culture-dependent), tree, wand, obelisk, and fruits/vegetables such as bananas, asparagus, and cucumbers.

Some female symbols are cauldron, cave, chalice/cup/the Holy Grail, circle, hole, holey stone,* moon (culture-dependent), ocean, shell, tunnel, Stonehenge,[1] and fruits such as pomegranates, peaches/nectarines/apricots, and apples.

Symbols of the union of male and female are the blade in the chalice, the Star of David (which is two triangles united), the ankh, the Christian cross, the broom, and a bell.

Although there is no hard evidence for it, the cave could very well be the oldest symbol of the Great Mother's womb, with the entrance symbolizing the vagina.[2] This brings a new meaning to cave paintings—they were not necessarily just placed there because it was a nice sheltered surface to decorate. The cave itself may have been used as a sacred space.† Entering it may have been a symbolic return to the womb, and leaving it a rebirth. In modern times, any underground passage can have this significance. Seeing your subway commute in a new light?

Fertility, as originally defined by historical religions, is no longer an overriding concern for most of us today. Our survival does not depend on how many offspring we have to help us hunt game or work the fields. If anything, we might do better to have *fewer* children—it would help to conserve our resources. Therefore, as NeoPagans, we must explore other definitions of "fertility."

---

*Stones with natural holes in them.

†It's also possible that the only reason we see paintings there, and no other place, is because the elements destroyed the outdoor ones.

According to the Merriam-Webster OnLine Dictionary, *fertile* can mean many things that have nothing to do with either plants, fruit, or reproduction:

1. Characterized by great resourcefulness of thought or imagination, inventive
2. Plentiful
3. Affording abundant possibilities for development
4. Capable of growing or developing

Remember, too, that the creation and destruction are both sacred; the Goddess may plant babies in our bellies, but she also rips them out. Abortion, both miscarriage and intentional termination, although tragic, are sometimes necessary.

Also, it is perfectly possible to be brimming with fertility all on one's own. Many Goddesses in history have been called "virgin." Although today we mostly use this word for someone who has not had sexual intercourse, the term has also, at various times, meant unmarried, self-sufficient, untouched, and/or pure. Virginity may also symbolize a preservation of power.[3]

Gods Who Have Sex

One of the unique things about polytheism is that the Gods have gender and that they have sex. Although the standard party line in Judaism, Christianity, and Islam is that God is beyond gender, it doesn't make much difference in practice, when the language they all use to talk about God is utterly masculine. The fact is that we live in a gendered world, and it's hard to talk about anything with a consciousness without either assigning it gender, calling it "It" like it's some kind of robot, or using New Age terms like "the Source" or "the All," which, while pretty, also make deity so undefined as to be impossible to grasp. So, many of us have been stuck with this Sistine Chapel image of God as a bearded old guy with great muscle definition.

Some NeoPagans, being tired of such an overused archetype that may have little spiritual significance for them, have adopted a feminine monotheist deity, "the Goddess," which many have justifiably called "Yahweh in drag." This is an improvement from a feminist point of view, certainly, because it honors women and women's bodies, which have been given such a bad rap by monotheism, but it simply turns the tables and gives the bad rap to men and the masculine. In my opinion, this is just as unbalanced a viewpoint and just as sexist. Biologically, diversity is critical for survival and reproduction for creatures who have gone past the single-cell stage. And for goodness' sake, fathers have the potential to be just as nurturing as mothers. The best Pagan solutions to this problem have been duotheism, polytheism, or the notion of a hermaphrodidic deity.

ANNIE SPRINKLE: *My deities morph constantly. My Goddess/God morphs. He/she can be very androgynous, male, female . . . although generally, if I have to choose one, I choose Goddess, just because I'm female, and I was brought up to believe God is within you, so if I go inside myself, it comes out female. But if I go into some Christian church, or to a 12-step meeting, which I enjoy doing on occasion, I connect with that male God, just to be friendly and go along with the program. I'm not attached to the gender of God/dess.*

DOSSIE EASTON: *My thesis of polytheism is that we don't know what the fuck God looks like. It is, like the galaxy, much less the entire cosmos, it is way, way bigger than us, and we may feel, I believe, that divinity flows through all of us all the time. I'm a Tantra practitioner, and . . . a lot of my practice is about connecting with Kundalini. So my notion about all these Gods and Goddesses is that we create images that we can sort of connect to with our minds, that are often anthropomorphic, but sometimes animals and sometimes rocks, and whatever, but a lot of times stuff in nature . . . and we use those as symbol paths.*

If God has gender, then that gender is made holy: male, female, and intersexed. If the Gods have sex, then our sexuality is holy.

JEZEBEL DAWN BLESSING: *My experience of sexuality has led me to explore further into the archetypes of different cultural myths in regards to sexual deity. This has greatly enhanced my understanding of the collective unconscious and helped me to embody the Gods and Goddesses in my own sexual nature.*

A Few Sex Gods and Goddesses

Just a word about these deities before I go into describing them: In doing my research, I was amazed by how many God/esses associated with sexuality also have a violent, destructive, or just plain scary side. I don't know what conclusions to draw from that, but it's a provocative element.

Aphrodite (af-roh-DY-tee) is the Greek Goddess of love, beauty, sexual rapture, and some say marriage. She is also a Goddess of gardens, mainly because the Greeks felt that there was a strong connection between fertility in humans and the fertility of the land.

One legend of her birth says that Uranus, the father of the Gods, was castrated by his son Cronus, who wanted to take over his position. Cronus threw the severed genitals into the ocean, which began to churn and foam. From the *aphros* ("sea foam") arose Aphrodite, a full-grown woman, and she floated to shore.

Zeus, afraid that the Gods would fight over her, married her off to the smith God Hephaestus: great for Hephaestus, but not so great for Aphrodite, who, less than thrilled with her sooty husband, took on many other lovers. She became fond of Hermes, but he wasn't into women at the time, so she grew a beard and partially transformed into a man to catch his eye. It worked, and the child they bore was named Hermaphroditus. In some myths, he is born intersexed; in others, he is born male and later fuses with a female lover. The God Eros, originally conceived as one of the eldest Gods, was later "demoted" to a child she conceived with her lover Ares. Aphrodite is also the mother of Priapus, who has a huge ever-erect penis and is magnetically attractive to women.

Aphrodite is a multifaceted Goddess, with many surnames that describe her different attributes. She has many lovers, divine and mortal alike. Her priestesses were and are sacred harlots, through whom men could and can worship her. Although Aphrodite is often portrayed in modern culture as a blond brainless bimbo (which irks me to no end), she must be fairly tough if she's lovers with the God of war. Indeed, she has a vengeful streak.

She is associated with the dolphin, dove, swan, and sparrow. Plants include lily, rose, apple, myrtle, quince, opium poppy, mandrake, pomegranate, and lime and myrtle trees. Her scents are fennel, myrrh, and cinnamon.[4]

Dionysus (dye-uh-NY-suhs) is the Greek God of fertility, vegetation, pleasure/ecstasy, wine, and the arts. Dionysus can bring joy and divine ecstasy, or brutal, unthinking, rage—as can both love and alcohol. He carries a staff tipped with a pinecone (phallic, of course!), which makes you insane if you touch it. He is represented as a man who is in touch with his emotions (more about Dionysus's androgynous qualities in chapter 5) and he has been lovers with Aphrodite and Persephone as well as Hermaphroditus and Adonis.

He is a shaman who walks between worlds, as were his ancient followers, who would drink, dance, and have orgies, entering altered states that sometimes tipped into madness. He is accompanied by Maenads (wild women wearing fawn skins) and satyrs. It was traditional to worship him in the woods, rather than a temple.

Because Dionysus died and returned to life (more than once, it seems), as well as journeyed to the underworld, and because grape vines must be pruned and then lie dormant before they bear fruit, he became associated with rebirth after death. Unlike the other Gods in the Greek pantheon, Dionysus is believed to dwell within his followers as well as outside them.[5]

The Horned God is not an ancient deity, but a NeoPagan conception which combines elements of several Gods. Horns have been symbols of power since prehistory because of their association with the animals who have them. Pan is the goat-legged God of nature, the arts, animals, sexuality, and terror (*panic* comes from his name). He is a trickster and indiscriminately lusty, chasing after shepherds, sheep, and nymphs alike. Though Pan was originally a minor God, the nineteenth-century romantic poets gave him more importance, to the point where he came to represent all of nature and especially the English countryside.[6] Ronald Hutton suggests that the "standard modern conception of the Devil as a being with cloven hooves, goat's horns, and pointed beard is a nineteenth-century creation, representing a Christian reaction to the growing importance of Pan as an alternative focus for the literary imagination."[7] By the 1930s and 1940s, Pan had become an archetype and was on his way to morphing into the Horned God. NeoPagans have blended him with other figures.

Cernunnos, a Celtic deity with deer antlers, is sometimes pictured with an erection, surrounded by men, also with erections, which suggests that he may be bisexual or gay. Herne is a folkloric figure in Britain, the Lord of the Hunt, also with deer antlers, and has a dark personality. Today, the Horned God is associated with the forest, lust, and passion. He is a symbol of the union of our human and animal natures.

Inanna/Ishtar and Dumuzi/Tammuz are a Goddess-God pair of the Sumerian and Babylonian pantheons, respectively. I've lumped them together because their stories are so similar, they are practically the same deities.

Inanna is a Goddess of love, fertility, and war—essentially, life and death—as well as the moon. She is most famous for her descent to the underworld, where she traveled with the intent to wrest control of the realm from her sister Ereshkigal. The gatekeeper, under order from Ereshkigal, had Inanna remove one article of clothing for each of the seven gates she passed through to enter the underworld. When Inanna reached Ereshkigal, she was killed, and all of nature stopped growing and died. The God Enki intervened and told her she could come back to life if she sent someone in her place. She chose her beloved consort, the vegetation God Dumuzi. She was sprinkled with the water of life, led back out through the gates, and given back her clothing and jewels. Dumuzi would from then on rule the underworld every half year. In a slightly different story, Ishtar went to the underworld to try and retrieve her lover Tammuz, after he died, but she failed.

They say that Inanna is fickle, first attracting men and then rejecting them, and Ishtar is an evil, heartless woman who was known for destroying her lovers—but one has to wonder if this is original myth or just patriarchal propaganda. She is depicted as richly dressed or naked. Her symbol is the eight- or sixteen-pointed star, her sacred number is 15, and her sacred animal is the lion (she is sometimes depicted riding a lion) or dragon. She is armed with a quiver and bow. Her temples had sacred harlots of both genders. As patroness of ritual promiscuity/prostitution, Ishtar is known as Abtagigi.[8]

Dumuzi/Tammuz is the Sumerian/Akkadian vegetation God, brother and partner to Inanna/Ishtar. Because Dumuzi is exchanged for Inanna in the underworld, he is a symbol of death and rebirth in nature.

Kali (kah-LEE), or Kali-ma, is not strictly a sex Goddess, but her name comes up in this book several times, so here she is. She's an aspect of the Hindu Mother Goddess Durga, who is the active aspect of Shakti. (Even Kali herself has different aspects, some more gentle and others more fierce.) Her skin is black, symbolizing her transcendent nature, and she is garbed with human skulls and arms. She was born from Durga's brow (kind of like the warrior Goddess Athena, coming out of Zeus's head, eh?) during a battle with evil forces. Kali got carried away in the battle and started destroying everything in sight. The God Shiva, her husband, threw himself under her feet and thus stopped her. She has four arms; one has a sword and one holds the head of a demon, but the other two bless and reassure her worshippers. Her red lolling tongue indicates her omnivorous nature—"her indiscriminate enjoyment of all the world's 'flavors.'"[9] She is linked with Tantric practices, in which she manifests as a Great Goddess, responsible for all life from conception to death—as such, she is tender and terrible at the same time, creator and destroyer.

Lilith (LIL-ith) is a figure who has changed over time, but has always been a troublemaker. In Sumer, circa 2400 BCE, she was a demonic seductress, a "harlot and a vampire who, once she chose a lover, would never let him go, but without ever giving him real satisfaction." By 2000 BCE, she had become a Goddess: artwork of the time shows her as a nude, shapely woman with wings and owl feet. She stands on two lions and is flanked by owls. By the seventh century BCE, she had changed back into a demon, sphinx-like, who was still seducing and torturing men, but also believed to endanger women in childbirth. In *The Alphabet of Ben Sirah*, a medieval Jewish work, Lilith is described as Adam's first wife, as a way of explaining the two creation stories in Genesis, as well as the myths about Lilith's demon past. She refused to lie beneath Adam while having sex, saying, "Why should I lie beneath you, when I am your equal, since both of us were created from dust?" Adam refused to give in, so she left the garden to have a grand old time with demons, bearing them more than 100 offspring per day. From about 600 CE, Liliths (she was now a category of demon) were believed to be a sort of succubus, lying with men at night, and also especially threatening to women during menstruation and in childbirth. Jealous of their lovers' human wives, they would cause barrenness and miscarriage and also murder the women's babies.[10] More recently, she has become a feminist role model because of her refusal to submit to Adam, and she is now revered by some as a dark Goddess.

Oshun ("oh-SHOON"), originally an Orisha from the African tradition of Yoruba, Oshun is now also a Loa in Voodoo and Santeria.* She is associated with sensuality, beauty, love, sexuality, romanticism, delicacy, sweetness, happiness, water, serenity, the moon, gold, flirtation, and lust. Oshun is a "party girl," swinging

---

*Orisha and Loa both mean the same thing: a God, Goddess, ancestor, or nature deity.

her hips from side to side, inciting men to jealous rages. Her partner is the storm God Chango (Shango), with whom she became
the mother of all. She rows a boat down the rivers of the world
every evening to take away the sorrows and misfortunes of all
her children. Oshun is especially called on by those who wish to
become fertile and who need money.

When she possesses dancers, their movements are those of a
woman who loves to swim, who makes her arm bracelets jingle,
and who admires herself in a mirror. Altars to her hold copper
and brass bracelets, fans, a pottery dish filled with white stones
from a riverbed, and dishes of omuluku (onions, beans, and salt).

Oshun is associated with the colors yellow and gold, and
amber, rose wood, and coral. She enjoys eating canistel (a tropi-
cal fruit), pumpkins, sunflower, capon goat, hens, ochin-chin
(spinach with boiled eggs and shrimp), raw honey, and oranges.
She drinks beer, champagne, and chamomile tea. She prefers Fri-
days and Saturdays, and the numbers 5, 15, 25, 35, 45, and any
multiple of 5.[11]

Shiva/Shakti (SHEE-vuh and SHAHK-tee) are the God/Goddess
pair who are revered in the Tantric tradition, which I mentioned
in chapter 1. Shiva is the most powerful God of the Hindu pantheon and the most complex. His symbol is the lingam, a stylized
phallic shape of stone or wood, which is covered with flowers
and ocher powder.[12] He has a serene appearance, wears his hair
piled high on his head, and the Ganges River flows from his
hair. Around his neck is a serpent, representing Kundalini. He
holds a trident with a small leather drum.

Shiva is responsible for death and destruction, but since it is
understood that there can't be new life without death, he is also
associated with creation. To reduce his destructive influence, he
is fed with opium, and so is called *Bhole Shankar*, "one who is
oblivious of the world." On his holiday, *Maha Shivratri*, worship-

pers drink *thandai* (made from cannabis, almonds, and milk), sing songs in his praise, and dance to the rhythm of the drums.[13]

The Encyclopedia of Sacred Sexuality tells us that "Shakti as goddess and symbol represents the ultimate female principle of energy and motion, without which there could be no manifested universe."[14] All women and their genitals are considered embodiments of Shakti, whose name means "cosmic energy"; as such, Tantric doctrine teaches men to hold all women in reverence. When we die, we enter into final union with her.[15]

The Hieros Gamos

The most important concept in most Wiccan and some Neo-Pagan traditions is the hieros gamos, the coming together of God and Goddess, Lord and Lady. This is symbolized by the athame in the chalice, which when brought together in ritual is also known as the "Great Rite in token." Unfortunately, we don't have any record of sexual rituals before the third millennium BCE, and by then the notion of the hieros gamos was well established—so we can only speculate as to its true origins.

MAGENTA: *I think, mythically, the attraction between the Goddess and the God is one of the building blocks of the Universe.*

RHOMYLLY FORBES: *Our wedding rings are engraved with* hieros gamos.

FRANCESCA GENTILLE: *Being raised Catholic, you have this sacred moment of the Mass, in the chalice and the wafer. It's this moment where you recognize this magical transformation . . . that this being, who is part divine and part human, sacrificed himself so that we could all be redeemed. . . . Well, in my perception, in the Wiccan service, the most sacred moment is the chalice and the blade. And the chalice and the blade . . . represent the womb and the phallus. They represent creation and creativity. In my belief, we are microcosms of the macrocosm, and*

55

every time we have sex, we are in a creative act. And every time we make love, we are like God, because it is an act of energetic creation.

HONEYBLOSSOM: *For me, the image of the Goddess and God uniting in sex is one of the central symbols of Pagan religion. . . . I think this is also connected to the Pagan idea that the mind-body earth-sky split is ultimately unhealthy—that is, that the body and spirit are not in opposition to each other, as much of the Judeo-Christian tradition would have it. Dirt, sex, body functions—all of these things can be holy for us. It's this idea of immanent divine, rather than transcendent divine.*

Although most traditions of Wicca place a heavy emphasis on cross-gender polarity, not all NeoPagans do.

OBERON ZELL-RAVENHEART: *I don't think that the [gender polarity, chalice/blade] thing is widespread through the larger Pagan community. It's not even in all branches of Witchcraft, just really every group or every tradition kind of makes its own statement on that subject. The kind of work that we do, that I've done magically, really isn't about that. It's about people finding the place within ourselves from which we can focus our power and energy individually. And the path that I've always followed is one which embraces the greatest possible diversity. We say that it's like weaving a tapestry. You want to have as many different kinds of threads as possible. And the fewer the colors of threads, the less interesting and more monochromatic the tapestry becomes. If you've only got one thread, you don't even have a pattern! We recognize the existence of polarity on countless levels, but the focus on just the gender polarity seems to miss the point. [*Jen: Or it's too restrictive.*] Right.*

*I regard all of this polarity stuff not as a conflict or a struggle, but as a dance, which is why I think the Yin-Yang symbol is such a nice one, because it's in motion . . . if it were two hemispheres—[*Jen: Like a cross*] Exactly, like a cross. It's static. It's conflicting motions. So that's kind of the way I see it. It's part of that ongoing relationship, but I have to be able to meet the Goddess and women in all aspects, and for* *the completion of Deity, at least in the Pagan perspective, all aspects must manifest. And the challenge in anything involving partnership, as in God/Goddess type stuff for Wiccans, or whatever it is, anything involving other things—the trick is to be able to match the dance, the moves in the dance. It's the foundation of courtship, and it's the foundation of magic.*

Gods as Our Lovers

The romantic, sexual love in the biblical Song of Solomon was said by rabbis to be a metaphor for the union between God and the soul of the individual. Later, the Christians whitewashed this same book even further to mean the union between God and church. There is a lot of religious literature about spiritual ecstatic union with the divine, but this is strictly a soul-level union; the body is not included.

In contrast, in a religious framework where you can have personal, intimate contact with deities, and where sex is sacred, we can relate to the Gods as more than just their children; we can relate to them as their lovers. This can make for some kick-ass fantasies. And in a magical framework, where you can manifest things just through visualization and the movement of energy, the line blurs between fantasy and reality. Are you just fantasizing about making mad passionate love with the Horned God, or are you really doing it?

> LEON: *I've had very intense "fantasies" about/with the Goddess Sekhmet.* At first I thought I was completely off my rocker. At the time I knew her as a Goddess of intense healing and occasional vengeance. After a few very intense "fantasies," I discovered she was also a Goddess*

---

*Egyptian Goddess of war and battle. She has a lioness's head.

of sensuality. If you like playful biting on the neck, you should try it with a lover who has six-inch fangs.

HONEYBLOSSOM: *I once unexpectedly fell into a trance while masturbating and had a powerful sexual/spiritual vision. I'm not sure I want to relate the details, but suffice it to say I have had a much stronger relationship with the God since then.*

KITTY: *[Do I fantasize about] Gods or Goddesses? Both! More than one at a time if I can! [*drools just thinking about it*]*

CAROL QUEEN: *The way that I was able, in a really biphobic lesbian environment, to begin to shift my notion of myself—not just my behavior, but my identity—was really through the erotic part of Wiccan liturgy or belief where the Goddess and the God are consorts, and the God is extremely important erotically. I'm not sure that I exactly fantasized him as my lover per se, but that meditation was very, very important to me at that point, and my spirituality in that period helped me transition around my public identity.*

I will be forgiven as a twenty-something lesbian being really impressed by the rampant Pan, but it could have been someone else, I suppose! [laughs] There's something about that image that just did it for me then, and you know what, I still get a little thrill when I see people dressed as Pan, at Pride parades, or Pagan parades, Burning Man, or wherever.

In *The New Bottoming Book*, Dossie Easton and Janet Hardy make the point that "fantasies have a lot in common with mythology: they are stories that people become attached to for a variety of reasons, they satisfy some sexual or psychological need or want in our (probably only partially conscious) minds, they are rich in symbolism and emotional texture."[16] Although most of us feel pretty comfortable making up our own sexual fantasies, even we creative NeoPagans might feel limited to using only established mythologies in ritual, meditation, spellwork, and liturgy. But the imagery we are drawn to is just as important as the content of our dreams. It bears attention.

Simply inviting a particular deity to be present with you when you make love, or dedicating your pleasure to him or her, can be a powerful experience.

PHIL BRUCATO: *By connecting with my Goddess through lovemaking, I can bring both my lover and myself to higher levels of pleasure.*

Although most deities have at least some sexual aspect, just like people, different deities have different flavors of sexuality. Aphrodite is usually seen as playful and passionate. Pan is more lusty and untamed. Kali is dark and dangerous.

Also, remember that we can always invite into our beds and become lovers with Gods and Goddesses *not* traditionally associated with sex. Death, prosperity, change, home and hearth, and even trickster energy can all be incorporated into one's practice of sacred sexuality. As polytheists, we honor the diversity and complexity of life. As sex-positive people, we must do the same thing for sexuality.

Finally, as nature worshippers, we can experience nature as a lover, too—symbolically or literally!

ANNIE SPRINKLE: *I have taught sex workshops for years. One of the things I would sometimes do is send everyone out into the woods to make love with something in nature. I'd tell them to lick a tree, eat a flower, caress that rock, rub your pussy on the rock, you know, so really making love with nature. People would come back to the group with the most incredible stories of having had some of the best sex they'd ever had in their lives. Beautiful magic happened. My specialty is just giving people permission to try things sexually. We're so often told what not to do sexually, lots of us need permission, believe it or not.*

Being Taken for a Ride

Many indigenous and shamanic religions incorporate elements of consensual spirit possession in their rituals. At these times, the individual offers up his or her body (and mind, to some extent) as a vessel for a God or other spirit to come through and move, speak, dance, or simply be present in a more physical form. The most well-known examples of this in the United States are when practitioners of Santeria and Voodoo are "ridden" by their Gods. It is usually a very dramatic and ecstatic experience for all involved.

Drawing down the moon or sun, in Wicca, is more closely descended from the spiritualist movement of the late nineteenth and early twentieth centuries than from shamanic religions, but the effect is similar. In this case, the priest or priestess traditionally invokes the God or Goddess into his or her partner, and then the deity is given the opportunity to do whatever he or she wants. This is also called "aspecting."

You need not see the Gods as literal entities in order to do this. They can be types of energies or even aspects of yourself; the effect will be largely the same.

MAGDALENE MERETRIX: *I view the Gods as symbols of particular currents of energy. So when I dedicate my sex work to the Goddess Babalon,* I am dedicating it to a particular current, not to a discrete external entity. When I channel the energies of Babalon, I am taking on a sacred role, much like an actress takes on a secular role on the stage, and allowing the current represented by the Godform Babalon to flow through me, influencing my actions and perceptions.*

---

*A Thelemic Goddess of sexuality.

In traditional Wicca, this sort of work is supposed to be something only for third-degree initiates—in other words, people who have been trained and are experienced in magic and energy work. But with the rise of eclectic Wiccan traditions and people who are self-trained, that restriction has flown out the window. Channeling and consensual possession is, in my opinion, higher-level type work. Some people may have a natural ability for it without training, but it's risky (psychologically, energetically, spiritually, and even physically) to share your body and mind with a discorporate entity.

LaSara Firefox: *There is a friend who is priest to my priestess self. When we are aspecting, it is nearly impossible to avoid being sexual, or at least sensual, with one another. . . . To aspect a deity is to take that deity on, to give that God or Goddess your body for his or her use. . . . For me, this practice is very intentional. Though I may vacate my body for long periods of time during the experience, I am nearly always very near by. And, I nearly always have the ability to stop a God from taking action with my body that I deem inappropriate. But it is still a learning process, and sometimes lines are crossed.*

So take it slowly and gradually. Inviting a deity to "be with you" is a good first step.

Sexually, we can channel deities or types of energies either consciously or accidentally; we may see our partners change and take on other faces and energies as well.

Magenta: *I frequently try to envision my partner as the God, and he envisions me as the Goddess. During or just after orgasm, we often say "Thou Art God" "Thou Art Goddess" to each other.*

Raven Kaldera: *I often envision my submissive partners as embodiments of All That Is Sacrificed That We May Live, and myself as the deity of death who receives that sacrifice. I am also a horse, in the*

Yoruba-faith sense that I loan out my body to deities who want to ride it (part of my deal with Hel*) and I have lent my body to a few for purposes of sex. And even being in the backseat, that was pretty awesome. Especially with Baphomet, who really knows how to have sex.

SHAI SHAHAR: *There are times when Cora and I are making love that she seems to shape-shift, where her face seems to "morph" into the faces of younger or different women . . . into "eternal" woman. It is as if she goes through all the archetypes, that I am making love to just one or more facets of the feminine divine. It does not always happen by design . . . in fact, for me, at least, it hardly works that way. Beyond that I can recall a . . . moment in my youth when the very same thing happened to me . . . when "she" became She. And that is about as best I can describe it.*

RHOMYLLY FORBES: *I know I've, at minimum, "shared my body" with the Goddess during intercourse on Beltane Eve . . . I know when Alex is sharing his body with the Dagda.[†] His eyes turn a really bright green, instead of the blue-gray they normally are.*

PHIL BRUCATO: *Quite often, I see [my partner] as my Muse—a tall, fit, barefooted woman with wild hair, fierce eyes, and a wicked smile. Most of my lovers have fit that mold to some degree, so they meld with that image in my mind.*

It doesn't have to be specific deities that come into you at these times. It can also be elements, hidden aspects of yourself, and/or animal energies.

DOSSIE EASTON: *I do a lot of shapeshifting when I play. One time I turned to an eagle when I was tied to a table. I want to tell you, that*

---

*Norse Goddess of death and the afterlife.
[†]Irish Earth and Father God.

doesn't work. Having your wings tied down is really peculiar. The wrong body type. And the noises are very hard on the throat. I turn into snakes, and usually lizards, because if I'm tied down, because lizards have appendages. A lot of times I feel Big Snakey* running right through me.

FRANCESCA GENTILLE: *I feel like there's a point in lovemaking, when I'm really open to the universe and my beloved, when what there is, is acceptance and flow, that there's a point where I'm not making love; I am lovemaking. I am the force of creation. And at that time, when I'm with my beloved, his face can shift. Like at one moment, I can see the child in him, and sometimes I might see a past life in him. It's like different visages drop over him.*

If only *you* take on God/dess energy, then you can enjoy the sense of oneness with that energy. Alone, you can pleasure yourself and worship the God/dess through your own body. With a partner, you can act in the role of sacred harlot, providing a link between your partner and the divine. If only your *partner* does so, you can be the worshipper, making an "offering" at your favorite altar.

WYRDOTTER: *[My partner is] a beautiful, full-figured, curvy woman, and it's easy to see some of the more bountiful images of the Goddess in her. For centuries, the Goddess was portrayed as plump, rounded, full-breasted, full-hipped, welcoming, and my beloved is all these things, so yes, occasionally, I can see Her in her.*

---

*Kundalini energy.

63

3. PAGAN RELATIONSHIPS 🌿

IF THERE'S SEX TO BE HAD, there's a relationship to have it in, whether a long-term committed monogamous marriage, a one-night stand, or something in between. After all, there are still frameworks, boundaries, decisions, labels, and negotiations.

Being in a relationship can easily be perceived as sacred or magical work—even an initiatory path. First of all, there's the work involved in the relationship's maintenance and repair. You are making yourself vulnerable, risking body and soul, and giving from your own personal energy to make something that wasn't there before. Second, there's the whole hieros gamos concept of fusion between opposites. You emerge from this experience changed, hopefully for the better. It's not hard to perceive relationship as sacred and magical.

But how can a one-night stand possibly have magic in it? Where other religions may give a nod to the holiness of sex—Judaism, for instance—it is only within a monogamous heterosexual relationship. And our secular culture teaches us that only monogamous, long-term unions have value. But looking into human history, we learn that "requirements for sexual fidelity to one partner are linked with sex-negative attitudes and attempts to control sexuality in the interest of society. 'Control' is the key word here—in particular the control of reproduction in the interest of primogeniture or other dynastic goals."[1]

The trick is to find the source of these assumptions: values that we have picked up from our culture or our religions of origin, which may or may not match what we believe is right. In practicing a nature religion, we look to the natural world for inspiration. Some animals pair-bond for life; some don't. Some humans are comfortable in a long-term relationship with one other person; some find it very difficult. To automatically judge our natural inclinations that do not conform to the accepted norms of conduct as a sign of psychological immaturity or "sex addiction" is to blindly accept what we have been taught.

"All acts of love and pleasure are My rituals," says the Charge of the Goddess. Looking beyond assumptions, we discover that there are actually a myriad of ways to express love and sexuality, and they can all potentially have magic and value. Any relationship between any number of consenting adults can fit nicely into the Pagan path, when entered into and conducted with respect and honesty.

> DON KRAIG: *I am a human and follow the path of humanity. I have been monogamous, polyamorous, polyfidelitous, and just about everything else that has/hasn't a name. The thing which is most important to me is honoring the partners I am with and the Goddess within them. Each act of love brings me closer to the divine.*

NeoPagans run the gamut in terms of our relationship structures. Many of us are quite traditional, dating only one person at a time, getting married and perhaps having children, and intending to stay together for a lifetime. Others may choose to stay single, or commit to more than one person, or have one primary partner and one or more other lovers.

Finding a Tribe

The usual alternative to a nuclear family is the single-mother home. Conservatives assert that this structure is less than ideal, and I agree with them. It's damaging to the mother, who is frequently overwhelmed and exhausted, and has no life of her own.

It's damaging to the kids, who must rely only on this overburdened person. They typically don't get enough time with the father—every other weekend, in my experience and opinion, is not sufficient. Single mothers without a support network are especially screwed. I was raised by a single mother with no support network who was clinically depressed throughout my childhood. I am a single mother myself, and were it not for my wonderful support network (and fantastic co-parents) . . . well, I don't even want to hypothesize.

The solution to the problem of the "broken home," for many conservatives, seems to be to cajole, guilt, and force people back into their idea of what a family is supposed to look like. Monogamous dyads can be wonderful, but are definitely hard to sustain for long periods. The result is that the more people strive for the ideal of the nuclear family, the more people get divorced.

And so, as NeoPagans, we look to the past for inspiration, and there we find the concept of the tribe, and/or the extended family. When we were hunter-gatherers, we lived in tribes, for cooperation and protection. In an agrarian culture, extended and large families were necessary to work the land. But with the industrial revolution, families became smaller and people more isolated. Living in our modern society, it's no longer necessary or even desirable to form tribes in the classic sense of small groups that function as a unit 24/7. However, we can form tribes in other ways, which provide the support and love that we need, combined with a flexibility that isn't found in the traditional family structure. One of the ways to create tribe is through polyamory.

Polyamory

In the 1960s, Morning Glory Zell was searching for a word to define her and Oberon's consensual practice of nonmonogamy.

But "nonmonogamy" was a negative, and she wanted a positive. She found it by combining the Greek word for "many" and the Latin word for "love": polyamory. It should be distinguished from "polygamy" in that it does not necessarily involve multiple *marriages* but rather multiple *loves*. Dossie Easton, independently, at around the same time, was crafting the path of "the ethical slut" (which became the title of her coauthored book in 1998):

DOSSIE EASTON: *It was kind of conventional back then [the late sixties], and I still think it is, in many places, where people are doing basically pick-up or sport fucking, to withhold affection until you were securely in a certain kind of relationship. And I decided that . . . since I needed love and affection in my life . . . I would be loving and affectionate in relationships that were not necessarily primary. It didn't protect me any to withhold it. It didn't do anything for me, and if I wanted a community that was as loving, and sweet and intimate as I wanted it to be, then I was going to have to write a new script for how we do affection, and love, and caring, and like that. So I did.*

As far as I know, NeoPaganism is the only religion that fully accepts polyamory as a legitimate relationship structure. Because of this, there is a fair amount of cross-pollination between Pagan and poly communities—Pagans discover polyamory, and poly folks discover Paganism.

The only thing polyamorous relationships have in common, besides the honesty and communication, is that they are not composed of a monogamous dyad. A polyamorous family may be composed of three or more adults who do not have relationships outside the group (also called polyfidelitous) and may be involved with each other in any combination. A single polyamorous person may have many "fuck-buddies," or sexual friendships. A married couple (as primaries) may each have secondary lovers, or only one of them might. A polyamorous person might even be celibate and define "many loves" in a platonic sense, although this is very rare, because, let's face it, most people want to have sex. Unlike standard monogamy, in which you are either single or "taken," polyamory opens up the spectrum to include a practically infinite array of possibilities, which can be made-to-order based on the individuals' needs and preferences.

> RAVEN KALDERA: *Right now I am married legally to my wife—we've been together for eleven years—and in a contract situation with my boyfriend. We all live together and sleep in the same bed. We are a mostly polyfidelitous family—by that I mean that they are both polyfidelitous with me by choice, and I have a couple of occasional outside fuck-buddies, so I'm technically polyamorous. We are all old hands at the poly thing, and we negotiate well, and all love and respect each other, so we do okay.*

Any type of limits, guidelines, or boundaries might be placed on polyamorous relationships, from no intercourse, to required barrier use, to no overnight guests, to "all new partners must be approved by the primary." Polyamory is about mutual respect, individual freedom, and being able to experience pleasure and connection with more than one other person.

Since most adults today have not been raised to be poly-amorous, they find themselves making a conscious choice to practice a different relationship style. People come to polyamory for different reasons. Some simply find themselves unsuited to monogamy; it feels more natural for them to be polyamorous.

> OBERON ZELL-RAVENHEART: *When I was a little kid, my first childhood crushes were with two girls simultaneously. I always dated at least two girls at a time, all the way through high school. My first year in college (1961), I read Heinlein's* Stranger in a Strange Land, *and thought the attitudes expressed regarding polyamory, line*

marriages, etc., all made perfect sense. I turned others on to Heinlein, and founded the Church of All Worlds based on those precepts. And I and many others have lived that way consciously (and conscientiously) ever since. And we've found that it works, if you do it with integrity and love. . . . [When] Morning Glory and I met . . . it was the Pagan romance of the century. And practically the first thing she said to me was, "As much as I love you, and know that you are my soulmate, I cannot be in a monogamous relationship." And we never have been.

JEZEBEL DAWN BLESSING: I was monogamous (serial monogamy) until I was introduced to polyamory by a new boyfriend, and I have been polyamorous ever since. I find that polyamory is my natural state of being and have been quite happy with the fruits of my labors. When I was monogamous, what used to make me so miserable was that I would meet someone new and like him enough to want to start an intimate relationship, but I would either have to cheat on, or break up with, my current boyfriend. But this was not how I wanted to conduct a relationship; I felt that these choices compromised my integrity, hurt the people that I love, and genuinely made me look bad in the eyes of my peers. So after a major break-up with my first live-in boyfriend (it had nothing to do with being unfaithful), I decided that I was going to remain single until I met someone that I really wanted to spend my life with. I met another man about a year later, but I did not want to become monogamous again, so when he said, "That's okay, because I'm polyamorous," I wanted to know what that was.

DANIEL DEL VECCHIO: I am polyamorous. To me it is like being bisexual. I have always been both, and it took me a long, long time to figure that out. The polyamory I practice is the kind I call "thelemic" after [Aleister] Crowley's Law of Thelema: "Do as thy wilt shall be the whole of the Law. Love is the Law; love under will." I refuse to be owned by anyone, and I refuse to own anyone, not sexually or any other way.

SHAI SHAHAR: *I'd describe myself as a former serial-monogamist who cheated a bit on the side. If I had to do it all over again, I'd do it honest . . . I'd do exactly what I did ten years later with Cora: show her an artist's rendering of a Pagan orgy on a postcard, and invite her to go there with me. "I will give you all that I possess—my strength, my faith, my heart, and my protection—if you will join me freely in this room to celebrate as they are celebrating." Since then, I've gone on to be a polyamorous but faithful "consort" who is very (and I mean very) committed to his partner. We swing and swap to be sure, but still prefer each other's charms and arms. Our hearts and minds are seriously intertwined.*

Coming to live, work, and play in Amsterdam, which is arguably the best city in Europe to experience Paganism as a lifestyle, helped me to throw off some of my American focus on the merely physical or one-dimensional view of sex. It also helped enormously in the shedding of my (Israeli sun-dried) Jewish guilt. When I got over guilt, I got over insecurity. When I got over insecurity, I got over my jealousy, too . . . and also found it less necessary to lie about intimate feelings and my penchant for involving myself with "fatal attractions." I came to realize that bodies are meant for sharing, along with love and pleasure. I felt a strong need to seek and provide that pleasure on a guilt-free basis. To connect. Mostly, I learned the value of self-respect over self-recrimination, and that freed me to enjoy the "totality of it all." And that's when life became "magical" again for me, the way it was when I was five years old . . . and thirteen. Full of erotic possibilities.

Between all the stories I've heard from clients and intimates, and all the science I've read concerning the biological imperatives of male and female, the behavioral patterns associated with mating, and the effects on sexual health and development of children raised in communal environments, I came to believe a polyamorous way of living is the most suited to our species and our times.

To many NeoPagans, polyamory is a way to build networks and extended family, creating a modern sort of "tribe." In *The Ethical Slut*, Easton writes, "It is customary, in my brand new culture, for one's lovers to welcome a new lover as, not competition, but an addition to the community."[2]

RAVEN KALDERA: *To me, [polyamory] really is about wanting a Pagan tribe. I think I come at being poly not just from being Pagan, but from being a queer Pagan, who is not necessarily going to breed. I mean, I did breed once, but neither of my lovers are going to breed, and the way that nonbreeding queers form tribes is through the bonds of sex. Not necessarily current sex—it could be your ex-lovers, or your lovers' lovers, and that sort of thing. Your tribe is this network of people who have mostly had sex with each other, to one extent or another. You could count less than six steps. And there is something very primitive, and very tribal, very primordial, about it. We're replacing blood kinship with sex.*

LEON: *We're both open to expanding our family by the inclusion of other adults, but we prefer quality to expedience. The concept of tribe is something that resonates across the Pagan spectrum. I believe that polyfamily models are one good way to make some of those visions a reality.*

Both polyamory and monogamy as relationship styles offer benefits, liabilities, and opportunities for spiritual growth. It has been argued that between monogamy and polyamory, one is more "natural" than the other.

SHAI SHAHAR: *I ask everyone not to underestimate the size of the human heart, how capable we are of loving many, and very deeply at that. Remember the times of ten-child families? If a mother can love ten children, is her heart not also big enough to love two men? Can a father*

*of ten not love two women, or more? Not only [do] Pagans say yes,
but so do the early authors of the Bible (and the Book of Mormon . . .
and the Koran). This idea that we are only suited for one partner "'til
death do us part" is against all that our instincts tell us is the natural
way of things. I believe we should trust our instincts and build a society
where they are our trusted companions, not our inherited demons.*

To my mind, this issue is moot. If your relationship style
requires superhuman effort to sustain, then it's not natural for you.
It's one thing to ignore your attraction to someone outside your
relationship so that you can focus on the dyad, but if you are
feeling constantly tempted and are becoming miserable because
of it, then there's a problem. If you are polyamorous, but keep
getting derailed by feelings of possessiveness, fear, and jealousy,
then there's a problem. The problem may be with the relationship
style, or it may be something going on within yourself—deter-
mining what's right for you requires serious self-examination.

The benefits of polyamory are fairly obvious: First, it's lovely to
have the opportunity to allow one's relationships to move in
whatever direction they want to move. If you're bisexual, or if
you have sexual needs that can't be fulfilled by your primary partner, this may be the relationship style that seems most comfortable for you.

> DAVE SYLVIA: *One benefit is that one partner may be better at doing a
> certain type of magic than another, and one may be more spiritually
> attuned than another, but you don't have to settle. You can have the best
> of all worlds!*

Second, the more people with whom you are intimate—emotionally and/or sexually—the more you have the potential to
grow as a person. Each partner has something unique to teach
and give you. (Of course, this is potential. If you're just having
recreational sex, then that's perfectly acceptable in Paganism and

poly, but there probably won't be much growth involved, except in your skills as a lover.) In many ways, polyamory is the ultimate "pro-choice" relationship. In a monogamous viewpoint, people naturally expect sex to be a part of a close and intimate relationship between people who are attracted to each other's gender. But in polyamory, although you are not expected to refrain from sex, neither are you expected to *have* sex. Opposite-gender platonic friendships can be deep and fulfilling, without the risk of a primary partner feeling threatened, as often happens in monogamy. Likewise, polyamorous partners may choose not to have lovers outside the primary relationship, for any length of time.

Polyamory rejects the notion that the ultimate goal of every relationship is to be the "one-and-only-until-death-do-us-part" kind of bond. No one expects you to live in the same town or work at the same job for your entire life; why should you be expected to have the same partner? Polyamory allows for lovers (and friends, too, for that matter) to remain in our lives for precisely as long as they should, whether that's for one evening or seventy-five years. It's a very organic relationship structure, nicely compatible with a nature-based religion.

LaSara Firefox: *Being able to love whoever I feel moved to, whenever I feel moved to, is an honoring of the divine in every person I choose to love.*

Magenta: *I think polyamory and polytheism are related; I can't imagine sticking to just one God or one guy.*

Diversity is valued and cherished in both polyamory and polytheism. When you have a multiplicity of relationships, you get to become close with many different kinds of people, who are equally precious. When you are with different partners, you show different faces of yourself—all equally precious. Yet in both polyamory and polytheism, there is also an underlying unity. Although someone may have a multiplicity of relationships, the same elements—love, respect, and passion—run through them all. And the center remains the individual. Whereas many people tend to lose themselves in a monogamous pair bond, in poly-amory, the individual is more likely to retain his identity. Many poly couples who cohabitate nonetheless each have their own bedrooms. Our culture gives us the message that we are not whole on our own and that we need a partner to complete us, to make us happy. When the center is yourself, you are free to have as many partners as you want, or none.

Of course, polyamory comes with its own challenges; it's not all one big free-love fest. Even casual relationships or encounters have ethical considerations.

DOSSIE EASTON: *I do not approve of fucking for reasons that are not about connecting with somebody, or that are not clean, or equal, or if somebody is being treated as a thing, or an object, or something that will give you more points in a status hierarchy. I don't disapprove of sport fucking; I have played with many people who essentially were one-night stands or whatever. But somewhere in my career I made a personal limit that I was not going to play with anybody that I . . . wasn't at least open to playing with again . . . because, doing that, I had wound up with too many people calling me haplessly on the phone, over and over, that I didn't want to see again. I figured out that it was unkind of me to take somebody home because we were having a hot time at a party, when that might have consequences for the other person.*

Because there are many different ways to interpret "poly-amory," it requires negotiation.

FRANCESCA GENTILLE: *Most Pagans, in my perception, whether or not they have ongoing multiple relationships, have situations that they consider "between the worlds," that don't count. So it doesn't count if*

74

we're at a Pagan festival, and I take another lover. It doesn't count if we're at the Renaissance fair, and I take another lover. It doesn't count if maybe it's one of my circle-mates. In the California area, there are several informal sort of sacred sexual communities—like "The Temple of"-this, or "The Divine Rites"-that—where people get together and have sacred erotic sexual encounters. And those don't count.

In any relationship, most of us encounter situations that make us jealous. Most of us can be possessive. We all require some negotiation, definition of boundaries, and communication of needs, wants, and feelings. Even if the relationship is a "casual" one, this stuff is necessary. To be in a successful relationship of any sort requires that people know themselves really well and be open to learning about their partners. The more people we add to the mix, the more complex and challenging this task becomes. In a group of three people, there are actually three pairs of relationships going on, within which all of these things have to be shared and discussed. It can be a lot of work.

LEON: *In a nutshell, if you're not good at relationships, you'll be horrible at being poly.*

MAGDALENE MERETRIX: *We got together while I was still active in sex work, so I had many sexual partners outside the relationship, and we both agreed that each was free to have sex outside the relationship . . . but . . . at this point (we've been together for five years), neither of us has actively pursued other sexual relationships (with the exception of my sex at work), because we both feel that keeping a relationship alive and vital takes a lot of time and energy, and we'd each currently rather put that time and energy into our relationship with each other rather than increase the amount of time and work it takes to also keep any secondary relationships healthy. . . . Between our relationship with each other, our work, our creative/artistic pursuits, and our mutual and individual friendships, we just don't have the time left over to court*

*others and maintain full-blown sexual/emotional relationships
with others.*

A responsible practice of polyamory forces us to take a hard
look at the very things most people try very hard *not* to see. It's
critical that poly people be extremely conscientious with regard
to safer sex. To this end, it's necessary to have very frank discussions about risk factors and safer sex precautions (discussed in
more detail later on).

> FRANCESCA GENTILLE: *Before the whole poly thing became so big,
> twenty years ago, I was looking at our community and saying, "Hmm,
> we're a group of really friendly people." [laughs] And there was a time
> period about twenty years ago, where one person got chlamydia, and
> within a month, forty people had chlamydia. And it just spread like
> wildfire throughout the community. And this is pre-AIDS and
> everything, so people weren't being very careful. So I think safer sex
> is really important.*

Likewise, it's good practice before becoming intimate to nego-
tiate what you would prefer to do in the event of an unexpected
pregnancy. Having to deal with these potentially scary and
embarrassing issues can be seen as another type of initiatory
experience—one that is challenging, but ultimately can change us
for the better.

On the other hand, challenges that may not have such positive
results are the ones that arise from the practice of a relationship
style that most of your culture regards as sinful and/or immoral.
People have lost jobs, lost custody of their kids, and so on. It's
worth asking yourself, if you are already a practicing Pagan, do
you want to take on even more stigma by being polyamorous,
too? Sure, you can just be discreet about who you date, but it's
tricky to be in the closet if you want to live in the same home as
your loves. Where there may be precedents and structures in

place to protect gays and lesbians from discrimination, there is nothing of the sort for poly folks. And you never know whose buttons your lifestyle is going to push. Someone who's perfectly laid-back about homosexuality may be disgusted and horrified by the notion of nonmonogamy. So tread with caution.

JUDY HARROW: *In 1993, at the Parliament of the World's Religions, Pagans were just sort of introducing ourselves to the larger religious community. It was described by some people I spoke to as our "coming out party." Covenant of the Goddess had a hospitality suite at the hotel. Apparently, the rumor went around that there were orgies going on in the CoG suite! So some reporters showed up at midnight, to find a bunch of fully clothed people, fatigued almost to the point of coma, sitting there staring into space, too tired to even converse, forget about orgies. Well, one reporter thought he was going to get a juicy sound bite out of me by asking, "What do you people think about adultery?" I knew what he was looking for, and I am, of course, polyamorous, so what I said to him was, "I believe in keeping my promises."* [Jen: Did he get what you meant?] *Not at all. The idea that somebody might have had a polyamorous contract, and be engaged in sex outside their base relationship, without in any way breaking a promise, was completely off the radar scope for him. He thought I'd said I believed in monogamy.*

As with any difficult task, polyamory provides abundant opportunities for growth. It promotes development of good communication skills. It forces people to become aware of their feelings, including negative ones like jealousy and possessiveness. It makes speaking up for one's needs absolutely critical. In that sense, the poly path can be seen as a path of initiation and magical challenge, with the potential for great reward.

KITTY: *One spiritual "problem" with polyamory, which is actually a great benefit, is that our hearts are challenged to open in ways and*

77

toward people that we otherwise might have easily avoided. The Pagan ideal of "Love is the Law" goes a long way when one finds oneself faced with a SO's (significant other) OSO (other significant other) that we simply don't like or get along with. Personality differences are not an excuse for hatred. When love is the law, all actions and reactions and decisions must be scrutinized with Radical Honesty (a personal term of mine),* and the heart and mind are given another opportunity to expand.

JEZEBEL DAWN BLESSING: Over the last six years, I have learned to conduct multiple simultaneous relationships by learning communication skills, schedule-juggling, and also by being genuine with my expression and emotional involvement. It might be difficult for some people to see the magical benefits of a polyamorous relationship, but I see that by conducting multipartner relationships, I have created pathways to understanding myself better, to creating and maintaining positive relationship energy, and it has helped my personal integrity and my overall feeling of well being. I have to be truthful, knowledgeable, and able to communicate my needs and desires clearly, as well as being happy or finding satisfaction with what I receive. These are all valuable skills if you are a practicing Witch, and greatly aid in my relationships with the Gods and Goddesses within myself.

OBERON ZELL-RAVENHEART: [Jen: What are the challenges you find in polyamory?] Just keeping everyone talking through everything that comes up, creating deep mutual commitments, mediating disputes toward the most harmonious and felicitous outcome for all, being deeply honest with ourselves as well as each other, and always working towards the manifestations of all our hearts' desires.

---

*It's also a book by Brad Blanton, *Radical Honesty: How to Transform Your Life by Telling the Truth.*

Of course, all this talking and negotiating can become tiresome.

LaSara Firefox: There is a tendency to overanalyze things in the Pagan community, and a tendency toward huge amounts of processing (up to three degrees removed sometimes, with the poly situation: like, my boyfriend's girlfriend's boyfriend wanting to process with me about the relationship situation). I don't often feel like I have the time, energy, devotion, or concentration required. I process with my husband, my kids, my parents, and assorted other near and dear friends. I already have my hands full without building a network of commitment through sex. In some ways I prefer the quick and dirty—or the easy, at least.

Does polyamory work? Sometimes! Relationships end for a huge variety of reasons, and only one of those possibilities is that the relationship style was a poor choice for the people involved. When a monogamous relationship fails, rarely do people blame it on the relationship's exclusivity.

I'd just like to note here that although polyamory may seem related to swinging, in reality, they are quite different. Swinging tends to be much more sex-oriented. Although poly people may have fuck-buddies, their relationships contain more potential to become romantic and emotional. Swingers tend to reserve that sort of thing for their primaries, placing their swinging experience in the category of recreation. Swingers are almost entirely heterosexual couples in which many of the women are bisexual but few of the men are (or admit it). Polyamory is pansexual, recognizing the wide range of sexual orientations from straight to gay and everything in between, and recognizing different gender orientations as well. Swingers almost always have sex as couples with other couples, as a straightforward swap. There are no such restrictions on poly folks.

The Magic of Monogamy

Monogamy may have been invented as a way to control women and keep track of progeny, but it has survived as a practice because it has a lot of things going for it. Spiritually and magically speaking, dedicating oneself to one person (whether for life, or for the forseeable future) is a very powerful act.

> ANNIE SPRINKLE: *Around the age of forty, I stopped being very promiscuous. To have sex with dozens of people became less interesting. I'd been doing that for twenty-three years. Suddenly, I became more interested in focusing all my energy into one person, and going as deep as I could go with that person. It became much more of an adventure not to be promiscuous. . . . One day, my partner and I might open it up and include sex with others, but for now, we are so totally enthralled and consumed with each other, other lovers would only detract.*

The benefits of monogamy include a sense of security and safety. You don't have to worry about feeling jealous or challenged in your relationships as much as the poly folks (although it's still going to crop up). You don't get distracted by all the potential partners, dating, psychodrama, and breakups. You have the opportunity to become very deeply intimate with one other person, giving him all your romantic/sexual time and energy, and receiving all of his. You also don't have to worry about using latex barriers, assuming you and your partner are disease-free. You don't have to worry about the implications of an accidental pregnancy with the "wrong" partner. And then there's the fact that your relationship style is the one vastly more accepted by the mainstream.

Some NeoPagans feel it's more natural for them to be monogamous.

ANAHITA-GULA: *I find I can be fond of many people and express this in myriad ways, but I can only find it in my spirit to share my body, mind, and soul at once, with one person (male).*

RHOMYLLY FORBES: *I am monogamous now, but was polyfidelitous for many years. Personally, I find a truer union with the other person and the Other during sexual activity as a monogamist. It has been my experience with polyfidelity that someone always, always is unhappy and gets hurt.*

WYRDOTTER: *I'm monogamous. It's a choice, in one sense, and honestly, since I met my beloved, I haven't wanted anyone else anyway. It's very important to us, not in a possessive way so much as there are so many pitfalls to multiple-partner activities, and you can never be completely certain of what that third or fourth person has on her agenda. Neither of us condemn people who choose nonmonogamous paths, but we are both happier being monogamous. Besides, there's enough to learn about one other person in a lifetime!*

Monogamy has plenty of its own challenges. It's hard to remain with one partner alone for your entire life, even when you discover things you don't like about him, and even when you become attracted to other people. Another significant hurdle is to overcome sexual ruts and boredom. And it's a challenge for many women to be part of a couple without feeling their sense of self submerged under that of their partner. One possibly unexpected difficulty is being "out and proud" as a monogamous person in an increasingly polycentric Pagan community!

The opportunities for growth within a monogamous relationship include learning to foster intimacy, accepting someone with all her faults, learning to be vulnerable and open when your partner gets to know you better than anyone else does, and also learning how to compromise and accept that your partner cannot fulfill all your needs.

> LaSara Firefox: *Monogamy can be an intensely powerful dedication. Vowing to be sexual with only one partner can be a deeply bonding experience that can lead to deep work, especially if the individuals involved are working with the Gods in their relationship. Trust is not an easily found commodity in this time and place, and sometimes true monogamy can bring one to that trust more easily.*

Leaving Room for Change

Ideally, we should leave ourselves open to have whatever kinds of relationships are right for us at the time. In the same way that polytheism can encompass monotheism, so polyamory can encompass monogamy. Any nature-oriented path must leave room for growth and change over time. There is no reason why a relationship style or structure shouldn't change according to the needs of the people in that relationship.

Regardless of whether you're strictly monogamous or a raving slut, magically speaking, it's important to make your relationship style a conscious choice, made with enough relevant information, experience, and self-awareness. Most of us choose monogamy because it's the only choice we perceive as available; this is not conscious choice. Likewise, some people feel pressured into polyamory because "all the other Pagans are doing it." This is also not conscious choice. Look into your own heart and look at your history. What went wrong in your past relationships? What do you hope to gain from, and give to, future relationships? What sorts of things do you value in relationships? Do not dismiss any of your personal realities as invalid. Having a high sex drive is a perfectly good reason to seek out multiple partners. You are not any less of a person because you like to fuck a lot. Likewise, being extremely insecure is a fine reason to be monogamous. You are not any less "evolved" because you get upset when you see your partner kissing someone else. Honor yourself by being honest with yourself about who you really are and what you really need in a relationship.

Partners: Pagan and Not

Interfaith relationships are common everywhere, and Pagans are no exception to this trend. It can cause problems, but it can also be an opportunity for growth on both sides. When both partners are Pagan, the shared sensitivity to energy can make for some amazing sexual experiences.

PHIL BRUCATO: *Although nearly all of my lovers have been essentially Pagan (in heart, practice, or both), my sweetheart Francesca actually is a sexual priestess. That's given a whole new sensua-spiritual dimension to lovemaking. We both actively integrate divine visualization, appreciation, invocations, energy work, and soul-sharing into our loveplay. The results have been incredible, even slightly addictive.*

HONEYBLOSSOM: *My last monogamous relationship (with a non-Pagan) was seriously rocked when my partner found out that I had practiced group sex in a ritual setting. I was monogamous with him, but he couldn't stand the thought that I had ever done that before. Clearly, it was a difference in attitudes about sex. I think that we both took it seriously, but we just had very different interpretations about the right context for it. I had also wanted to be polyamorous, and he wasn't comfortable with that.*

WYRDOTTER: *My Beloved still has a lot of issues from her particularly repressive fundamentalist upbringing (according to the church in which she was raised, she's going to hell just for having her ears pierced, never mind that sleeping-with-a-woman part!). Sometimes, that early indoctrination still causes her to have problems with inhibitions and intimacy, but she's been working on it for as long as we've been together, and there has been amazing growth. Not that just agreeing with me constitutes growth, but growth in recognizing when she's being ruled by those old lessons instead of her own feelings, and learning how to go with what her heart tells her, not what her old pastor told her.*

Partners who are sympathetic and supportive, even if not Pagan, can still participate in sex-related rituals.

JEZEBEL DAWN BLESSING: *I have spent all night in sexual marathon with a partner to dedicate my temple to Ishtar; we did anything and everything that pleased us, and that temple held that charge for months after I had left and moved on.* [Jen: Was your partner also involved in the magical work, or was he participating only as your lover?] *He was participating in the magical act more as a vessel for the energies and as a catalyst for my magic. He does not share the same beliefs as I do, but he was willing to recognize and worship the Goddess within me.*

Safer Sex

Since the Stone Age, sex and death have been intimately linked. Not only was sex possibly a first step toward death—giving birth at that time was certainly a huge risk—but the two were linked just by virtue of their places in the cycle of life. In this time of AIDS, the connection between sex and death has become even more literal: Sex can kill you. There are gay men who respond to the fear this induces by going out of their way to get infected with HIV, and some who simply choose not to use protection, resigning themselves to catching the illness eventually. Others simply prefer to exist in willful ignorance and just not think about it. Some people respond to these risks by shutting down sexually. These choices can be very destructive. The NeoPagan viewpoint is to be aware of the risks, accept the dark side of sexuality, and proceed to enjoy one's sexuality educated and protected.

I asked the folks I interviewed whether it was their perception that most Pagans practice safer sex. I got about a fifty-fifty split between "Yes, I think so" and "No, not in my experience."

SHAI SHAHAR: *I wouldn't know or claim that Pagans practice "safer" sex, like in the standard "we use condoms and wash often" context. But I would venture to say that they practice more "conscious" sex . . . and that means Pagan sex-practitioners and practices are probably safer.*

RHOMYLLY FORBES: *It has been my experience that the really spiritually connected ones do [practice safer sex], and the ones who use Paganism as an excuse to fuck-at-will tend not to.*

Of course, monogamy or polyfidelity between STD-free people is a great way to avoid having to use latex barriers.

JACQUI OMI: *There was a young woman who wanted to have sex with my husband, before we were married, and he was just nuts about her, and I said, "Fine, as long as you protect yourself. Don't let me get in the way," because I never want to dictate how anybody else practices his sexuality. But he sat down [and listed] just the partners he knew that she'd had, and the partners he knew they'd had, and came up with fifty-nine, and he said, "I'm not willing to take that risk."*

Some Pagans are of the perception that using latex barriers "kills the magic," either literally or figuratively, and for that reason they get lax about safer sex.

RAVEN KALDERA: *Part of Paganism is this whole bucolic "sex in the woods" fantasy, this sixties free love thing, which is nice and everything—I mean, the spirit of Beltane, you know, run off in the woods and have sex, and people want to live that, except rubber gets in the way. It really does, and a lot of them are willing to dispense with the rubber "just this time, just this once, it probably won't matter, it's a low-risk kind of thing," in order to get that, because it's so important to them. A lot of them come out of really repressed situations. This is what I think they're saying to themselves: "I really want and need this experience, and I'm willing to risk my life for it."*

Some Pagans have the stupid idea that God/dess will protect them from disease, which is stupid—God/dess created viruses just like she created you, and she likes them just as well as she likes you. There was a rumor going around that if you do it during sacred sex in a cast circle, via the Great Rite, that you can't get diseases. There was an article about it in Green Egg *with some safe sex educator getting up and saying, "You people are idiots!" and totally refuting that. I was horrified that it needed to be refuted.*

FRANCESCA GENTILLE: *I really have been sitting in a room where people have said that they practice intuitive safe sex: "If I intuit that you're healthy, and that you have no virology that could be negative to me, then I'm not going to worry about it."*

No, they didn't have latex barriers in the "good old days" of pagan Europe, but they sure as hell had STDs and unplanned pregnancies. Hey, let's not overromanticize the past. Things were cold, dirty, and very unpleasant in many ways in ancient pagan times. And now we are happy to avail ourselves of the blessings of modern life, yet we are reluctant to make some of the compromises that modern life entails. Fortunately, we know how to avoid catching STDs. Unfortunately, getting in good with the Gods isn't one of them. There is no reason that latex barriers can't be used in any sacred sexual practice.

The other part of people's aversion to safer sex, in my opinion, comes from a very narrow viewpoint of what "sex" entails. Most of these diseases can only be transmitted by genital-to-genital contact. A few of them can theoretically be transmitted also through oral-genital contact, but it's less likely. Now, you say, "If I can't have my dick in someone's mouth," or "If I can't have some-one's dick in my pussy," what on earth is left for you to do? And I say unto you, "Think outside the box." You may be pleasantly surprised.

ANNIE SPRINKLE: *I had a lover, Marco Vassi . . . who got AIDS. We wanted to continue having sex, but we stopped having intercourse, or oral sex. Ultimately, we had better sex, more profound, deeper, more intimate sex . . . because we became more creative and learned how to be really intimate without fucking and sucking.*

All my nonmonogamous interviewees were stringent about safer sex precautions with anyone other than their primaries.

DAVE SYLVIA: *My primary and I use condoms with everyone except each other. We are also conscious in general about not rushing into a sexual space with new partners, until we have had time to check them out and ask some questions about their sexual history. It's important to have boundaries that create safety for the people involved, so that one can relax and open up to the magic.*

DANIEL DEL VECCHIO: *I am in a condom pact with my primary alone. We both agree to use condoms for vaginal or anal penetration with all others. I sometimes use condoms for oral sex with men who I don't know extensively yet. I carry condoms (including flavored ones and my favorite types) with me everywhere (you just never know . . .).*

FRANCESCA GENTILLE: *In my particular group, we'll have safe sex meetings among six, eight, ten people, to talk, and get huge whiteboards out [laughs] and talk about, "Okay, who's lovers with who, and how many lovers, and where are you fluid-bonded, and where aren't you, and are you practicing frottage or not, and do we think that frottage is okay?" And we'll have huge discussions, and people will go to the CDC and research the statistics of different kinds of behaviors and how high risk they are. And we'll come up with consensus about what's safe and what's not safe.*

MAGDALENE MERETRIX: *While I respect other people's beliefs, I do think that unprotected sex with someone other than a committed partner is irresponsible, and I don't believe that irresponsibility and magery go well together at all. Being a mage is about self-discipline and responsibility (among other things) and so my personal feeling is that a mage would only have unprotected sex with a trusted, committed partner.*

HONEYBLOSSOM: *I practice safer sex with all people that I have sex with, except for my primary partner. By safer sex, I mean barriers for intercourse and oral sex, sterilizing penetrative toys or covering them in latex, and gloves if there's a high risk associated with an activity (such as anal penetration) or a person (who, for example, has an STD or has been exposed to one). I think that responsible, consenting safer sex and birth control choices are crucial to a magical/spiritual practice of sexuality. Consenting, in this case, means that your partner must agree to whatever you are proposing, and in order to do that, your partner needs to have all of the information about your sexual history, etcetera.*

RHOMYLLY FORBES: *I think not killing anyone with HIV is a good spiritual practice.*

It's worth noting that no barrier use is 100 percent effective. Latex rips and slips. Part of responsible safer sex means getting tested regularly (ideally, every six months) for all the STDs that one can.

One way to think about safer sex magically is in terms of shielding, protection, and/or casting a circle to enclose energy.

RAVEN KALDERA: *We are body fluid polyfidelitous, which means that we don't share body fluids outside of our circle; everyone else gets full latex. This reflects not only on issues of safety, but our feelings that our body fluids are sacred, and only to be shared with each other and not wasted on casual sex.*

LASARA FIREFOX: *I practice safer sex outside my primary relationship. With strangers it's kind of nice, as I feel more protected psychically as well as physically. With long-term lovers it's more difficult to stick to the safer sex, though I do. Sometimes it takes all my strength to do so. I just want to merge, to taste, to consume, to digest and comingle and become one with him or her. I think that with new partners, or one-timers, safer sex is great. It sets boundaries. Once one really stops desiring those boundaries is when the troubles arise.*

JUDY HARROW: *I'm a huge believer in "condom compact," which is what we have here in my family, and even in making that a matter of sacred vow. We care for each other, and so we take care of each other. By practicing condom compact, we protect the intimate family unit, the primary unit, not just each of us separately as individuals. It's like casting a circle. One theory about what happens when you cast a circle is that instead of having individual auras, for that period of time, you open your personal auras and instead create a collective aura for the people that are gathered. At least for the small, intimate type of circle, that model works for me. I perceive condom compact as something similar, like drawing a circle around a group, a family of lovers, rather than an individual. In this case, it's a circle of physical safety, of health, a circle of care for the people who are your closest lovers.*

4. SEXUALITY IN THE PAGAN COMMUNITY ❧

IN THE MODERN NeoPagan community, sexuality is in many ways part of public life. Whenever there's more than one Pagan in attendance—at large festivals, smaller gatherings, and in Pagan households—you'll find that the rules for behavior regarding sex are considerably more relaxed than in mainstream society.

Generally, among average Americans, when coupled folks are friends with members of the sex to which they're attracted, it's regarded with suspicion—much more so if they're affectionate. In the Pagan world, this is no big deal, even for the monogamous folks. In mainstream society, public nudity is unacceptable for anyone older than about age three. Nudity is quite easily accepted in the Pagan community. Many festivals are clothing-optional, and most Pagan households, in my experience, tend to be as well. In mainstream society (to differing degrees), even *talking* about sex is considered in poor taste. And among Pagans—well, it's quite different.

Of course, these are gross generalizations, and I'm sure there are plenty of very modest and conservative Pagans out there. In fact, some in the community perceive a trend back to more conservative values. Don Kraig senses a rebirth of monogamy and prudery, which he thinks is linked to solitary practice. Solitary practitioners, he says, are not faced with as many challenges to their assumptions and preconceptions. This trend may also be linked to AIDS education, which has created an inexorable link between sex and risk in the minds of many young people.

DON KRAIG: *In my experience, the previous generation of NeoPagans have, in many cases, evolved into monogamous relationships without denouncing either their earlier sexual freedom or the sexual freedom of others. . . . Many in the younger generation of NeoPagans have been so scared and terrified by sex education in school, which stresses terror, fear, and illness, that they have become more selective with their partners.*

FRANCESCA GENTILLE: *I am shocked by the number of Pagans who are almost sex-negative and body-negative. I was posting on my Pagan list about some of the classes that I teach around sacred sexuality . . . and I had people e-mailing me, saying, "Well, what does sexuality have to do with Paganism?" and, "We don't want to hear about sex parties." This is not what I'm teaching. There's not even any sex going on! I was actually barred from posting my workshops on the list. The feeling I got was that they were threatened by the idea of sexuality.*

One of the unfortunate side effects to this seemingly wonderful explosion of personal freedom is that the more conservative members of our community are feeling uncomfortable and threatened. Monogamy is becoming a minority behavior in some groups, to such an extent that it's assumed "if you're Pagan, you're poly." Any counterculture group that sticks around long enough is bound to establish its own set of norms, but it's unfortunate that we are still excluding some people because of their relationship style. Even poly folks who may think they are being all cool and accepting may not realize that they are inadvertently stomping right past people's boundaries.

ANAHITA-GULA: *My one real "squicky" point is the flagrant "sizing up" of people by some polyamorous people. Whenever a new person walks into a room, some poly people can be visibly open about assessing*

the new person as a possible bedmate. I find this quite threatening. If I
want to be in a meat market (say, a pick up bar) I will go to one.
(I call this "Predatory Polyamory.")

It may come as a surprise to some, but not all polyamorous
people like being so aggressively courted, either. This is an area
where it's necessary to perceive some shades of gray. If a person is
monogamous, then she's off-limits; that's simple. But if a person
is single, or poly, it doesn't necessarily mean that she's an utter
slut, either. A sign I saw at a gay pride march read: "Bi, poly, and
still not interested in you."

LaSara Firefox: *When I was younger, I didn't interact sexually with*
many Pagans [because] . . . I felt that if I slept with one person, there
would be a line of expectant suitors waiting, and I didn't want to hurt
anyone's feelings. I felt that if I slept with one person I'd be somehow
expected to sleep with others, or people would end up feeling rejected. It
felt easier to reject everyone, and limit my sexual exploration to the
outside world.

Nudity

Most of us have grown up in a culture that condemns social
nudity, so being nude around other people (with whom we are
not sexually intimate) may be something that takes some adjust-
ment. Of course, there is no reason we should have to force ourselves to be socially nude, unless we want to join a coven that
practices skyclad. But if we accept the body as sacred and beautiful, and nothing to be ashamed about, then we inevitably come
to the conclusion that any shame around nudity is something we
have been taught, in which we no longer believe.

PHIL BRUCATO: *As a kid, I never liked feeling exposed. I wasn't raised with the whole "body is bad" thing; I just didn't feel comfortable with my shirt or shoes off. My parents weren't nudists, but neither had issues with being barefoot or (in Dad's case) shirtless . . . I now realize that I was hypersensitive to energy, eroticism, and sensation. I often felt exposed even when I wasn't. . . .*

Thankfully, puberty pretty much demolished this prudishness. My involvement with theater (high school), and fondness for heavy metal rock and heroic fantasy (a little earlier) wore down my timidity around flesh and sensation. By then, though, I felt I'd constructed an identity around self-concealment. So I began adventuring out long after dark, climbing out my window in the time-honored tradition of American teenagers, to walk barefoot and shirtless through the woods around my neighborhood. I realize now that I was getting in touch with my Pagan heart; back then, I just thought I was being weird.

By late high school, I had largely overcome my shyness. (Four years in theater will do that to you.) My emerging sexuality and increasing comfort with my own skin intensified when I got involved in medieval re-creation the summer of my eighteenth year. (Fighting in sweltering heat while dressed in armor and surrounded by half-naked girls will do that to you, too.) That fall, I started the theater program at college; my shyness to being exposed lessened as I got into good shape. My sophomore year, I decided to blow the doors off that prison, and began nude modeling. I also got into punk rock, and started dating girls who rarely wore shoes even on city streets. So much for my sensual inhibitions!

Since then, I've become an advocate for naturism, barefooting, and sensual meditation. I realize that my earlier prudishness was based on fear and caution. As I've grown more comfortable with my self and all its sensations, I've deepened my connection to that Pagan part of my soul, and to the world in general, as well. These days, I try to help other people get more in touch with their sensuality, inspiring confidence and adventurism through my writing, sacred work, and example. At clothing-optional festivals, I like to go nude or nearly so; I nearly always go barefooted, and often take time wherever I am to sit back and savor the sensations of my current time and place.

OBERON ZELL-RAVENHEART: *When I was a kid growing up, I had this total obsessive modesty. One of the ones that used to just drive me nuts when I was a kid is, I would sleep with pajamas, but the fly is just wide open on those things, and I was terribly afraid that my mother might come in in the morning to wake me up, and somehow I had tossed and turned and flung off the sheets to be lying there somehow exposed. And upon a couple of occasions I inadvertently glimpsed my mother nude, passing from the shower to the bedroom or something, and it was terribly embarrassing. I would avert my gaze and try to just blank the thing from my mind. I have no idea why I had this, but it was really very obsessive stuff.*

At some point I discovered a pile of old black-and-white nudist magazines under my father's bed. . . . I managed to spirit off a couple of copies, to see what it was that girls really looked like, which was amazing, of course, because they all looked like Barbie dolls, in that the nipples and pubic areas had all been airbrushed out in the photographs. I didn't know about airbrushing and stuff, it was just that there was nothing there. It also fit with the pictures I saw of Greek statues and so on, where there is no pubic hair, or pubic areas, and nipples are pretty much non-existent. So I had a very strange idea of female anatomy.

HONEYBLOSSOM: *I used to be less comfortable with nudity, but the "fake it till you make it" approach worked okay—I just acted as though I felt fine and perfectly comfortable when I thought I ought to feel comfortable, until I actually did.*

Not all people have to work at becoming comfortable with nudity, though!

JEZEBEL DAWN BLESSING: *Nudity is wonderful, and I prefer to live in a clothing-optional household. I think bathing suits look ridiculous, and clothing only needs to be worn when it's too chilly to be naked. I am a clothes horse (or whore); I love to dress up pretty and prance around, but nudity is sacred. I have always wanted to have a wedding/commitment ceremony where the betrothed appear naked to one another—no artifice, no fancy trappings; what you see is what you are committing to.*

MAGENTA: *I never understood clothes except as a social construct, and to protect against the weather.*

Most Pagans have no experience with public nudity until they start going to festivals, and it may take some getting used to. Not all are clothing-optional, and not all are warm enough for it to be a blessing, but Starwood, for instance, takes place in upstate New York, in mid to late July. It gets quite hot during the day. When I attend, all I wear is a flowy skirt and sandals. It's wonderful. (Then, when I come back to the mundane world, it seems strange to see all these women wearing shirts in such hot weather.)

LEON: *In my early twenties, I developed an attitude toward nudity reflected in the statement, "I don't mind your nudity if you don't mind my staring." It wasn't a very mature attitude, but it was honest. As I've seen more and more (and MORE) naked people, it no longer surprises me. . . . not a lot, at least. I am extremely grateful for this aspect of the Pagan community . . . I can't imagine swimming or hot-tubbing with clothes on anymore; it just seems unnatural that way. I've become much more accepting of my body and of others'. I don't feel as vulnerable when I'm naked now, though I'm most comfortable*

*in a sarong—it's all I wear around the house and at festivals (as
weather permits). I've come to a point where I can see a beautiful woman
(of any size or shape) naked and truly admire her body, and not
have it be all that sexual. I suppose the same is actually true of a man
as well.*

Many people use festivals as an opportunity to decorate themselves with body paint and to show off their tattoos and piercings.
Another nice thing about public nudity is that it helps to undo
the cultural conditioning that nudity equals sex. The Pagan pre-
dilection for nudity may be one reason why the mainstream thinks
of us as licentious beasts, and to be fair, it does imply a greater
degree of personal license. But as anyone who's been to a nude
beach knows, nudity is often less arousing than someone in a
bathing suit or lingerie. Any initial arousal often quickly fades to
a more aesthetic appreciation: something more calm and less lusty.

SHAI SHAHAR: *I have always been in favor of nudity, although I did
not get a chance to experience the joys of communal nudity until my
late twenties. No doubt being raised in Philadelphia had a lot to do
with that. Here in Europe, however, we are exposed to an awful lot of
bare-breasted advertising, even to sell things like bottled spring water,
and there must be at least a thousand nudist/naturist camps within the
EU where families congregate under the sun. I think in America there is
an assumption that nudity automatically inspires or incites people into
sexual shennanigans. In Europe, nudity is viewed as a natural state,
liberating to be sure, but not licentious. I cannot think of a finer way to
(re)connect with nature, and feel bound up in the great circle, than to
walk naked through the woods or along a sunny beach, wind in the
hair, free, and unashamed.*

This is all great fun if you're into it, but discomfiting if
you're not.

OBERON ZELL-RAVENHEART: *I remember, back in the mid-sixties, I visited a nudist camp in Florida that was dealing with a local lawsuit situation . . . because some woman had managed to climb up on top of a stool in her bathroom, and over the very top of her bathroom window's curtain, could barely peer over the top of the eight-foot fence surrounding the camp, and was therefore complaining that these people were offending her. And the police basically said, "Well, then, don't get up on the stool."*

PHIL BRUCATO: *In terms of social nudity, I favor responsible displays of flesh and sensuality. Taking other people's comfort level into account is vital. I have no problem being nude at home in front of Francesca's son because he's been raised with nudity as a natural thing—inside the house! By the same token, I would never walk down the street naked; even if it were legal, I just don't think many people could handle it. Sad, but there it is. Within a society, it's respectful to take your fellow citizens and their feelings into account. It's also safer than whipping out one's dick in public.*

Unfortunately, many Pagans, just like everyone else, internalize the media standards of beauty, and some folks are too uncomfortable with their shape to be willing to show it off.

WYRDOTTER: *Gravity and age being what they are, my willingness to be nude drops as my body sags. I don't have any problems with the concept in general, and don't mind flitting around the house wearing only what I was born with, but you probably won't catch me traipsing around the . . . festival grounds in the buff. I still have too many body-image issues to go that far. Besides, I try to consider those who may not be comfortable with seeing my pear-shaped, fluffy form in the altogether.*

Gardnerian Wicca has always mandated that coveners hold rituals skyclad. The tradition is validated by a line in the Charge of the Goddess: "You shall be free from slavery, and as a sign that you be truly free, you shall be naked in your rites." This line is taken directly from Charles Godfrey Leland's *Aradia: Gospel of the Witches*, but as it happens, Leland mistranslated the Italian, and the original text doesn't even mention nudity.[1] Regardless, since Gerald Gardner himself believed in the therapeutic power of sun-bathing and thus was a naturist, he might have instituted ritual nudity even if he'd read an accurate version. He also believed that clothing hampered energy flow, and he also wanted to do away with the trappings of class distinctions—something especially important to British society—in the context of sacred space.

It's a powerful symbolism to strip off the pretenses of the out-side world to appear before the Gods as they made us (and are continually reshaping us).

JUDY HARROW: *I think that the real reason for ritual nudity is [to be] worshipful. It's a symbolic statement of the theology of immanence, a celebration of the beauty and sacredness of the body.*

Ritual nudity helps to put us in a different and magical frame of mind, and it helps to break down the barriers between covenmates, creating a more intimate space. It seems doubtful, however, that the pagans of old would have been naked for a ritual, for instance, in the middle of the winter. Required nudity, season-round, is def-initely a modern concept, demanding heated space. To me, it seems natural to be naked when making love, when it's hot, or when swimming or bathing, but not for its own sake—and I think that's more the way it would have been done "in the old days."

Pagan Gatherings and Sexuality

Pagan festivals and other gatherings are often quite sexually charged. At spring and summer gatherings, the lusty overtones may just be part of the seasonal vibe getting into people. In other cases, it may just be the general sense of freedom from social conventions that tends to release people's inhibitions. Amazing things can happen at festivals because of this.

LEON: *The weekend directly following my initiation as a Witch, my covenmates and I, as well as a few others, were putting on the first "Beltane Witch Camp." I had brought no companion to help warm my tent. Everything was so very magical that whole weekend, I was greatly disappointed that I hadn't found anyone to help me celebrate Beltane in the good ol'-fashioned way. It just seemed proper and fitting that on this particular Beltane, my first as a Witch, that I should engage in sex as a sacrament. As I lay unsleeping, grumbling to myself and all the Gods about my predicament, I heard a gentle scratching at my tent door. I quietly asked, "Who's there?" with no small amount of surprise. It might have been the Goddess herself—it was, after all, a very magical celebration out in the woods apiece—and in a manner of speaking, it was the Goddess herself. "A little fairy," came the reply in a youthful, very feminine voice. We cuddled and talked quietly for hours before I built up the courage to ask for more. The rest, as they say, is history. It was a very good Beltane indeed. I have not yet been able to reconnect with my Beltane fairy; it's been years since then. I don't know that I would recognize her today; we've both aged. I sincerely believe it was supposed to be like that, though. It was a sacrament for both of us. Plus, I had direct evidence that the God and Goddess answer prayers and take care of their children. I felt cherished by my divinity and my community.*

Some people regard festival space as "between the worlds" and not subject to the same limitations as the mundane world. Because of this, as Francesca mentioned, they may relax their relationship rules to allow for new partners, just at festivals. This is similar to what folklore tells us about the observance of Beltane in the British Isles. Marriages would be null and void just for Beltane

Eve (May Eve), and people could couple with whomever they liked. This encouraged lots of sex, which, through sympathetic magic, was believed to encourage fertility in the crops.

People who tend to be sexually private may feel awkward at festivals about setting personal boundaries in regard to their own comfort levels about public sexuality. Again, this is an area where we as a community need to remember that the acceptance of all growth-affirming paths, includes those that may wind up appearing mainstream in some aspects. (Gods forbid!) We're not really giving people the freedom to be different, if it's different in the exact same way as everyone else.

> ANAHITA-GULA: *I stopped attending Pagan festivals some years ago because I got tired of the high level of pheromones in the air . . . the under-twenty-five crowd who felt fests were an excuse to find a rock by a swimming pond and "go at it" all weekend.*

Just because the rules of social conduct at Pagan gatherings are different from those of mainstream society doesn't mean no rules exist. They're just a little harder to puzzle out, and they may not be consistent.

> DOSSIE EASTON: *I think that predatory cruising is a problem. And sometimes, it's been interesting to me, when I've been outside of my own community, here, and somebody has come on to me, more in S/M than anything else, but with that same kind of predatory energy, and I'm like, "No, no, that's not how it happens. First we get equal, then we make some agreements, and if I decide that the agreements are suitable, and you decide that they're suitable for you too, then you get to play predator. We've got to get this straight." [laughs] There's things that have to happen first. I know it sounds kind of counterintuitive, but that's how it works in my universe. And I don't like that kind of energy, although I enjoy a good predatory come-on. But "good" for me means*

*that there's some sense of respect and consensuality there, too. I love
playing predator and prey. "Victim" is one of my favorite roles. But
that is not who I want to be in my life full time.*

My friends tend to be very physically affectionate—not necessarily in a sexual way, but just with cuddling, backrubs, playing
with each other's hair, that sort of thing. After a party with a different crowd than my usual one, I discovered that what I perceived as a backrub has been considered "making out" by some of
the guests, who had felt uncomfortable about it. In a much more
extreme example, a friend told me about a small gathering of
BDSM-ers at a friend's house. They were just hanging out and
chatting, when all of a sudden one of the dominants ordered his
submissive to lick his boots. Then another one followed suit by
demanding a blow job from his sub. Although all the people
there were folks who normally enjoyed public play, this sort of
behavior was inappropriate for the casual tone of the gathering.
People were offended and left the room, and their esteem for
these "gentlemen" dropped several notches.

ANAHITA-GULA: *I have noted with a few polyamorous people (and to
me this is a minority thing!) that they have the attitude of having a
right to be very physically affectionate with anyone, at any time, and
if you don't like it, it's your problem. Those who may have survived
sexual assault can find this very threatening as an attitude. Like
everyone else, poly people need to be sensitive about feelings of those
around them (an' ye harm none . . . did I say that before?) and exercise
a modicum of decorum in a mixed crowd.*

As NeoPagans, we are in the process of creating a subculture
different from that in which we have all been living for decades.
We can't take things for granted any longer. And the Wiccan rede
is a little too general to serve as a universal guideline for Neo-

101

Pagan etiquette. It falls to the individual to use common sense and a dash of intuition to decide what behavior is appropriate. And part of our responsibility is to politely and constructively speak up when we are uncomfortable with a certain kind of public behavior on another's part. If we have any question about whether a behavior is appropriate or not, then it's our responsibility to ask. The solution may not be as clear-cut as one person being right and the other being wrong, but these kinds of ambiguities are something you have to live with when you practice a religion that you get to make up as you go along.

> OBERON ZELL-RAVENHEART: *Personally, I think it's charming to see people engaged in PDA. Very romantic; makes me feel warm all over. If you don't like what you see, look elsewhere. My basic principle in all of these cases is, "If you don't like it, you can't have any." If it is allowed that people can simply say that something somebody else is just being or doing makes them uncomfortable and therefore should be prohibited, that's a very slippery slope.*
>
> *If I were involved at a gathering . . . or were running one, where somebody came up to me and said he or she was offended by somebody going around doing something or other, I would say, "Well, let's sit down together with those people and have a talk about it." What offends me and what offends somebody else, there's probably a vast gulf between those arenas. I think that this is a better thing for dialogue, rather than prohibition.*

In case all this gives you the impression that Pagan festivals are meat markets—that's not accurate. Most festivals are very family friendly, and all this adult stuff tends to go right over the kids' heads. Activities, parties, or workshops with explicit content are restricted to those over eighteen. Some festivals are entirely adults-only.

The Obligatory Section on Orgies

Sacred orgies are a historically proven aspect of ancient paganism, so it's reasonable that it's something some NeoPagans might like to revive. But I'm sure there are many of us who would never dream of attending such an event. Ronald Hutton, in researching his history of NeoPaganism, found no one out of hundreds of covens in the United Kingdom who would admit to doing such a thing. "If there are Pagan covens in Britain which engage in sexual orgies . . . then they have not merely escaped my notice but that of the vast majority of witches, and other Pagans, who operate in this country."[2] But I don't think that odd at all; I'm sure if there had been any groups who *were* having orgies, they wouldn't be about to tell Mr. Interviewer about it. Paganism has a hard enough time being taken seriously by the general public and the media, that there's no point in our marginalizing ourselves any further.

That being said, I will now gaily go on to talk about orgies, because, heck, it's a book about Pagan sex, and you *know* you all want to see this part. I'm sure it is a minority of Pagans who attend what are generally called "safer sex parties" or "play parties." But because we tend to view sexuality as normal, healthy, and something that should be enjoyed without shame, there is apt to be a fairly significant percentage of us at such events. Carol Queen's Queen of Heaven—named after the Goddess, not Carol—now running for twelve years and going strong, is one such party. It is held in sacred space.

CAROL QUEEN: *From one vantage, [Queen of Heaven] just looks like a pansexual play party, but . . . we always do a ritual, we call the Quarters, we usually call the Goddess and the God, and people don't need to actively participate in the ritual, but . . . we always, always find that whether people are Pagan-identified or not, they speak well of this ritual and the way it makes the space feel. . . . They're like, "What did you do? This is cool!" [laughs] . . . And we also always find that even if things were sluggish to get going in a sexual context, the ritual makes it happen. It's a very interesting thing. From a distance, it doesn't look like we're performing actual sex magic at all, but the two things, superimposed with each other, always seem to work.* [Jen: Well, you're creating a safe space for people.] *Yes, and we're creating a space, probably most importantly, where erotic behavior that people choose to engage in is called "sacred." People rarely get that in this culture; in fact, most people get quite the opposite, so that's the healing we know the party can accomplish, and everything else is people finding like-minded others, and having a good time erotically, and all of that.*

In *The Ethical Slut: A Guide to Infinite Sexual Possibilities*, Dossie Easton and Catherine A. Liszt write, "We believe that it is a fundamentally radical political [Jen: I would add *magical*] act to deprivatize sex. So much oppression in our culture is based on shame about sex: the oppression of women, of cultural minorities, oppression in the name of the (presumably asexual) family, oppression of sexual minorities. We are all oppressed. We have all been taught, one way or another, that our desires, our bodies, our sexualities, are shameful. What better way to defeat oppression than to get together in communities and celebrate the wonders of sex?"[3] Indeed, group sex can bring about a very positive transformation for many people.

SHAI SHAHAR: *My "borders" have shifted in that the presence of other men around me watching or commenting while I'm fucking doesn't bother me like it used to. And I find that when they are participating in having sex with my woman it does not disturb me anymore. I've gotten to the point where I quite enjoy it, actually. I got over it by getting over myself and my dick obsession. I stopped looking at sex as an Olympic event or arena . . . as something to do to prove myself. I lightened up . . . and learned to relax and enjoy myself . . . I feel empowered now in my sexuality and empowered by the sexuality of my woman . . . my Goddess. Paganism has allowed me to revel in my gender and my orientation . . . to give it purpose and meaning without the attendant guilt and shame issues getting in the way.*

CAROL QUEEN: *Being in a group sex space . . . fucks with people's ideas of "Well, we do this, and they do that, and we're different from them," because when a whole bunch of people of varying orientations and desire patterns start to do what they do . . . you start to see essentially the same acts repeated in all kinds of configurations. It's a profound anti-homo/hetero/biphobia tool, at least for the people who are ready to have that experience.*

DOSSIE EASTON: *When you see somebody whose body type is "wrong" (the way you imagine yours is, right?) being ecstatically turned on, having an orgasm, waving their legs in the air in some ridiculous position, that happy person is radiant—perfectly gorgeous.*[4]

The safer sex rules at these parties are generally very strict. This is another thing that tends to differentiate the poly crowd from the swinger crowd. The only barrier you'll ever see at swing parties is the condom. Pansexual safer sex parties use gloves, dental dams/plastic wrap, and condoms for any type of contact that might potentially involve sexual fluids. Even fluid-bonded couples are not exempt. This irritates some people.

CAROL QUEEN: *Sometimes people are put off by [the safer sex rules, saying]: "But we're fluid-bonded, we don't have to do that." The answer is, "You have to do it here, and the reasons are that, one, someday you may need to be the safe-sex advocate or instructor for somebody in your*

*life, and we want you to know exactly what it is when you're telling
your little cousin how to put a condom on, or something. Two, we want
everyone from every need-to-protect and walk-of-life, to feel safe and
welcome in this space, and others to feel safe with them, and if we are all
safe, we don't have to start asking for each others' HIV registration
cards, or [to keep track of] other problematic barrier-lifting activities
and groupings."*

Sexual Manipulation in the Community

It is unfortunate but true that there are predators out there, who,
in the name of Paganism or Wicca, will manipulate others to get
sex. NeoPaganism may be an ethical religion, but that is no guar-
antee that someone calling him- or herself a Pagan is ethical (it
doesn't work for any other religion; why would it here?). According to Kellen's Internet article on "Sex and Paganism," when
someone advertised looking for "13-to-20-year-old female initiates," it was Pagans in the community who reported him to the
police and the FBI.[5] In this way, the community tends to be self-
regulating, by excluding people who act harmfully.

LaSara Firefox: *Many Pagans seem lacking in the realm of
boundary awareness. This makes it difficult to feel safe being an openly
sexual person in the community. Also, many newbies have fallen prey to
the "Oh my God, I'm in love with everything!" sense of awe that
spiritual openness can bring, and then end up feeling bad about
exchanges that occurred because of a lack of safety or care on the part
of those initiating the newbie into the fold. And, there have been some in
the community who I feel have actually preyed on this moment of
expansion. The feeling of "no rules" that newbies find, when they can't
recognize rules, because the rules they are faced with are unfamiliar, can
also be a problem.*

PHIL BRUCATO: *One of the reasons it's hard to feel "respectable" about sacred sexuality is because so many folks simply use the idea as an excuse. Under the guise of "free love" and "sexual empowerment," a lot of people manipulate, deceive, dominate, and dump their lovers, then justify their actions with "I'm just taking control of my sexual power." . . . I'm sure you've encountered such folks yourself . . . supposedly "enlightened practitioners of sacred sexuality" who are little more than addicts with a good pickup line. This sort of bullshit erodes the trust and openness that's essential for people to share a sacred sexual bond, and to maintain public credibility for our practices. (My roommate, no prude herself, has said, "These girlfriends of yours keep talking about how healthy and powerful they are, but their actions show just the opposite.")*

I feel, at times, that the NeoPagan community falls victim to an attitude of "It's all good—no judgment." That's crap. A person who misuses his/her sexuality as a drug or weapon is hurting others and degrading him/herself. In those cases, I feel it's perfectly proper to confront such a person, offer help and compassion, but potentially avoid or exclude him/her if the person chooses to continue sexually abusive or reckless behavior. It's not the sex that's being punished here—it's what someone does with it. I feel a community has a certain responsibility to call people on destructive bullshit; a community that doesn't do so won't last for long.

One of the unfortunate liabilities about being a small religion is that people can pose as leaders and elders, and they can assert anything about the Pagan or Wiccan path, and there's no way to call them on it. Sure, there are plenty of books out there, but no one authority—no Vatican or rabbinical council—to lay down the law. I think most of us would agree that this is a *good* thing, but it also leaves it up to the individual to intuit whether someone is up to trouble. Secrecy oaths don't help matters. Many covens require initiates to promise not to reveal details about their rituals or initiations, which can be a very solid magical practice, but is also a great way for them to get away with shit. If anyone says that you must be polyamorous to be Pagan, that you must have sex with them if you are ever going to learn the Mysteries, or to practice sex magic, or to be initiated, or that you must "share your body with your coven brothers and sisters," *it is a lie, and this person is manipulating you.*

Sexual initiation is a topic that generates a lot of controversy in the community. Used ethically, it can be an extremely powerful event. But it's tricky here, because where sex and power are involved, people's boundaries can get very fuzzy. Something that may seem comfortable in one context may get very much not so in another, and than it can be too late to do anything about it.

RHOMYLLY FORBES: *I think that sexual initiation is unnecessary. Assuming a third-degree initiate is pledging to serve the Gods and his or her fellows for the rest of this lifetime, what the hell has that got to do with fucking? Yeah, yeah, Great Rite and all that—but there are other ways to get the point across that don't involve Tab A and Slot B. I've known a lot of people who suffered pretty horribly as a result of this requirement. The Pagan community has lost a lot of good people because of this, which is a shame.*

ANAHITA-GULA: *In traditions with secrecy oaths, there is always the uneasy fact that some high priestesses or high priests use sex as a lever, in the manner that Starhawk would call "power-over": "You must have an actual sexual Great Rite in order to move to the next initiation . . ." or "I will teach you if you have sex with me." . . . As with any other religion, there are pitfalls. Paganism, having such an intertwined path between sex and religion, walks a careful balance that can be easily upturned.*

WYRDOTTER: *I don't see any reason for a sexual act (other than symbolic) to be required for initiation. I wouldn't want to be a member of any coven that would demand sex acts for membership. There's something going on there that borders on being exploitative and manipulative.*

Even those who support sexual initiation say that the bottom line is for initiates to be informed and to feel that they have a choice.

JUDY HARROW: *There are some traditions that quite honorably practice sexual initiations. I think that some of the things that make it honorable are, number one, letting candidates for initiation, at least—if not the general public—know in advance, not springing it on them when they're already in that headspace. Secondly, for those groups, at least, minors are off-limits. And thirdly, being very sensitive about candidates' marriages or intimate relationships and to the commitments or agreements they have made. Some people are monogamous; others are on condom compact, etcetera.*

CAROL QUEEN: *I don't know that I think [sexual initiation] is inappropriate, but . . . particularly knowing that spiritual practice and initiation has always been a place where people playing with power have gone, they seem to be, in my opinion, a little unclean sometimes about that power. I've seen it happen more in other religious systems than in Paganism. . . .*

I don't think that having to have sex to do anything *is a really very good idea, if it feels to people as though they don't have a choice.* [Jen: So they would need to be told about it right up front.] *Right, and in addition, to say, "And other covens do things differently." Because certainly I could see somebody stumbling in to the community of a coven, finding it highly attractive and meaningful, but*

*not knowing that down the road there's somebody who doesn't [do
things that way]. Full knowledge is sort of a hard thing to impart . . .*
[Jen: I can see why someone would be loath to mention it
right away, because it seems like a Mystery.] *Right.*

*I can look back and think of a time, myself, when [sexual initiation]
would have been an enormously strong thing for me to be offered.* [Jen:
But your attitudes toward sex are not the norm.] *That's true.
I'd have to pull that situation into a really specialized situation, and
then by the time I got to that point, I'm not sure that I would believe that
any given individual would impart anything to me that I couldn't have
myself. And that's the other piece of it. It's like, "Why you?"* [laughs]

Sexism and Sexual Discrimination

What, did you think we were perfect? No, unfortunately, just
because you're Pagan does not mean you're free from social pro-
gramming and sexual hangups.

DON KRAIG: *I knew one very beautiful woman who was single and
studied hard to become a member of a particular coven. . . . Most of the
members of the coven were married or at least coupled. She received
several "no" votes and was not allowed in. I talked to the high priest
and asked about this. I figured that some of the women might be jealous
because she was so beautiful and would take the attention from them,
perhaps leading their partners "astray." He told me that the women had
all voted to accept her. It was the men who had voted her down. . . .
They were afraid they might become embarrassingly erect during
skyclad rituals as a result of her beauty. Now personally, considering
that . . . NeoPaganism [is inspired by] early fertility cults, I would
think that this should be a positive thing. My assumption, though, is
that the men were still being influenced by their upbringing, and while
talking about "Great Rites" was good, actually showing that you
might be aroused was bad.*

This is really sad in two respects: one, that the woman was being discriminated against because she was attractive, and two, that the men in the coven were embarrassed about showing arousal.

Because the NeoPagan movement has been in large part influenced by American feminism, sexism more often tends to tip the other way and go against men.

LEON: *I'm certain we've all heard some allegedly enlightened supposed "elder" proclaim glibly that "all men are assholes," usually right to the faces of sympathetic and caring men who are listening to her . . . I really don't tolerate that anymore; no man should, no person should. I'm not going to make some bizarre attempt to "reclaim" the term "asshole"; that's just dumb. I've actually read* Drawing Down the Moon, *so I understand how our current community evolved from the feminist movement. I have a great deal of admiration for early feminists; what they did was tough. Factually, by many definitions I might be called a feminist. I'll even grant that there is some much needed healing to be had by women from Moon Lodges and Dianic circles, [but] that healing should never come at the cost of anyone else.*

I've been in more than one Pagan circle where I was made to feel [that] . . . somehow, because I had a penis, I was responsible for every bad thing ever done to anyone by everybody else who happened to have a penis. How fucked up is that? Here I am, discovering a place where I seem to fit in (for pretty much the first time in my life, I should add) and then I'm somehow completely unfit due to a cosmetic accident of genetics? It didn't matter that I was sensitive; it didn't matter that I was magical; nothing else mattered. Now, with the wisdom of a little age, I see those attitudes for how skewed by pain they must be. But . . . I want to let men know they don't have to accept that; they can expect to be respected (assuming they're worthy of it). I just want women to know that not all men are assholes, and they can reinforce that by not assuming the worst.

A lot of attention has been paid in our community to healing the inner Goddess, of tapping into Goddess energy and Goddess power. Now it's time for the gentlemen, and the God(s), to step up. If we don't explore this side of things, then our community will flounder in everything it tries, because if only the women are empowered, or everybody is empowered in a feminine way, then we're only running on half our cylinders, only half or less of our potential power.

HONEYBLOSSOM: *I've heard men in the Pagan community talk about feminine energy getting too much focus. But too often it seems like, "Oh, I'm so oppressed; nobody in the Pagan community appreciates masculine energy, and do you want to go to bed?" Even if it were true—and I'm not convinced—wouldn't it be a good thing to have one small corner left in the world where women are still on top? Something's got to balance all that patriarchy!*

What to Teach Our Children About Sexuality

It *should* go without saying that the idea of child sexual abuse is completely abhorred among NeoPagans as a whole—with whatever isolated exceptions might be found in any group of people. But unfortunately, in some people's minds, NeoPagan groups (especially those that start with "W") are associated with Satanism, and (as "everyone knows") Satanists perform child sexual abuse as part of their rituals. I have no knowledge of what Satanists do, although I suspect that this stigma is undeserved. I do know that in my seventeen years as a Pagan, I have never once heard of any kind of child sexual abuse ever taking place in our community—much less in any kind of ritualized fashion.

Because NeoPaganism is a philosophical and religious framework that tends to be permissive about sexuality, our kids are being brought up with less baggage and shame around the subject. They are also being given the kind of thorough and practical sex education that might ultimately save their lives, and the lives of their lovers.

Riane Eisler says, "If we stop to think about it, what is immoral is *not* to educate young people about sex. Because for no other matter of importance in our lives—and sex is obviously of tremendous importance—would anyone think of advocating ignorance. Not only that, it is well known that all forms of repression have first and foremost relied on ignorance, which has throughout history served to maintain every kind of power imbalance."[6]

JEZEBEL DAWN BLESSING: *Our puritanical culture fears the corruption of its children, but what they do not realize is that withholding information can be even more damaging over the long span of our lifetimes.*

Even within NeoPaganism, there's a wide diversity of approaches to teaching kids about sex. This leaves parents to set their own rules and boundaries about how much they feel their children ought to see, hear, know, and do. In my experience, this seems to work remarkably well: Pagan kids seem comfortable with themselves and their bodies, yet do not tend to go overboard in that "Jenny Jones: My Teen Is Dressing like a Whore" way.

ANAHITA-GULA: *I do find myself uncomfortable with complete nudity around children under the age of fourteen or so.... The school system punishes little children who try to take off a shirt or pants because they "itch" or [their clothes] are "tight"—it becomes confusing to sort out when nudity is appropriate and when it is not.*

FRANCESCA GENTILLE: *If I'm changing, and Dylan walks into the room, I just keep changing. You know, I treat it as "bodies come naked and they come clothed." And sometimes—Harbin Hot Springs is a clothing-optional hot springs—sometimes we're in a naked place, and* we run around naked. Sometimes clothing is the way to go, and we're running around in clothes. But there's nothing wrong with the human body naked. [Jen: And is he okay with that so far?] Totally.

One time, Dylan walked in on one of my lovers and me. Oopsie! And I just looked up and said, "What do you need, honey?" Because you know, as a mom, they walk in, they need something. [Jen: What exactly were you in the middle of doing, specifically?] Having intercourse . . . I actually think he watched a little before I realized he was there. So I said, "What do you need?" and he said, "Apple juice," or "Cheerios and milk," or whatever. And then he said something like, "Mom, what are you doing?" And I said something like, "We're making love, honey." He goes, "Is this sex?" And I said, "Yes, sweetheart, this is sex." [laughs] And he said, "Does he have his thing up your butt?" and I said, "No, honey, there's a special spot." And I said, "You've seen Mama put in tampons and take out the tampons," and he's like, "Yeah," and I said, "Well, it's that place." And I said, "Is there anything else?" [laughs] And he said, "No," and I said, "Well, then I'd appreciate it if you'd leave now, and I'll get your apple juice in just a minute." And he said, "Okay."

The key thing is that I treated it like it was normal. Like, if you saw two dogs making love, if you saw cats, or horses, and your child said, "What are they doing?" You'd say, "Well, they're having sex" . . . or whatever, and hopefully it would just be normal. . . . If I had been shocked, if I had been hurt, if I had tried to hide it, if I had yelled at him, then later, when he's seventeen or eighteen or whenever, then that would shade his own view of his sexuality, that there was something abnormal, that there was something that had to be hidden, that there was something that was wrong. [Jen: Did you pick up where you left off, or what?] I can't remember. What I'm going to actually default to is that, if Dylan needed me, then we probably disengaged, I probably took care of whatever it was he needed . . .

and then we got back together and kept going! [Jen: What was your lover doing all this time?] *He was just there. He's a dad, but he's already raised his kids, and he raised his kids much more conservatively, so he was just kind of looking at me, going, "I wonder how she's going to deal with this."*

The bigger question is how kids deal with having parents whose sex lives are outside the norm, such as being gay, polyamorous, involved in BDSM (no, these things are not always something you can keep "just in the bedroom"), and even working in the sex industry. Let's face it: most of us don't want to think about our parents' sexuality any more than we have to.

OBERON ZELL-RAVENHEART: [Jen: How do your kids, now grown, feel about having been raised in a multiparent, polyamorous household?] *I think that they've all said that they regarded this as a source of valuable lessons and insights in their growing up. I've stayed up very late at night, having conversations with the kids in our tribe, about that very question: How do you feel? Were we turning you into pink monkeys by giving you all this stuff? And basically what the young people have said was that they really valued having grown up in this community and these circles, where all this stuff was treated naturally. It took the spookiness out, while still retaining the magic and the sacredness. So they consider that to be good.*

I grew up in the fifties. I grew up in "Pleasantville." So perhaps I tend to be a bit conservative when it comes to kids, projecting my own upbringing. It's a funny thing. There's a part of me that is very shy, modest, etcetera, and that seems totally absurd to anybody who observes me outside, but I tend to be concerned with not wanting to expose kids to things that are just too far out there. For example, Pagan gatherings these days have an increasing number of really out-there people with the piercings and S/M stuff, and all, and I'm a bit uncomfortable about exposing the kids to all this. But I look around and I watch the kids, and they seem to handle it just fine, so I figure, "Well, okay. . . ." But it's not something I would have wanted to introduce my kids to when I was raising them.

I'm not quite sure how to deal with it, because kids are being exposed to all kinds of stuff that I'm uncomfortable about, and a lot of it is Internet stuff, but most Pagans, for example, really oppose all these controls and stuff on the Internet that don't allow kids to be exposed to certain stuff. Maybe in the issue of free speech, there may be a case here, but I kind of think that there's stuff kids shouldn't be exposed to.

PHIL BRUCATO: *My main lover is quite open with her son about her sexuality, and from what I've seen, she has raised him with healthy ideas of both passion and propriety. I've seen Pagan people who either dump their full sexual baggage in the laps of their kids (not a good idea!), or lock the doors and pretend nothing's going on (perhaps even worse). Not being a parent myself, I'm still trying to figure out the ideal space between those two extremes, but Francesca's respectful openness provides a good example.*

When you're not only Pagan but also a sex worker, it poses even more of a challenge to your kids.

SHAI SHAHAR: *Our daughters share the blessing and the curse of having been reared by sexually honest elders. (Un)luckily for them, we were not prepared to be hypocrites. Perhaps it would have been easier if we had lived a life of anonymous Paganinity and held nine-to-five jobs, or lived in a commune far and away from urban reality and public pressures. But all three of us who can claim to have had a hand in parenting Aida, Cora's daughter, are quite public personalities: local sex and performance art celebrities, authors, and "counterculture" icons. We*

116

are always being interviewed for magazines and newspapers, seen as guests on chat shows and variety TV, not only here, but in other countries, including Israel, where my daughter Keren has lived more than half of her life, and where she is living now. So there was an awful lot of what I would call discomfort which I'm sure they endured while dealing with peers and teachers at school after one or both of us had been demonstrating sexual techniques, talking of sexual adventures, or advocating sexual (Pagan) principles on the tube the night before. And we deeply regret the moments when they were forced to choose between defending their parents or distancing themselves from us and our "message."

However, now that they are both at the very end of their puberty, each a knowing and nubile eighteen-year-old goddess, I am proud to say that they are two well-adjusted, sexually healthy girls, with open minds and a true sense of their own value. They are both very open with us about the sex they are having and with whom. They respect their bodies and we respect their choices. And I doubt that there is anything about our sex life they don't know, and didn't hear from us first.

Adolescents coming of age in the Pagan community will be vulnerable to the same sexual issues as the adults in that community. The kind of freewheeling sexuality typified by the community can be liberating to adults, but intimidating and confusing to teens. And when our tribe is also our "chosen family," sexual boundaries get fuzzy.

LaSara Firefox: *As a person who grew up in the Pagan community, I can say that we haven't figured out how to be a multigenerational community yet. I experienced a lot of gray area around family versus tribe versus clan, etcetera. . . . It was confusing to have sexual vibes intermingled with the familial, as can be expected. There are some taboos*

117

that make sense. . . . There are certain cases where it is important for a budding puer or puella* to feel safe in developing his or her sexuality.

For a young man or woman to be encountered sexually by someone he or she has a complex relationship with can be confusing, and there can be elements of the misuse of power that are not obvious, even to the older, wiser one. I have been on both ends of the older-younger relationship spectrum, and I do feel that there are times that an age difference is totally all right. But there are also circumstances that make an age gap more profound, like assumption of an authority role, or close family ties, by marriage, or even divorce, or even just having grown up around a person for all of your life.

We NeoPagans are in the process of crafting (pun intended) our own community. Since that community's social mores about sex are so radically different from the ones with which most of us have been raised, and since we don't have a rule book to which we can turn for ethical and moral guidelines, we need to give serious thought as to how we want to handle our sexuality as a group. The bottom line appears to be consent and respect.

---

*A Latin term meaning male or female youth.

5. GENDER AND QUEER PAGANISM ❧

IN ANY FERTILITY and nature religion, gender and sexual orientation are going to play a central role. But for many of us, those things are inextricably intertwined with cultural and personal assumptions. At this point in the gay rights movement, and with gender roles being continually challenged in the mainstream as well as the Pagan community, we can't take the same things for granted as we could perhaps fifty years ago, in NeoPaganism's infancy.

Gender roles, whether socially constructed or biological, exist—and in a more pervasive way than may be immediately obvious. Unfortunately, many of them set up impossible goals for us, as we try to become living archetypes of what we've been taught equals maleness or femaleness. Riane Eisler says, "Men can never meet the exaggerated expectation that they will provide all meaning, content, and purpose in women's lives. Women can never meet the exaggerated expectation (their own and those of men) that they will be eternally beautiful, young, pliable, and pleasing."[1] Fortunately, since gender is a big part of our theology in Paganism, this gives us a chance to think about these things and change our outdated attitudes.

Of course, we can't ignore biology. There are certain hormones that affect male and female behavior and that always will.

RAVEN KALDERA: *[The masculine/feminine idea is] copied from present culture. There is a certain biological truth to it . . . I think we attribute things to the biology that are not necessarily true, but . . . having had both estrogen in me and testosterone in me, they're different. They feel different. They make you do and think differently. . . . People who go around saying, "Oh, hormones really don't affect behavior," they aren't talking to trannies.*

SHAI SHAHAR: *I am robustly male. I have come to accept that estrogen, progesterone, and testosterone are the Holy Trinity of sex hormones and that testosterone sure has a way of influencing one's sexuality, behaviorally speaking. At least it has for me.*

Although gender plays a significant role in NeoPagan magic and worship, that paradigm gives us a lot of leeway to form our own interpretations. Polytheism gives us femme Gods (Dionysus) and butch Goddesses (Athena) to emulate and enjoy. As a feminist religion, NeoPaganism gives men a break by freeing them from many of the internalized gender roles—they aren't judged if they're emotional, affectionate, creative, and so forth. It also helps to counteract the prevalent female-negative sexism in our culture.

JACQUI OMI: *As a child, I prayed and wished and asked constantly that I be male, because that's the only thing that worked for my parents. They wanted to have six sons, and my mother was raised to feel that women were very inferior, and she always reminded me that I was extremely inferior. So my Paganism has given me the desire to be a woman, and enjoy it, and body acceptance, and [the idea that] you don't have to have a penis to have brains. It's been wonderful.*

The Taoist yin-yang is a useful symbol for gender. Each side has a bit of the other, and they are fluid, moving, ever-changing. No matter what your sexual orientation, there will be times to be yin—to receive pleasure, and there will be times to be yang—to give pleasure. No matter what your gender orientation, you have both male and female elements within you, dancing together.

LaSara Firefox: *I feel that getting to bring my inner "guy" out has given me some real insight into my own wounded image of men and maleness and has also given me a very palpable awareness of some of the cultural issues of maleness. I have cross-dressed and passed as male, and it was a very lonely, isolating experience. People were afraid of me, because I was not a very approachable-looking guy. Girls totally ignored me when I talked to them, even to the point of walking in the other direction. I got some respect from guys, but got no love from the girlies. It really gave me a sense of compassion for men who are not exactly the standard pretty thing. But mostly, getting to play out my own male demons and see who was caught in there was really growth-producing.*

Queer History in Paganism

Certainly, there have been homosexuality and bisexuality as long as there has been sexuality. In some ancient cultures that practiced sacred sexuality, such as the Hindus and Greeks, homosexuality was perfectly acceptable. And in prehistory, when heterosexuality was revered for its capacity to create life, it's conceivable (no pun intended) that gay folks created rituals to sacralize their sexuality as well. Cave art in Italy dating to 10,000 BCE shows an all-male ritual in which the participants are wearing bird masks. They have erect penises and there are lines connecting them to each other's buttocks and ankles. The lines, it is speculated, could be cords or even semen. The man who discovered this art believes it depicts a homoerotic initiation.[2]

Greece is known for its association with homosexuality, and no wonder. Ancient Greece, in theology and culture, was very

121

gay-friendly. The Greek Gods Dionysus, Hermes, Pan, Zeus, and Apollo are all bisexual. (Dill seeds are supposed to represent Hermes' semen—so go enjoy that pickle.) The Amazons were likely bi as well.[3] Festivals for Artemis, since she rejected traditional marriage, included same-sex eroticism for both women and men. Eros, according to Christopher Penczak, author of *Gay Witchcraft: Empowering the Tribe*, "is the patron and protector of homosexual love," and "as patron of success in battle, he was called upon by warrior/lovers before a fight, because many in the Greek world believed the love men had for each other would unite and lead them to victory."[4]

Transgendered people have had a special role in many indigenous religions throughout time. They may be seen as representing the union of male and female in one body—a walking Great Rite, as it were—and also may be honored for their in-betweenness, a characteristic important for any shaman. This has been true with Native American Navaho, Mohave, and Hidatsa tribes. Eisler says that the Minoans, men and women both, cross-dressed for special ritual events.[5] As the Greek God Dionysus was characterized as somewhat androgynous, being delicately built and wearing women's dresses, his worshippers particularly loved to play with gender. His female worshippers, the Maenads, wore men's clothing. The word *hermaphrodite* comes from Hermaphroditus, the child of Aphrodite and Hermes. The Semitic Goddess Astarte is sometimes pictured as hermaphroditic. Athena has the ability to transform into a man. Baphomet is not an ancient deity, but was first conceived during the Middle Ages in Europe; he is both male and female, human and animal (goat).* The Voodoo Loa Baron Samedi, a God of the dead and magic, wears a combination of men's and women's clothing.

---

*Baphmet was thought to be associated with the Knights Templar.

As evidenced by the books *Gay Witchcraft* and *Hermaphrodeities*, as well as the recommended *Encyclopedia of Queer Myth, Symbol, and Spirit*, there is a buttload (so to speak) of gay- and transgender-themed material in ancient paganism, more than I have the room to do justice to in this section. So, go and study.

In the Edwardian era (1901–1919), Pan was perceived as the patron of "forbidden" (i.e., gay) sexuality, and indeed, Aleister Crowley's lover and working partner Victor Neuberg wrote poetry about rapturous union with the God. Crowley performed sex magic rituals with both men and women. In 1913, he conducted the Paris Workings—three and a half weeks of sex magic and Dark Eros work—with Neuberg, in the process remembering a past life in which Crowley was a hierodule (sacred whore) priest/ess of the Goddess and Neuberg his male lover. They decided that one is more apt to be gay or transgendered after recently changing sex from the previous lifetime. They also concluded that, while heterosexual energy is directed outward for the conception of children, homosexual energy is more suited toward magical and shamanic practices.

Early Wicca was extremely heterosexist, maintaining a balanced boy-girl ratio in covens at all times, only initiating cross-gender, and so forth. In the 1970s, the Dianic and Minoan traditions were started; Dianic covens were and still are for women only, and the Minoans, although being open to both sexes as a tradition, work in single-sex covens. The Radical Faeries were founded in 1979 as a "loose affiliation of gay men weaving the principles of queerness, ecology, anarchy, community, transformation, paganism, and self-love into a wonderful whole."[6]

There are still plenty of Gardenerian and other covens that operate within a strictly heterosexual framework, but the huge growth in the Wiccan and Pagan population since Gardner's day has brought with it a broader range of lifestyle. Today, there's apt to be a tradition out there for anyone across the spectrum of gender and sexual orientation.

The Magic of Sexual Orientation

It's not surprising that the Pagan community today is extraordinarily accepting of the wide range of gender orientation and sexual orientation (and those are two distinct things). NeoPaganism is one of the few spiritual paths that wholeheartedly accepts the diversity of sexual orientation (the Society of Friends and the Unitarian Universalists are others). Admittedly, in some ways it's difficult to reconcile the basic beliefs of a fertility religion with a sexual chemistry that is not linked to physical fertility. In order to do so, we need to look beyond a strictly duotheistic theology and into the heart and soul of Pagan practice as nature religion. Any arguments about a sexual orientation being "against nature" are absurd; if it exists, and if it is something humans want to do, then it is part of nature. Humans do what comes naturally, and that includes bisexuality, homosexuality, transgendered sexuality, and masturbation. (It also includes BDSM, but that has its own chapter.) As long as no one is being manipulated or harmed, it's all good.

Almost everyone I interviewed perceived the Pagan community as very welcoming to those of different sexual orientations, but that is by no means a universal experience.

RHOMYLLY FORBES: *I've found that bisexuals are (a) sneered at by the gays and lesbians and (b) considered kinky aberrations by the heterosexuals in the Pagan community just as they are outside of it. I've been accused of being an oathbreaker by former friends in the Pagan community by choosing to have sex with both men and women in one festival weekend.*

Stories like this indicate that we as a community still have some distance to go before we can say we are truly accepting of sexual diversity.

Self-Loving

In the late 1950s, sex researchers William H. Masters and Virginia E. Johnson discovered that virtually all their subjects who described their sex lives as "satisfactory" had one thing in common: they masturbated.[7] I asked the folks I interviewed whether their Pagan path has influenced their experience of masturbation. Most of them said that their beliefs had allowed them to be free of guilt about it—a major relief.

> WYRDOTTER: *I never felt guilty about doing it, but at least as a Pagan I stopped feeling like I should feel guilty about doing it.* :)

Various creation myths involve the primordial God or Goddess making love to him- or herself to create the universe. According to the ancient Egyptians, as the first "thing" in the midst of nothingness, the God Atum relieved his loneliness by masturbating. His ejaculation resulted in the appearance of the first God and Goddess, Shu and Tefnut, who in turn parented the rest of the world. In one Sumerian myth, the creatrix, Tiamat, fertilizes herself. The Tigris River was said to be the ejaculate of the Mesopotamian God Enki. And Hermes taught Pan to masturbate to relieve his frustration.[8] If the Gods masturbate, why then, it must be fine for us to do it as well. And who knows what we might create?

Our society grudgingly accepts masturbation as a second-place substitute for "the real thing," intimating that pleasure should ideally come from another person. But when we choose to give ourselves pleasure, we are choosing to be that much more self-sufficient. We do not need a partner to make us feel good; we do not need a partner to complete us.

JEZEBEL DAWN BLESSING: *I think my Paganism definitely had a hand, so to speak, in my choice to begin loving myself. Paganism taught me that the body is a wondrous gift, and that ignoring it or feeling that you must overcome its urges in order to become "holy" is missing the point. To become one with the universe, you need to know how to unite body and soul by treating your body as a sacred vessel for the divine. This means exploring all of the sensations that your glorious vessel has to offer.*

My very first clitoral orgasm was an offering to the Goddess and magical moment of acceptance in union with Her. I was twenty years old and masturbating for the first time, when my orgasm hit. I had this wonderful image of hot sexual union and then I was filled with the overwhelming acceptance into the sisterhood of sexually aware Goddesses. I remember crying with joy and thanking the Goddess for the wonderful gift of my body.

I practice sacred sexuality by making myself my primary source of sexual exploration and experience. This may sound slightly strange at first, but think of all of the people that you know who experience sexual pleasure only in the context of giving or receiving with others. I have used masturbation in the Great Rite when renewing my vows between my feminine and masculine selves. There is really nothing like being your own best lover and your own Sacred Union. I endeavor to make myself a sex Goddess in the way that Inanna, Ishtar, and Aphrodite were in myth—secularly singular, autonomous, and self-sufficient—by living my experiences to their fullest, and creating a universe of my own pleasure. I find that this practice, whether it is through education, body exploration, energy work, or meditation, has helped me develop a sacred practice of getting and giving pleasure in life.

DAVE SYLVIA: *Once I became aware of the energetic aspect of masturbation, I became much less interested in porn, since it felt like I was throwing my energies away to someone I did not know and would never meet.*

MAGDALENE MERETRIX: *Because of my spiritual beliefs and experiences, I see masturbation as more than a pleasurable activity. (Though it most definitely is that as well!) I see it as a way to raise spiritual energy, clear chakras, build upon my ability to experience more love, heal myself, others or the community, and help others learn more about sexuality and the female body (through demonstration of masturbation). Additionally, my sex work has taught me to view masturbation as a fully satisfying form of sex itself rather than a poor substitute for sex, which is how many people describe masturbation to me, which makes me sad. I wish I knew a way to help people with that attitude unlock their capacity for self-love and sexual joy, but I haven't a clue yet, other than to serve as a positive example that it is possible to have a satisfying sexual relationship with one's self as well as with others.*

FRANCESCA GENTILLE: *I said to one of my teachers that I was so in love with my partner, and that when I looked at him, I would just have that feeling of bliss and euphoria, you know that rush that you get, especially when you're newly in love? And it's like your whole body is being flooded . . . with some wonderful drug, and it's actually phenylethylalamine—and I was just saying, "Oh, I have this bliss and transcendence when I look at my beloved, or when I touch him," and she said, "You know what? I want you to have that when you look at a flower. I want you to feel like you can have that anywhere, at any time, and that it's not dependent on a person, or a person doing some specified numbers of tasks, before you can have that sense of bliss and wonder." So when I look at my practice . . . and my spiritual practice, of which, to me, sacred sexuality is just embedded in that, [my question] is: How can I have that sense of appreciation, compassion, and wonder, just in my life?*

This can be taken one step further. Besides giving folks permission to pleasure themselves, NeoPaganism can provide sexual fantasy material.

PHIL BRUCATO: *I freely confess that my wild imagination and love of primal fantasy inspired (and still inspires) my Pagan devotion, and vice versa. I find the Amazonian heroines of Pagan myth and heroic fantasy to be much more appealing subjects for self-pleasure than Photoshopped models or haughty cheerleaders. The settings and circumstances of my fantasies are often Pagan, too—glorious couplings amidst fire and woodland, deep under the sea, or in the middle of a wild rite.*

And then there's my taste in women, which is Pagan in all the right ways. I've always favored spirited, defiant sensualists—partners rather than playthings. In the NeoPagan realm, I meet a lot of women who fit my desires. My lust for barefoot dancing witch-chicks makes the NeoPagan subculture a natural ground for both dating and self-loving fantasies. Other guys jack off to beer commercials; I masturbate to visions of hot Beltane celebrations. And unlike those other guys, I actually stand a good chance of realizing my fantasies!

Heterosexuality

As the "default" setting for most of humankind, heterosexuality fits easily into just about any spiritual practice. Since NeoPaganism is at heart a nature and fertility religion, heterosexuals can very easily make their love lives symbolic of their belief system. Heterosexuality is important in traditional (Gardner-derived)

Wicca; the union of God and Goddess is a central focus of liturgy, ritual, and meditation. Initiations are conducted between the sexes. Once upon a time, you couldn't join a Gardnerian coven unless you did so with your opposite-sex working partner.

ANAHITA-GULA: *I can choose to use sex as a Great Rite, honoring the Goddess through my body, and that of my chosen male partner as the God.*

OBERON ZELL-RAVENHEART: *I'm heterosexual pretty exclusively these days, though I have explored many paths. Again, I never particularly gave it a thought. I love women; I love the Goddess; I love Goddesses; I'm a Pagan artist who sculpts images of Gods and Goddesses, and I work with live models. I go to a lot of Pagan gatherings, and I encounter a lot of lovely naked Goddess women. Works for me!*

LEON: *Being straight makes issues of sexual polarity clearer in some ways. Paganism . . . provides a context wherein I can be a hetero male, and that is appreciated. Yet, I can still be sensitive and caring, and not be less manly for it. I love to show that a man can be confident, even randy, without being slimy or overly insistent. (Or at least I hope that's what I'm doing when I'm flirting!)*

PHIL BRUCATO: *My love for women fuels my love for the Goddess, and vice versa. My taste in strong, sensual women makes Paganism an obvious choice for me. And my spiritual beliefs allow me to show women that a man doesn't have to be a controlling prick to be a compelling lover.*

Even the heterosexuals who I interviewed are extraordinarily comfortable with homosexuality. Some have absolutely no interest in members of the same sex, yet don't feel threatened by gay folks.

SHAI SHAHAR: *I'm a pretty "straight" hetero, but I would claim a healthy "pro-active" tolerance and acceptance (indeed an appreciation)*

*for bisexuality and homosexuality as valid sexual options and
lifestyles.*

ANAHITA-GULA: *The Pagan worldview on sexuality allows me to be
far more accepting of alternative sexualities and the open expression of
love between people.*

Some have experimented with same-sex love; others, although
they've had no experiences in that area, acknowledge that possibly they just haven't met the right guy or girl yet.

LEON: *I've been mostly straight all day, all day yesterday and the day
before. I'll probably be straight tomorrow, but there's a very small
chance that I'll meet the right guy or change my mind for some other
reason. I'm open to the possibilities.*

There's not much more to say about heterosexuality. Sorry
folks, but you've had way more than your share of airtime already.

Bisexuality

"Bisensual" is a term I hear a lot around the NeoPagan community. It generally means being affectionate with members of
the same sex, but nothing overtly sexual. In mainstream American
culture, although women are expected to hug and kiss each other,
straight men aren't supposed to show any more affection than a
slap on the back. This is obviously a sign of a deeply internalized
homophobia (and a double standard, I might add).

DAVE SYLVIA: *I coined the term "bisensual" to describe myself, as I am
heterosexual, but comfortable with hugging, massaging, and even
kissing certain men. It helps me to be open-hearted and willing to
exchange energy with both male and female magical partners, whether
sex is involved or not.*

FRANCESCA GENTILLE: *I feel like being bisensual honors my loving my own self and my own gender and my own body, so if I truly love myself, if I'm truly self-loving to my body, then I'm going to have at least a sensual appreciation for my own gender. That's my belief.*

For some people, being sensual with members of the same sex indicates a willingness to play a bit more.

PHIL BRUCATO: *I'm heterosexual but pansensual. I play with men in group settings, but am not sexually aroused by men beyond the obvious sensual enjoyment of texture and energy. (And yes, I've "tested" this at various times. Guys just don't turn me on.)*

True bisexuality fits right into a religion that emphasizes polarity. When we acknowledge God and Goddess as each dwelling within us, it stands to follow that each of them would be inclined to reach out for their complement in the world—and lo, we find ourselves yearning to join in love and/or lust with both men and women. This becomes a self-perpetuating cycle: Expressing ourselves sexually in a way that seems to us "other-gendered" gets us more in touch with the gender within us that may be neglected, and then we start to express it more.

JEZEBEL DAWN BLESSING: *My Pagan path has helped me to achieve the Great Rite or great marriage within myself of my masculine and feminine sides. I feel that I am a gender-balanced person, and I would not have achieved that, had I not pursued my interest in Paganism.*

JACQUI OMI: *Just as I worship male and female, I express my regard for both of those body forms here on earth. And I think that's real special. I never, ever, ever, would have been bisexual if I hadn't been Pagan; I am absolutely positive of that, and that's mostly because I thought about it for many, many years. This is my first female partner, and I'm fifty-six. Even as a teenager, I never went through any of that.*

Many years ago, I thought about how awful it would have been for my daughter for me to be a lesbian, because she would have that to deal with, too, along with my being such a weird person. And it turns out, when I told her [I was bi], she was the most supportive of anyone.

MAGENTA: *I see myself as partaking of both male and female, Goddess and God; thus, bisexuality seems natural and normal, at least for me.*

Many of the NeoPagans I interviewed who do not restrict their sexual interaction to one gender chose to call themselves "sexual," "pansexual," or "omnisexual," rather than the usual "bisexual." Some of them gave the reason that they do not believe there are only two genders—rather, there is a continuum between male and female.

SHAI SHAHAR: *I would like to see a climate emerge in which this preoccupation with one's sexual orientation . . . heterosexual, bisexual, homosexual, transsexual, etcetera could be replaced with the acceptance that we are all "sexual."*

JEZEBEL DAWN BLESSING: *I am sexual, whether it is with men or women; I'm just sexual. So I guess if you had to orient my sexuality you would call me a bisexual.*

RAVEN KALDERA: *I'm pansexual, and so are my lovers. That means that bodily configuration has nothing to do with what we are attracted to in human beings. I will sometimes call myself bisexual when talking to ordinary folk, but "bi" means two, and there are way more than two genders, and I've fucked them all.*

I am capable of having a perfectly decent relationship with all sorts of genitals. They don't matter, as long as I can have sex with them. What's upstairs matters. Monosexuals, or even the sort of bisexuals who like their men manly and their women womanly, they don't get it. They are restricted by being hung up on primary and secondary sexual characteristics. They can't touch a soul without playing with some kind

132

of roles. For those of us for whom it doesn't matter, we can dispense with roles. That in itself is a special, sacred perspective.

MAGDALENE MERETRIX: *For convenience, I use the term* bisexual, *but I consider it a flawed definition since, as I said, I don't believe that sex is a dichotomy. (And since I've had sex with intersexed people in the past and thoroughly enjoyed it, "bi" is a partial definition at best.) I've found freedom in the term* bisexual *even though it hints at a simple dichotomy that I've long since discarded. Like most symbols, the word* bisexual *is an icon that depicts a transcendent reality, a meaning too large for that symbol to effectively capture and box away. When I label myself bisexual, I am calling myself open. Open to possibilities, open to the ebb and flow of people past the shores of my life. Though the word* sex *is contained within the word* bisexual, *to me it's about so much more than sex (a vast realm itself!). It's about opening my heart and my life to the winds of time and learning to love as much as I can, as long as I can, as full and deep and wide as an ocean.*[9]

The gay community has worked hard to instill the idea that "sexual orientation is not a choice," but this also tends to imply that sexual orientation is something you have from birth and it is unchangeable. In reality, folks who are comfortable with their sexuality may experiment and even slide back and forth on the Kinsey scale* through the course of their lives. Bisexuality is about being open to change and exploration.

CAROL QUEEN: *[At Queen of Heaven], we have seen a couple of pretty stellar sort of bisexual conversions—or comings-out, really, because you don't take an adult who's never ever had any desire and*

---

*Developed by Dr. Alfred Kinsey and his associates in the late 1940s and early 1950s, the Kinsey scale was a seven-point continuum through which people could define their sexual orientation: zero was exclusively straight, six exclusively gay, and three completely bisexual.

instill it in him or her suddenly. That's not how it works. You make a place where it's safe, and then the person acts on it or doesn't. Of course, the first part is our job, and that is especially meaningful to us as bisexually identified people.

It's also meaningful to us because we know how much homophobia lives in straight male culture—even in really benign, good straight male culture. Like in the Tantra community, for example, [it's accepted] for men to get much more emotional, to embrace one another, to get really close, to sit around with their arms draped around each other, or their heads in each other's laps. Do they turn around and suck each other's dicks? Not too often, at least, that we know of. In this context, we make space for a more full erotic response.

We've also seen it happen in the other direction, with same-sex identified people saying, "Oh, what the hell, I feel safe here. I always wanted to try this." So I think that's a pretty fundamental place for experimentation to live. When somebody's worn-on-the-T-shirt sexual orientation has a place to be fluid, we're just the kind of people who think that's a positive space.

Homosexuality

Paganism provides a safe haven for gays and lesbians who come from cultures and religious traditions that refuse to accept their sexual orientation.

WYRDOTTER: *When you're gay and everyone tells you "God" hates you, you have to make deliberate and studied decisions about your spiritual path; you can't just plod blindly down the same path as your family or other group. On the other side, if your spirituality says sex is a good thing, a positive and connecting experience, then you can't help but have a more fulfilling, positive sex life.*

134

Unfortunately, although mainstream NeoPaganism is socially very accepting of homosexuality in its culture, Wicca in particular can be downright dismissive of it in terms of theology and liturgy. It's all about the Goddess and the God, the Great Rite, yin and yang, fertility, the great pregnant mother Goddess, and so on. But first of all, "all acts of love and pleasure are her rituals," and that includes *all*. Second, if our path is polytheistic, and the Gods have sex, well then it must follow that at least some of the time the Gods are having sex with other Gods of their own gender. So much for the standard Great Rite. The Wiccan tradition of the Oak King and Holly King as the two Gods of the waxing and waning light, respectively, can provide a good substitute for gay men to the usual "Lord and Lady" deity pairing.

CAROL QUEEN: *There's a very hetero-balanced Paganism where you've got to have a priestess and a priest, you've got to be honoring the Goddess and the God. The notion of the Great Rite is powerful, but the way we usually hear about it is pretty powerfully heterosexual. That might not be very spiritually meaningful to somebody who's queer-identified. In fact, it might feel downright oppressive to some people who are queer-identified.*

As I was pretty young, and coming into being truly Pagan-identified, I would find the kind of "British Witches in the fifties sneaking off into the woods and doing the Great Rite" kind of stereotype literally off-putting. Today, to me, it's just "Why wouldn't somebody, in a group of people who were primarily heterosexually identified, or who value and respect the profound connection that a woman and a man can have, why wouldn't they want to go and do that?" That's fabulous, of course. It just can't end there, in terms of what the spiritual system provides for people. There have got to be other equally strong visions and images that will be meaningful.

As mentioned earlier, there are traditions, covens, and books that specifically focus on single-gender work. These are, as one might expect, very friendly to gay folks. One of the earliest Wiccan traditions is Dianic Wicca, which is very female-focused; Wiccan lesbians have long had a tradition to call home and a mythos that validates their experience. Gay male Wiccans, although they have the Radical Faerie community and the Minoan tradition, have not had as much of a place and voice in mainstream NeoPaganism, but that is slowly changing. Being gay, of course, is no obstacle to worshipping the God and the Goddess. Even those who don't like to sleep with opposite-sex people still have both a mother and a father. And the point of the Great Rite, really, is *alchemy*—not heterosexuality.

> ANAHITA-GULA: *Sexuality is central to much of NeoPaganism, but its not the end-all and be-all of ritual expression. The "Great Rite in token" or "in truth" can be used as metaphor for the commingling of creative juices between any human beings, whether they be gay, bi, homosexual, trans . . . etcetera etcetera! It is both metaphorically and literally a pivot point of NeoPaganism, IMHO.*

Certainly, on a literal, physical level, it takes a sperm and an ovum to create a new human being (although cloning and experiments with parthenogenesis may date this statement someday). In that sense, there is still something unique about a man and a woman coming together. But although it's wonderful and nice to make a new human being, there are many other things that also need to be made in this world.

As the gay rights movement continues, hopefully we will be able to craft a new way to look at gender in the context of traditional fertility religion. Some mental-health professionals, and even folks who are supposedly experts on sacred sexuality, still insist that in homosexual relationships, one person acts in the role of the "man" and one the "woman." Putting aside the fact that this comparison falls short in relationships comprised of more than two people, it's worth asking the question, what does it mean to "act in the role" of a man or woman? Yes, hormones are real, but not all men act the same, and not all women act the same. Furthermore, certainly opposites attract, but sometimes like-attracts-like as well. Even straight folks need to have *some* things in common with their partners. We need not get trapped in an overly simplistic paradigm.

Drag and Transgender

As mentioned earlier, transgendered folks, as boundary crossers and shamans, have enjoyed special ritual/religious status in many indigenous cultures over history. Unfortunately, however, mainstream NeoPaganism tends to employ a very clear-cut approach to gender that excludes such folks.

CAROL QUEEN: *I don't believe we should separate sexuality into female and male energies. The notion that there are binary female and male energies in the universe is fine, but there is also a whole spectrum inside and outside the male/female yin-yang notion. Even though I embrace the idea of the God along with the Goddess, I don't believe there must always be a man and a woman in any sexual or spiritual context. Our energies meet, connect, and swirl around on a lot of different levels, and the notion that there are rigid ways to be is wrong. Rigidity, binary identities—those are all constructs to help us think we have a handle on the world, when life is really so much more complex!*[10]

The symbolism of the hieros gamos can be taken too literally.

RAVEN KALDERA: *In most traditional religions, like in Hinduism . . . they emphasize that the whole point of the heterosexual dance of male*

137

and female is to bring them together into one being, which can never happen. It's why you have the hijira at weddings, the tranny priestesses. They symbolize the two-in-one, and therefore in cultures like that, the two-in-one are sacred, because they are the ultimate. We are the goal which heterosexuality is doomed to always fall short of. So modern NeoPaganism, because it's being practiced by people who came out of a Judeo-Christian situation, they miss that point. They are incredibly uncomfortable with that point.

Certainly, a nature religion should honor and celebrate maleness and femaleness as distinct entities; after all, genders are part of nature. But a nature religion should also honor the wide diversity of body types and gender identities that occur *naturally*. When a baby is born with "ambiguous genitalia," the common modern medical practice has been, and often still is, to perform "corrective" surgery. It's much easier to make girl parts than boy parts (as transfolk well know), so female is the default. This practice often causes great emotional pain and sometimes sexual dysfunction during the individual's lifetime, in ways that are far too complex and extensive to describe here—but I'm sure you can imagine.

RAVEN KALDERA: *I did not come out with ambiguous genitalia. I have a secondary condition. Mine showed up . . . at puberty. And it's probably lucky. Sometimes I feel like, "Oh gee, it would have been nice if I had intersexed genitalia at birth," but I'm glad I didn't, because I wouldn't have been allowed to keep them. . . . Knowing my parents, they would have hacked them off.*

Why is this surgery still performed, when it's so obviously a bad idea? Well, most people are very uncomfortable with gender ambiguity. Psychological experiments show that people have a strong need to separate individuals into categories of male and female. In my opinion, this position stems from a disconnect with nature, where things are not so clear-cut. All human embryos start out appearing androgynous, then become female, then some continue morphing to male. All of us have both estrogen and testosterone within us. All of us exhibit some traditionally male qualities and some traditionally female qualities, and the ratio and flavor of these things change and morph over the course of our lives. It is physiologically impossible to be 100 percent male or 100 percent female; those are labels we have created for our own ease of classification. Being born with ambiguous genitalia is not a condition or a disease; presuming all the excretory parts work, it causes no physical harm. It is a natural variation that needs no "fix."

Those who feel a contradiction between the genders of their mind/spirit and body may choose to use surgical and medical means to correct the situation. One may argue that this is "going against nature," but it is their *own* bodies that they are choosing to modify, and they have the right to shape their bodies in a way that makes them the most comfortable, just as anyone has the right to get her own ears pierced or hair cut.

One of the great aspects of the NeoPagan community is its willingness to cross and play with gender boundaries. It's common to see men wearing sarongs and skirts at festivals, and women need not act or look traditionally "feminine" to be seen as sexy— hairy legs abound.

DANIEL DEL VECCHIO: *I really love it that Pagan men* [sometimes!] *kiss one another on the lips in greeting. I love wearing skirts and sarongs and whatever else I feel like. I feel that, at least in the Pagan community, I can celebrate my feminine aspects openly. That, in turn, leaves me feeling confident that I know what sort of person I am.*

MAGDALENE MERETRIX: *I live in a very female body, but I do not identify as female or as male. "Transgendered" is not an accurate*

139

description for my gender self-perception, because "trans" means "across," and I don't feel myself to be the wrong gender or a gender-bender, so much as that gender itself feels like an alien concept to me.

I don't consider sex to be a binary concept, since there are so many different ways that intersex people can manifest. I consider sex to be more of a continuum (much as I've seen gender depicted) that presents as an inverted bell curve, with most people being either definitely male or definitely female, but plenty of room for variation in between.

As laid-back as the Pagan community is about gender, there is still a discomfort with transgendered folks. For those of us who have been trained in a duotheistic Wiccan framework, to try to absorb transgenderism into our theology can be at once an unsettling and hugely liberating paradigm shift. "Genderfuck" happens when someone expresses stereotypical aspects of both male and female genders at once. The Radical Faeries are especially known for this; they often sport beards with their frilly drag. Genderfuck is intended to be shocking—to jolt us out of our old assumptions and habits. But transgendered people are not making the choice to be shocking—they are just being who they are, and, as evidenced from my interview with Raven, large segments of the Pagan community need to buy a clue.

RAVEN KALDERA: *I wrote* Hermaphrodeities: The Transgender Spirituality Workbook *because I kept finding transgender mysteries in ancient myths and practices, and I could see how they could be applied to modern transfolk. I was also appalled by the nastiness directed toward Pagan trannies, and I wanted to create something that would show how sacred we are. That, and the transgender gods kept calling to me. . . . I'm FTM, married to an MTF, and my boyfriend is also FTM. We're an all-trans household. We know all about the trans mysteries—they're ordinary to us. Around here, it's normal to be both at once. There is no sexism in our household, our relationships, or our religion. We may be the only ones for whom this is true.*

I love nudity. Having naked people around makes me happy. I'm often naked in my own home. However, I am a transgendered intersexual, and I don't go naked in front of people who are not my family and lovers, because my anatomy is so different, and I'm a freak show every time. Bella and Joshua mourn the same thing. Being a freak show, having to educate everyone, knowing that a certain percentage of people will be visibly horrified by your naked body, that's wearing on one's soul. We can't go fully naked, even in Pagan space, and that's harsh.

At the worst, they stare and gawk, and maybe do things like deliberately get our pronouns wrong. If somebody looks at me, and is convinced I'm a guy, and then I take off my clothes, showing that I don't have a dick, and that person starts calling me "she," what the fuck is going on? Clearly, people like that have big issues. At worst, they'll come up to us and tell us that we've mutilated our bodies. Being trans is extremely uncomfortable for a lot of people. They're like, "What, you really think that you're a. . . ?" A lot of it's about sex. A lot of it's this total fear of, "If I get attracted to you, and I find out that your anatomy is weird, it'll fuck with me."

Traditionally, the NeoPagan Beltane maypole ritual has the women standing around the hole and the men inserting the pole—a very literal interpretation of the sexual symbolism. In *Hermaphrodeities*, Kaldera writes about being in a group of trans-folk at such a ritual who felt excluded and marginalized. Their solution was to form a human chain to bring the pole to the hole, demonstrating the way they form a bridge between male and female. At the Rites of Spring festival in western Massachusetts, organizers solve the problem in a different way. Those who feel that they are in a receptive time in their lives gather around the pole, and those who feel that they are in a proactive time fetch and insert the pole. It has always seemed to me to be a fairly even ratio of men to women in each role. I myself have played both roles.

Celibacy

There may be times in one's life, when, for various reasons, it makes sense to take a break from some aspect of sexual contact or practice. This could be defined in many ways for different people: no intercourse, no sexual contact with another person, no masturbation, and/or no orgasm. In a religion that accepts all forms of sexuality, celibacy and related sexual limits are rarely, if ever, mandated or even expected; as a result, they can only arise from a personal choice and need.

Refraining from sexual contact with others can give the individual a chance to turn inward and to save energy for himself that he might otherwise be giving away to his lovers.

MAGDALENE MERETRIX: *I've gone into celibacy when I've felt that I needed to sort things out inside, and spend time focusing on and nurturing myself, rather than nurturing others around me. Choosing to spend time in celibacy has given me a chance to examine my relationship patterns without the distraction of a current relationship to sway my thinking. Time spent in celibacy has given me insight, strength, and self-validation. If you are defining celibacy as refraining from any sexual action, including solitary sexual action, then no, I haven't ever practiced celibacy, but I do believe that it can be a valid practice.*

JEZEBEL DAWN BLESSING: *Periodically, I need to recharge my own sexual batteries, get back to center, and find my inner spark. During these times, I will refrain from sexual contact with other people. It usually only lasts a few weeks, at most. I love to flirt, and it's my favorite way to make people feel good, regardless of whether I'm actually going to sleep with anyone. I also like masturbation, and think it is an excellent mode of negative energy release, but if my goal in being celibate were to retain all energies, then I would refrain from self-pleasuring as well (I don't think I could make myself stop flirting). I think that celibacy is a very valid practice if it is not used as a tool to renounce the sexual self. You can be a sexual being without having sexual contact with others, but I find that when a negative stigma is placed upon sexuality or sexual human nature in the name of chastity, then those urges can become twisted and painful.*

Celibacy can also be a way to store up energy for later release or to restrict it to a sacred context. Historically, chastity was "often used as an instrument to prepare for heated and passionate sexual union during fertility festivals and ritual orgies or similar celebrations."[11]

ANAHITA-GULA: *There are rare times when one must charge up and turn inward, whereas in my experience, sexual magic is a building up of energy in the short term (during foreplay), culminating in the release and channeling of the energies (orgasm) outwards. . . . It is perfectly allowable to choose any sexual path if one is Pagan. If I choose to find that no man measures up to what I want in an embodiment of the God. . . . I can choose to choose no one.*

RAVEN KALDERA: *I think [celibacy] can be a very valid practice, especially for people who are trying to purge their sexuality of the detritus of collected issues. I think that the Pagan movement does itself a disservice by rejecting monasticism in all forms. The way that I visualize Pagan monasticism, it wouldn't necessarily mandate celibacy, but it might mandate something like: Sex only for wholehearted service, and for sacred ritual sex. It might also mandate that one couldn't have*

143

sex about which one felt ambivalent, or which triggered old negativity, and for some people, that might mean a long, long period of celibacy, until they could cleanse themselves of those problems. And some people just have a low sex drive, and that needs to be taken into consideration.

Even many of those Pagans who would never practice celibacy themselves can still see the value in it.

SHAI SHAHAR: *If someone can find peace or God/dess through abstinence, I see no reason to spoil it for them by saying they are doing it wrong, just as I would resent a "religious fantatic" of any persuasion telling me that overindulgence cannot lead to salvation. I believe people should be allowed to live according to their own lights in this matter, and to honor God/dess as they see fit. My God/dess has never intimated to me that sexual abstinence was desired or required, and I respect Her for leaving my dick and the decision of what (and whom) to do with it in my hands.*

Some Pagans have a hard time finding anything redeeming about celibacy, viewing it as an unnatural state that is either imposed on others or a way for someone to deny him- or herself the basic necessities of life.

JACQUI OMI: *I would never be celibate. Yuck! That would be terrible. I've known so many people who practice celibacy. [For years], I was very close to the gal who runs the Kashi Ranch in Roseland, down near Sebastian, Florida. She's actually married, and still celibate. She comes from a Hindu background. She only allows any of her people at her place to have sex when they are trying to get pregnant; they can't have sex any other time. [She says that] you need to take all your drive and use it for your spiritual development, not for anything else. "It's distracting; it keeps you off your path." I think it's nuts. I am totally opposed to forced celibacy. I think if a person's celibate and wants to be celibate, that's his or her business. . . . I'm really against religious dogma.*

OBERON ZELL-RAVENHEART: *There are five elements: earth, water, air, fire, and spirit. We are composed of all of these, and we need to take them all in to fully live. We take in earth via the food we eat. We take in water via the liquids we drink. We take in air via the air we breathe. We take in fire via the heat we must absorb from the sun, fires, etcetera. And we take in spirit through sex. We can live a few minutes without air; we can live a short time without heat; we can go a few days without water; and we can last over a month without food. And it's possible, I understand, to live an entire lifetime without sex. But why would anyone want to? All I can see is that it leaves one spiritless.*

Both celibacy and ebullient sexuality can be seen as opposite extremes, each expressing a kind of passion. In one, the energy is directed inward, and in the other, outward. Both states are natural. We breathe in, and then we breathe out. We take energy in and we release it. It is impossible to have sex twenty-four hours a day. There are always resting times, recharging times. In NeoPaganism, where many of us are still reveling in the freedom that our path brings, it's easy to forget the magic and value of saying no, of practicing restraint, of relating to people from the heart instead of the genitals—yes, of doing that "higher chakra" thing. Either sex or celibacy may be healthy or damaging, depending on the individual and the situation, and one may cycle through each many times in the course of one's adulthood. The only way to know what is right for us is to know ourselves intimately and without passing judgment.

In terms of sexual orientation, there seems an obligation to pick one path and stick to it—lest we be labeled "confused." But nature is in a continual state of change, and so people change, naturally, over time. There is no reason why our sexual orientation, any more than any other aspects of ourselves, must be static.

ANNIE SPRINKLE: *I made up the term "metamorphosexual," which basically means "always in a state of change": day to day, week to week, month to month, year to year. Some people may have very simple, straightforward sexuality, but not me. My sexuality is always in flux, with different interests, different likes, and different issues at different times. My sexuality is so multifaceted. It's like a kaleidoscope. I can never narrow it down to a "sexual orientation."*

6. BDSM
AND DARK EROS ❧

BDSM STANDS for three pairs of terms: bondage/discipline, dominance/submission, and sadism/masochism. Usually, D/S has more to do with mind-play and S/M with sensation or pain play.* B/D can be anywhere in between. BDSM is also called "leather," as in "I'm into leather," and "the leather community," because it's associated with the leather fetish. Although there are distinctions between dominant and top, and submissive and bottom (see the glossary), for purposes of simplicity I use them interchangeably here. "Dark Eros" is used here to signify the use of BDSM techniques in a ritual context, with the goal of achieving some form of personal transformation or magical goal. It is a reference to a "darker" aspect of the Greek God Eros.

I must stress a few key points:

- BDSM has nothing to do with abuse, rape, or any kind of nonconsensual activity. The submissive has the option of ending the activity at any time with a "safeword."

---

*"Play" is a term often used as a verb to describe BDSM activities. Dossie Easton: *"Play" has more than one meaning. There's play like little children playing, there's play like I'm not real serious, then there's play like drama and theater, and there's play like psychodrama. And there's play like dancing with the universe.*

- BDSM can involve pain, but it is not all about pain.
- BDSM is about a power exchange between two or more people, who are nonetheless fundamentally equals.
- BDSM is not just something practiced by a fringe group of perverts. "According to the 1990 Kinsey Institute New Report on Sex, 'Researchers estimate that 5 percent to 10 percent of the U.S. population engages in diverse sexual practices for sexual pleasure on at least an occasional basis, with most incidents being either mild or staged activities involving no real pain or violence.'"[1]

BDSM can be titillating or transformative and anything in between. In a magical and/or sacred context as Dark Eros work, it can be used for personal transformation, to achieve trance or other altered states of consciousness, for worship, and as a form of sex magic (details on the latter are covered in chapter 8).

Don Kraig: *Many people think that BDSM is just waling the bejesus out of someone because the abuser is a sick puppy who gets a thrill out of harming another. While there are probably people who do this, it is certainly unrelated to the BDSM community. BDSM is about sharing power, extending boundaries, working with magical energy, and—as surprising as it may sound to those who actually pay attention to movies and novels—caring for their partner. (Look at what mainstream novels and movies say about the Craft. Most of it is wrong. So why think that their descriptions of BDSM are correct?)*

Shai Shahar: *BDSM, when practiced carefully and with respect for the other, is all about healing, strange as that may sound. It is about trust.*

Illness or Sexual Variation?

Both within the Pagan community and on the larger scale of our society, people hold diverse opinions about BDSM. Mental-health professionals and sexual experts cannot agree about whether it is just another variation in human sexuality, or whether it is an unhealthy practice. At the very least, "[a]ccording to the American Psychiatric Association's Diagnostic and Statistical Manual of Mental Disorders [DSM-IV] . . . S/M per se is NOT a mental disorder. In their diagnostic criteria for both sexual masochism and sexual sadism, the DSM-IV states that S/M only becomes a diagnosable dysfunction when: 'the fantasies, sexual urges, or behaviors cause clinically significant distress or impairment in social, occupational or other important areas of functioning.'"[2]

Riane Eisler approaches BDSM from a feminist viewpoint. Although she admits that it might "bring [power imbalances] to consciousness" and expand consciousness through role-switching, she still believes that *any* power imbalance, in act or relationship, hearkens back to the "dominator culture" model of the male having power over the female and that power imbalances, whether real or symbolic, are something to be avoided.

I disagree with both these points. First, to see every dominant in the "male" role and every submissive in the "female" role is to force a variety of situations into a rigid binary that, most often, is simply not applicable. As for power imbalance being negative, Carol Truscott in *Leatherfolk* points out that we give up power simply by being part of our society, accepting decisions made by government. "We have given these groups the power to tell us when we may cross streets, when a restaurant may be operated, who can manufacture or sell things, how fast we may drive our cars and where. . . . Any relationship in which one person wants something the other has is a relationship with an exchange of some degree or some kind of power."[3] In a romantic relationship, there will always be times when one person has more power than the other. A constant perfect balance is unrealistic. My boyfriend cooks better than I do, so I accept his criticism when he looks over my shoulder in the kitchen. I've had partners who had no fashion sense, so I told them when they really needed to change clothes. Even a static power imbalance, though more challenging, can potentially be healthy. The criterion should be whether both partners are happy and fulfilled.

Responding to the assertion that BDSM represents trust, Eisler responds, "[T]he problem is that this way of expressing trust is itself a reinforcement of the notion that the powerless should trust the powerful, and thus willingly submit to their bondage."[4] BDSM is indeed an expression of trust, but it is not only on the submissive's part. Yes, she must trust that the dominant will not cross her boundaries. The dominant, on the other hand, must trust that the submissive is being honest about those boundaries and that she will speak up if there is a problem.

MAGDALENE MERETRIX: *Because I trance out so easily, I have to be able to trust my partner not to damage me. I'm not in a condition amenable to assessing personal levels of damage when I'm in a trance state . . . I am not into S/M in order to be damaged or harmed in any way—I am into it because I enjoy the experience of being in trance state, and the insight and healing it often provides me with. Very skilled S/M artists can take me to trance space for hours without a visible mark on my body the next day.*

In a very real way, the deep level of trust required for S/M play is as much a spiritual experience as the intense sensations and trance state. There is something purgative and healing about being able to trust another human being to that level, and something validating and reassuring when that trust turns out to have been well-placed. S/M is a dual-edged sword, however, in that badly executed S/M, or S/M with a person who should not have been trusted can do intense damage—S/M can be as damaging as it can be healing, and because it is such an intense experience, it cuts deeply no matter which edge of the sword comes into play at any given time.

Interestingly, later in her book, when talking about men's sexuality, Eisler says, "[I]t is the ability to give up control—to let go—that is basic to a full orgasmic sexual experience, as it is to a peak spiritual experience."[5] But is it only okay for *men* to give up control, not women?

Even among Pagans, folks who are normally very sex-positive and accepting, there are a variety of opinions about BDSM.

HONEYBLOSSOM: *A surprising number of Pagans don't support BDSM. They say things like "The Goddess wants us to love each other," and "The link between sex and violence is a patriarchal construction." I find that really frustrating, since many BDSM techniques are similar to what is used in shamanic cultures over the globe to induce altered states. It seems like BDSM and the Pagan community ought to go together better than they do.*

Certainly, BDSM relationships can be unhealthy, just like other types of relationships.

FRANCESCA GENTILLE: *There's been a feeling in me that BDSM could be used very, very therapeutically for trauma victims and people to kind of work through being molested, and raped, and everything, but that it's not normally used that way. It's my perception that a percentage of people can get stuck, sometimes reenacting that they were molested as a child. You know, if their daddy spanked them and then fucked them, then they reenact that their whole life, and their sexuality is limited to being spanked and fucked. And I've seen it sometimes where people are using sensation like any other drug, to leave their bodies. They're not actually present with their partner. It's a drug, it's a high, it's a rush . . . and . . . I worry that a percentage of [BDSM play] is a way to avoid integration and avoid working through one's pain, or one's issues.*

PHIL BRUCATO: *Personally, I've known a lot of damaged people claiming to be "healthy" in that lifestyle. I enjoy the shadow side of my sexuality, too, but I don't break other people's spirits with it. I've seen too many folks in the BDSM community who do.*

OBERON ZELL-RAVENHEART: *There are people who wish more than anything to control and dominate others* against their will *(an essential caveat), people who wish to really hurt others and inflict genuine suffering. And when such people use sexuality as a vehicle for this drive to control, dominate, and hurt, that's what I call the shadow side of sexuality. I consider rape—in all its permutations—to be the "original sin."*

The bottom line is that if a practice is enriching your life and the life of your partner(s), if it's not keeping you from getting the stuff done that you need to get done, if it makes you happy more often than not, then it's good for you.

BDSM in Religious History

Although the term *sadism* is a nod to the Marquis de Sade (b. 1740), he didn't invent kinky sex. Eisler blames Christianity for eroticizing violence by vividly, through words and paintings, associating forbidden sexual practices with the tortures of hell. Early Christianity used images of violence toward nude women to represent female saints being martyred, sinful women being bodily punished in hell, and accused witches being tortured. Whether or not such paintings exist from that period depicting the lurid, nude suffering of *men* is beyond the scope of this book (and apparently Eisler's as well—she makes no mention of it), but the important thing is the artists' fixation on the combination of sex and violence.[6]

Certainly, although all this may have contributed to turning modern people kinky, the practice of erotic power exchange and erotic pain has earlier origins. Vases from ancient Athens show satyrs beating hetaerae, forcing fellatio and having anal sex with them (which was apparently humiliating to the recipient).[7] The ancient Hindu sex manual, the *Kama Sutra* (circa 300 BCE to 400 CE), includes bites, slaps, and punches as part of lovemaking technique, along with various "sounds of pleasurable anguish which correspond to the different types of blows."[8] The Indian Sidhus have been practicing the "ball dance" for over a thousand years as part of the Hindu Kavandi ceremony; the skin is pierced in several places, and small balls or fruits are hung from the piercings. When the dancer moves, the balls bounce. The resulting endorphin rush* sends him into an altered state. The Lakota Sun Dance and the Catholic flagellatory orders are other historical examples of pain used for spiritual transformation.

Mythology is full of what might at first glance be perceived as nothing but barbarous violence. But since this is myth and not reality, the violence can be taken more metaphorically to symbolize destruction, submission, anger, and so forth—all things that may be healthy. In one Babylonian myth, Marduk created the world by dismembering the body of the Goddess Tiamat.

---

*Endorphins are neurotransmitters, the body's natural opiates that it releases in response to pain.

When the Babylonian Goddess Innana descended into the underworld in search of her lover Dumuzi, she was stripped of her clothing—stripped of her pride, her adornments, and her ego. The Roman Goddess Cybele's lover Attis castrated himself and bled to death—quite a fitting image for a man who is submissive to women. In the Greek myths, Hades, the God of the underworld, kidnaps Persephone. She is brought to the underworld, in a symbolic death, and eventually returns, wiser, and with the seeds of darkness within her. The Hindu Goddess Kali is also a particularly good example of healthy, necessary anger or destruction.

JACQUI OMI: *I used sex as part of a spell when I was going through the legal battle (Church of Iron Oak), that whole idea of raising Kali energy, because Kali is very cunnilingual. Her whole concept is heat, and she's powerful, and she's scary.*

NeoPaganism has a more recent history of sacred and magical BDSM. Aleister Crowley practiced Dark Eros, and he used it in sex magic. Gardnerian Wiccans use a scourge (flogger) in ritual. It is associated with the Goddess in her crone aspect and is a symbol of power, domination, suffering, and purification. The strands are made of silk cords and are intended to be used so lightly as not to cause pain. The idea is that it will alter blood circulation and thus consciousness, but in my opinion (as someone who has felt both a traditional scourge and a real flogger), it is entirely symbolic. Gardnerians sometimes also bind participants by the neck and wrists.

CAROL QUEEN: *When I was reading my old Pagan stuff in the seventies and [asking myself] "What's my entry? How am I going to relate to this? Do I want to find a coven? What does that mean?" one of the things that I noted with some interest was the binding and scourging part of the ritual, and I was all like, "Those Brits are just*

doing S/M!" And in fact, perhaps, that's just what they were doing!
[laughs] So "binding and scourging," well, allrighty then. I don't
know what else you call that, people. [Jen: I wonder if that being
part of early Wicca helped to create such a big crossover
between the S/M and Pagan communities.] *I wouldn't be*
surprised. My understanding about pre-1970s S/M was that people
had to look long and hard for a partner that they could do what they
wanted to do with. And any little space where the symbolism of that
kind of desire was brought in, in an acceptable context, might have been
a place where people gravitated on purpose, hoping that, well then, they
would find an appropriate partner there.

Aidan Kelly, in his book *Crafting the Art of Magic*, suggests that
binding and scourging were included in Gardnerian rituals solely
because such things were sexually exciting to Gardner. Hutton,
however, asserts that there is no indication Gardner was into S/M
in any other aspect of his life (he had an erotica collection that
was quite vanilla*); the binding and scourging was likely just a
unique way to affect blood circulation and achieve a trance state.
It also may have been an alternative to ecstatic dancing for Gardner, as he had asthma.[9]

Historically, there has been resistance to the merging of BDSM
and Paganism, from both communities. As I write this, Raven
Kaldera is trying to find a publisher for his book on just that
combination—the kink publishers think it's too religious; the
Pagan publishers think it's too kinky.

Dossie Easton: *During the politically correct era [the eighties] . . .*
there were a lot of people who were really appalled that we should call
our S/M explorations "spirituality," and they felt we were invading

---

Vanilla is a term meaning sex with no BDSM elements.

their turf when we insisted that we were a valid part of women's spirituality, our sexuality and S/M both. So it was not exactly an easy transition to make. There were a lot of people who really didn't want us to go there. . . . At that time, I was living in Santa Cruz, and I was "femina non grata" in all the women's spirituality circles. I'll never forget the time somebody invited me to her party. . . . I was very glad to come, [but] oh, my God, that was when I realized there were all these feminist spiritual whatevers running around the party going, "How did she get here?" And so I was isolated from women's movement circles for a long time.

At the same time, within S/M, the spiritual ritual stuff had been going on, but was kind of a secret submovement. . . . There was some resistance to doing that within S/M land. But meanwhile, friends of mine, one of whom is now a priestess of Oshun, another who is Fakir Musafar, were showing up and doing ritual and teaching about it, and so on, and so I became a member of Black Leather Wings about ten years ago.

BDSM and Paganism

Raven Kaldera is an expert on this subject. If you're not kinkily inclined, try to keep an open mind as you read what Raven has to say. He's rather . . . uh . . . intense.

RAVEN KALDERA: *I've been assuming that I ought to write something sweet and New Age about sexuality being sacred, and the body being sacred, and we should all just find new ways to love each other, and all that. Screw that. That's not what my sex life is about . . . I'm a pervert. I'm a sick fuck . . . I am incapable of getting it up for anything vanilla. In order to be sexually satisfied, I have to have some sort of real violence or pain or domination going on—if only in fantasy . . . I am a serious fucking sexual sadist, and I've got a decent masochistic streak in there as well. . . . No human being is ever more attractive to me than when they are so frightened and turned on that they don't know whether to shit themselves in terror or come really, really hard. Even among BDSM aficionados, I'm one of the edge-players, the folks who the "ordinary" leather folk look at funny and talk about behind one's back. . . .*

And how can that possibly be sacred? . . . Because I am also a shaman, I have died and come back (literally; I've had a near-death experience, a series of divine visitations, and a sex change, and that's about as severe as a shamanic rebirth gets in our modern culture) and everything I do must be channeled toward the sacred. I am as much a slave as my boy is, and my Mistress, my dominatrix, She Who Owns My Ass, is Hel, the Goddess of death, to whom I am oathbound. And She is one mean fucking top. If I don't do what She wants, She will kick my ass from here to Niflheim. And She makes sure that I stay ethical, and in spiritual service to my people and my tribe.

I have great power over another human being, of the sort that most people are convinced will inevitably result in corruption and abuse . . . and yet I don't have the option of being less than rigidly ethical about it. I can't abuse him, or Hel will come down with her spiked boots and kick my ass. Using power wisely is a lesson that is to be driven home to me in this lifetime, and I can neither screw up nor refuse the gift.

BDSM, as a variation on lovemaking, fits comfortably into the Pagan viewpoint of sexuality as sacred. It has been my experience that most people who have a strong interest in BDSM have been so inclined from early on; it's similar to sexual orientation. However, just as a straight person may enjoy occasional bisexual encounters, so someone who is mainly vanilla may dabble in BDSM.

As Dark Eros, its potential widens. It may be considered an initiatory path, in which the dominant challenges the submissive in a way that helps him work through various emotional and spiritual challenges, to emerge transformed. The consensual, erotic pain of BDSM can also be used as a method for raising energy in sex magic. Pain play in specific has the potential to alter consciousness, both through psychological "ordeal" and the impact of endorphins. In this way, erotic pain may be considered analogous to drugs and alcohol as a method of altering one's consciousness: In the same way, it can be used just for fun, but can also (when done with moderation and forethought) assist the individual in his spiritual path. In the same way, it can be dangerous.

Where good sex is often described as being attained through relaxation and just "letting things happen," BDSM is much more about intent. "Often, S/M has been described as an Apollonian way of reaching the Dionysian state—in other words, a controlled, skillful, and thought-out process for reaching the intuitive/ecstatic state."[10] In that sense, it has even more in common with magic than with your standard lovey-dovey sexual encounter. It is a ritualized and controlled method of sexual alchemy, intended to produce a transformative experience for its participants. On the other hand, BDSM, like vanilla sex, can sometimes become very intense of its own accord. Things happen, people are transformed, magic is released into the world—all accidentally.

There are plenty of Pagans who have no interest in BDSM.

JACQUI OMI: *I have never done BDSM. It is never anything I've wanted, because . . . I already felt that because I wasn't male, I should be dominated, so I certainly am not attracted to being in either the dominant or submissive role. I think sexuality should be a very gentle and sacred and warm and loving thing. That's my opinion. That doesn't mean I haven't had a lot of friends who are [kinky], and I have no trouble with that; that's entirely up to them. I've been to women's events where there was lots of that. Fine. And I've counseled people who were very heavy into BDSM, and that's fine. Whatever an adult wants to do.*

DAVE SYLVIA: *I personally do not believe in "cross-wiring" the pain and pleasure centers of my brain, and feel it is healthier to keep them separate.*

WYRDOTTER: *I have absolutely zero desire to whip or beat my beloved in any context, so it doesn't arouse me. What can I say? I'm the gentle, tender, moonlight-and-roses type.*

FRANCESCA GENTILLE: *I had friends that were in BDSM, I didn't know anything about it, and I was told to get the book,* Screw the Roses, Send Me the Thorns. *The first time I started looking through the book, and just kind of skimming, and looking, and reading . . . this wave of outrage came over me, and what came up was a past-life memory . . . of being in a temple, and using these practices of pain and stimulation and sometimes sight or sound deprivation and things like that, as a way to achieve altered states in ritual, and that they were very, very sacred, and that they were very secret practices, and that they were never meant to be disseminated in the general public as "toys." It's almost like taking the statue of the Goddess and making her a Barbie doll. It's like, "How dare you?" If you were from, like ten thousand years ago, and the statues that you had were sacred representations of the Earth-birthing mother, and then suddenly—Here's Malibu Barbie— You might be so outraged, you might think, "Never, never was the female form supposed to be used like this!" And it was that kind of a feeling.*

Dark Eros Therapy

According to some psychologists, every romantic relationship and act of lovemaking is an unconscious effort to return to the perfect and unconditional love between infant and parent, and/or an effort to correct bad experiences with one's parents. But because BDSM is generally much more carefully planned than vanilla sexuality, it can provide a unique opportunity to "set right" the things that went wrong. If someone carries the pain from a parent's abandonment, she may choose an older dominant who takes care of her in a paternal way. If someone carries anger from an abusive or overbearing parent, he may choose to scene in ways that will put him in control and allow him to call the shots.

Psychotherapists may argue that such play does not actually make the baggage go away. But as Dark Eros work, it actually might. "The games we play have the power to bypass our customary psychological defenses, giving us access to amazing experiences and awareness."[11] BDSM may get at the heart of the problem where talking just glosses over it. And it's so much more fun than going to a therapist.

> SHAI SHAHAR: *I can attest to the fact that [BDSM] feels a lot different in practice than it looks to observers. I can also swear to its beneficial side effects: the ability through role-play and sensory stimulus (or denial of same) to help people break through some serious personal issues.*

BDSM can actually enhance people's ability to speak up for themselves. How often do vanilla lovers ask for exactly what they want, sexually, and outline precisely what they will not do? In addition, playing with power in such a blatant way can teach you how to notice power plays in everyday life and to protect yourself against them. When you consciously allow someone to have power over you, you sure as hell notice when you are not allowing someone to have power over you and yet he is taking it anyway.

Playing with Power

Although BDSM may involve servitude, humiliation, and all sorts of ways in which one person may appear to be "above" the other, these are roles that are negotiated in advance between equals. To borrow Starhawk's terminology, BDSM is an example of "power-with" rather than "power-over." It may appear that a submissive is giving up his power—but wouldn't it be a powerful act to acknowledge that, however politically incorrect it may be, you would enjoy receiving erotic pain, and then to go about finding just the right person to give it to you? And of course, you can't consciously lend someone else your power without first owning it yourself.

Just as earth-centered religions challenge the concept of things "higher" being better, so terms like "top" and "bottom" are not intended to imply any value judgment. The top is doing something very big and important, certainly, in implementing the scene, making sure the bottom stays safe and is fulfilled through his skillful technique. But the bottom is doing something just as big and important: trusting someone enough to lend her power to him, and challenging herself to explore her own personal limits. This dynamic mirrors the roles of lover and beloved in the Great Rite in token. Of blade and chalice, neither one is of higher value than the other. They are simply the principles of giving and receiving. Although the submissive may be put in the position of worshipping the dominant, he is not holding her up as a deity per se, but in a way, bowing down to and honoring the deity within her. Of course, the submissive also has the same inner divinity; plenty of Gods and Goddesses have been put through some kind of ordeal and emerged transformed.

Just because someone is sexually dominant or submissive does not mean that he will be that way in all aspects of his life. Usually, it's quite the opposite. The best dominants I know are very soft spoken and kind. The best submissives are uppity, strong, and proactive. BDSM gives people a chance to alter their perspectives. Mixing up the traditional roles, some people call themselves "submissive sadists" or "dominant masochists." In a Wiccan context, where the magic of the Great Rite is in the balance of give and take, switching sides can be a magical and significant task.

Power exchange can happen without physical exchange (say, through speech, looks, or body language), and some people are interested in sensation play where there is no power exchange at all.

> MAGDALENE MERETRIX: *I am neither a dom nor a sub, and prefer egalitarian play, where one person might top while another bottoms (and roles might switch at any time with mutual agreement), but the focus is on playing with sensations and experiences, not with power exchanges. Power dynamics between people are already far too complex for me as it is, so I derive no pleasure from augmenting or exaggerating those dynamics.*

The Magic of Submission

Submission to the will of another person, a deity, or the universe in general can be a challenge to Pagans and Wiccans. When you have the option of using magic, it's tempting to conclude that consciously manipulating reality is the solution to every problem. But there are times when the best thing to do is to flow with the river of things rather than pushing it. This is actually more common in Eastern paths, including Zen, Taoism, and even Islam (a word that means "submission"). Loss of ego and control, and a sense of becoming one with the universe, is something that happens to mystics in an ecstatic religious experience, as well as to submissives in good scenes. A good submissive, like a spiritual person, knows how to go with the flow. This is not only useful for kinky sex, but for standard vanilla sex, as well. You can't *will* an orgasm. When a submissive really gives in, it's referred to as "sub space." This is probably similar to the "alpha state" of trance and meditation.

Pain is the least understood aspect of BDSM. Of course, no one enjoys stubbing her toe or having intestinal cramps. Erotic pain is carefully controlled and only applied in ways that the submissive has consented to in advance. In this case, it becomes another kind of sensation; perhaps an intense one, but a sensation nonetheless.

> DOSSIE EASTON: *I used to think that I was a wimp, and I used to think that I wasn't into pain: I preferred to think of it as intense stimulation. But some turning point came along in there. I was at this party, and someone introduced himself to me, saying a mutual friend was going to introduce us, because I was into pain. And I said, "Well, no, I'm not, but you won't be able to tell the difference."* [laughs] *And that's when I began to realize that indeed, I was doing something different with pain.* [Jen: Because you saw it as stimulation, or as sensation instead of pain?] *Well, yeah. I mean, if you do it right—and these are carefully selected forms of pain, mind you, in carefully selected circumstances—but if you do it right, it opens everything up.*

When endorphins are released, they minimize the pain itself and can fill the individual with a feeling of floatiness and well-being, which is sometimes called "flying." An endorphin high or rush can be a kind of altered state and can be used for the purpose of communing with the divine, meditation, divination, magical workings, and the release of ego. When someone is off flying, however, it may make the scene a bit less interesting for her partner.

> MAGDALENE MERETRIX: *So long as I trust my partner, and my partner is reasonably skilled in S/M technique, I go into a trance very quickly and easily. Some people don't like to play with someone who goes into trance, because they don't find it as "interesting" as a partner*

who squirms and squeals and otherwise engages them. . . . Someone who doesn't enjoy topping a person who goes easily into trance will intentionally alter their technique in ways designed to keep them out of trance. I prefer to go into trance—that's the whole point of S/M play for me!—so I try to avoid selecting partners who are uncomfortable or bored with allowing me to spend a lot of time there. In exchange for allowing me to spend a lot of time trancing out, I try to provide my partner with whatever suits his or her needs, be it sex before or after the S/M, or topping my partner in a way that pleases him or her, or whatever (within my personal limits and boundaries, of course).

Just as pain can send us flying out of the body, it can also put us back *into* the body. When we're comfortable and intellectually distracted, we often lose touch with our bodies. But a mildly painful sensation, like a moderate spanking or flogging, can increase blood circulation and body awareness. Although ritualized pain is often associated with mortification of the flesh, it can actually lead to honoring and more completely accepting the body. The more we become aware of our bodies, and the more we fully inhabit them, the more we are able to accept them.

Depending on the person, combining pain with genital stimulation may either be an incredibly powerful cocktail, or could be a recipe for a bad scene. BDSM is certainly erotic, but it need not include standard "sex" at all.

MAGDALENE MERETRIX: *I do separate S/M and sex, though many people don't. There is something about the blending of orgasmic energies and pain energies that does not please me, and instead of surrendering to and enjoying the intensity of one or the other I find that both together are too distracting and overloading for me. So not only do I have to trust a potential S/M partner implicitly, I have to find an S/M partner who is not displeased with my choice to separate sexual and S/M energies into different "playtimes."*

164

Many submissives see a scene as a way for them to test, show, and improve their power and strength. They may be working to conquer an ordeal as a warrior, or learning to give in, to trust, and to become vulnerable—even perhaps both in the same scene. Both require bravery. The challenge may have to do with pain, but not necessarily. It can be the submissive learning to handle embarrassment, managing to be patient as he sits there in full-body bondage, or simply by remaining still and composed while his dominant is doing something to him that feels really, really good.

> DOSSIE EASTON: *When I'm being flogged, early on I often come to a place where I need to stretch to take in the intense sensation, where I struggle and wonder if I can take it all. That struggle seems to make me stronger, and soon I feel intense energy running through me, as if all the force with which the whip is thrown at me is injected into me—becomes my energy to play with. While my tops throw the whips at me as hard as they can, I take in their power and dance in the center of the storm.* [12]

If it's working the way it should, a dominant should function like a trainer for an athlete, by giving the submissive challenges that will temper his metal and make him stronger. In *Leatherfolk*, Pat Califia writes, "A bottom goes into a scene expecting to experience a combination of physical sensations, psychological and emotional stimulation, and suspension of disbelief that will ultimately result in a feeling of being purified, transformed, and healed." [13]

The Magic of Domination

Those new to the concept of BDSM may have a hard time understanding how someone could cause another person pain in a loving way. I compare it to the difference between loving, consensual sex and rape. Both involve a penis entering a vagina, but they are vitally different. Likewise, pain need not be something given with the intent to harm. If it is a sensation the other person enjoys, then it is no more harmful than a hug or backrub—perhaps *less* so, because it is fully negotiated beforehand, which is more than we can say for most hugs. I've heard it suggested that eroticizing violence could lead to the individual becoming more violent in other aspects of his life. But does having consensual intercourse make one more likely to commit rape?

One might think that the only way someone can derive pleasure from "tormenting others" is if he does not feel empathy. This would make sense, if the person being "tormented" were not deriving pleasure from it. Quite the contrary; in a good BDSM scene, there should be an endless cycle of pleasure between top and bottom, in which the pleasure of one feeds the pleasure of the other. Dossie Easton and Janet W. Hardy write, "As tops in role, we are often called upon to present ourselves as cold, cruel, and unfeeling, when in fact we are getting our rocks off on an empathy so profound that it can approach the telepathic."[14]

> DON KRAIG: *I think there is a symbiotic (for lack of a better word) relationship of building energy for me as a bottom goes deeper into sub space. As the bottom's pleasure/transcendence/bliss increases, so does my own. All of this energy can then be directed. For me, this requires a great deal of energy. Not simply physical exertion from pitching, but mental exertion from riding the waves of my catcher, being attuned to what they need through nonoral communication, and being able to take them one little step more, increasing both of our energy creation/direction abilities. When working this way, it has required practice with the same partner. . . . It is a play off of each other.*

In the same way that submission can be a powerful rush, so can domination. It's rare for any of us to get the chance to be utterly in control, to have a chance to play with someone's body and see what kinds of nifty things you can make it do, to play with someone's mind and send her into a state of ecstasy. Just as submissives can enter a trance through stimulation and ritual role play, so dominants find themselves being transported to a different headspace.[15]

> HONEYBLOSSOM: *As a domme, in the best of my scenes, I frequently feel that I am channeling something larger than myself, something divine and old. Paganism has a lot of great models of Goddesses that are both loving and warlike, like Inanna. (They're some of the few positive models that female dominants have to draw from in our culture.)** *Sometimes, while in scene, I've gone into a trance state and then felt myself filling with a divine tenderness/compassion for my partner that goes beyond the usual human affection. In these times I am often able to perceive changes in what my partner is feeling almost before he or she does. Time seems to slow down. Usually, these scenes are among the very best of those I do, but they are also very exhausting.*

Much of the focus of a scene tends to be on the submissive, and so dominants don't often get a chance to have much attention paid to them, or to get any sexual pleasure. Depending on the person and the scene, this may not be necessary. Sometimes, the rush from the power exchange is all the release they need. On the other hand, they may want some sexual attention paid to them afterward. This is something that needs to be negotiated.

The way the energy tends to move is from dominant to submissive, and then it returns to the dominant magnified. In their books on BDSM, Easton and Hardy write, "S/M is sex magic, and you [the top] are the magician. The bottom is the cauldron in

---

*I know I've used Inanna as an example of a Goddess being submissive, but I guess She's a switch.

which you perform your miracles."[16] The submissive takes in the dominant's energy, blending it with his own, and returns it back as "something stronger, sharper, brighter than either of you could generate alone."[17] Because of this, the dominant has some responsibility for shaping and directing the energy—either toward a goal, or just in such a way that no one gets overwhelmed or drained. This isn't the kind of thing that can be explained in a book, but is learned through practice.

BDSM as Initiation

As expertly explained by Robert H. Hopcke in *Leatherfolk*, the ritual and practice of BDSM has many common elements with the standard format of initiatory practices in indigenous societies—most often initiation into adulthood. The three initiatory phases are: separation (the initiate is temporarily removed from the community), transition (he undergoes rituals or trials to strip away his old life and challenge him), and incorporation (he is welcomed back into the larger community as a new person).

In Wiccan initiation, these phases are largely symbolic. The initiate is separated from everyday life by elements such as a ritual bath, nudity or special dress, and entering the circle. The transition is a moment of truth where the initiate is compelled to state her intention unequivocally. There is generally no actual physical ordeal. In incorporation, the person is presented to the coven and Gods as a newly initiated Witch or Nth degree.

Pomp and circumstance can be beautiful and moving, but when these initiatory phases are made more physical, they can have a particularly profound effect. In BDSM, the dominant separates the submissive from his everyday self through elements such as a clothing change (being naked or wearing specific items), restrictions on speech, and/or specific positions and movements that express his submission. All these things conspire to strip away the submissive's ego-identification. They also make him feel much more vulnerable—a critical step in any process of transformation.

The transitional phase involves one or more challenges, as mentioned earlier. In typical BDSM play, these activities do not need to be anything but arousing for the submissive, although most submissives like to have their limits pushed slightly. If BDSM is being used as a transformational experience, they *must* be pushed—without physical or psychological harm, but with some real difficulty. The judgment falls to the dominant as to how far to go and with what. If it is predetermined that the submissive will succeed, we're back to pomp and circumstance. Here, "failure" would be the submissive's use of a safeword to call off the activity—nothing shaming, but not going all the way, either.

The final stage, incorporation of the initiate back into the community, is quite neglected in BDSM play. In indigenous societies, once the initiates return from their ordeal, there is a big celebration. They have the respect of the community and a new set of privileges. In Wicca, the person is presented as a new initiate and is embraced by his covenmates, with all the same good stuff to follow. But in BDSM, the best you can usually hope for is a cuddle and some take-out. Of course, not every BDSM scene is Dark Eros work, and they need not all be treated as such. But when partners plan to do some heavy work, it would be good if the dominant put some thought into the incorporation step at the end.

BDSM in the Pagan Community

Why are there so darn many kinky folks in the Pagan community? The most obvious connection is ritual. Both BDSM and Pagan ritual employ symbolic clothes, gestures, and words intended to change one's point of view. Sacred space may correspond with scene space: in both cases, we are leaving our everyday worlds and selves behind to become something other. So when one is well versed in one type of ritual, it's easy to switch to a different sort.

NeoPaganism and BDSM take religion and sex, respectively, one step further. Many Pagan traditions, and particularly initiatory paths like Wicca, are a way for individuals to step out of the church pews and into otherworldly realms. It's a religion of exploration. So Pagans may be more open to erotic exploration than most.

> RHOMYLLY FORBES: *There is a hell of a lot of crossover between the BDSM and Pagan communities. I think it's because of the need for intensity. Most Pagans aren't content with an-hour-a-week fed-to-them-like-baby-food spiritual practice; they want something more. BDSMers, same thing. Plain vanilla sex all the time isn't enough. Kinky people and Pagans tend to like to think for themselves on important issues like sex and spirituality.*

As a sexual variation, BDSM in particular is a way to take an erotic adventure, to push one's own limits, to take the instrument that is one's body and, rather than just playing chamber music, hook it up to an electric amp. Sometimes that means pushing one's own boundaries and venturing into scary territory. Pagans are not afraid of shadows; we seek them out and, in fact, embrace them. Having sex is not always making love. Sex can be dark and scary, and even fierce. And fear can be arousing.

> PHIL BRUCATO: *Sex is an extreme sport, and an even more extreme form of worship. "Safe sex" is an illusion. Sex isn't supposed to be "safe"; by its very intimate nature, it cannot be "safe." Passion seethes in our veins, occasionally grabbing us by the neck and fucking us till we scream. And we like it! We're supposed to! The AIDS adage "sex is*

death" is incomplete. Sex is life. But life does not exist without death. In that realization, we can find intense pleasure as well as intense damage.

I think that's one of the things we NeoPagans appreciate more than most folks: the idea that life and death are both sacred, both essential, both joined. While many people spend their lives trying to escape mortality, we try to embrace it, not with a sense of doom but with a howl of ecstasy. In general, we don't fear death so much as we fear a life that is not lived.

In one of my stories, I wrote: "They loved each other with fierce tenderness." That apparent paradox stands at the heart of sex's shadow. We crave tenderness, often so badly that we'll bite through a lover's flesh to get it! Within the slippery union of soft skin and vulnerable souls, there are ravenous beasts who want and take and have without mercy. And given the intense vulnerability we experience in sex, those inner beasts can hurt our lovers—can hurt ourselves—with the intensity of their need.

No contact is as profoundly intimate, physically or otherwise, as sexuality. No other communion feeds us so deeply yet wounds us so harshly. From sheer self-preservation, then, we need some degree of protection from sexual passions. Our relationships, our society, our bodies themselves would break from the strain of total sexual abandon. And so we set boundaries to shield our selves and societies from too much passion. Problem is, we don't know when to quit setting those boundaries. And when we do set them, there are people and diseases who just won't fucking care about them. Either way, sex remains dangerous, intoxicating, a glorious razor-ride between control, immolation, and utter transformation.

Every Pagan festival I have attended in the past few years has included at least one workshop on Dark Eros or straight BDSM— and sometimes play parties as well. The standard Ren Faire– inspired festival garb now exists alongside leather, collars, chains, and floggers. Because most of my friends and I are either kinky or supportive, I haven't spoken to anyone who has admitted being "squicked" by the new element at gatherings. But I'm sure they're out there.

CAROL QUEEN: *I think there's a squick factor [in the community's response to BDSM], yeah. There are so many roots by which someone might come to Paganism, and there are definitely more conservative, and sexually conservative, Pagans than others. I don't think there's any question about that, so in the same breath that somebody might not understand themselves as homophobic but present a spirituality that's inacceptable to gays and lesbians, certainly I think there are plenty of people who are like, "Eww."*

Also, often, Paganism is presented as an especially woman-friendly and feminist spiritual space, and of course many feminists have not been at all comfortable with various kinds of sexual behavior, very much including BDSM. That's a little more of a seventies and eighties phenomenon than it is a contemporary phenomenon, but there is still plenty, I think, of that kind of discourse going around. [Jen: Especially with maledom/femsubs.] *Especially there, right. Plenty of people are willing to make an exception for a pro domme Goddess, [laughs] you know, who has a submissive man crawling behind her like a worm. It's like, "Oh, that's nice, that's good." But when you see the exact same set of desires and behaviors acted out in an other-gendered way, it freaks people out profoundly.*

BDSM is all about the process, the journey. There is no goal or destination. It is not about being the most outrageous or taking the most pain or being the "best" top/dominant or bottom/submissive. As with other spiritual journeys, the most power may be found in the smallest, subtlest things. Beware of ego.

PHIL BRUCATO: *The ritualistic elements of BDSM—often played with a combination of campy snickers and robotic boredom—turn me right off. I'd love to stage a "scene" with one of my more voracious lovers, and show those primping poseurs that you don't need a rack and three-grand worth of gear to have some savage fun!*

Don Kraig: *Besides having another tool to generate and direct magical energy, [BDSM] helps you to learn more about yourself. For me, magic is about power . . . power over yourself. The more you know yourself, the more you can work with that power. So any self-knowledge is a positive thing.*

7. Sex Work ❧

Before launching into this topic, I want to acknowledge that there is a world of difference between sex work as an educated career choice and sex work because there *is* no other choice. In *Whores and Other Feminists*, Jill Nagle suggests that the distinction between voluntary and coerced sexual exchange is "every bit as salient and problematic as that between consensual sex and rape."[1] There are many sex workers in this country who are being abused, who live in poverty, and/or who are addicted to drugs. There is nothing sacred or holy about their situation—it represents a damaged part of society that needs to be healed. Likewise, just as sexual acts in and of themselves are not necessarily infused with magic or holiness, so sex work itself is not necessarily a sacred calling. To some, it may be just another job. This chapter deals with the sacred aspects of sex work: those that lead to healing and transformation for both worker and client.

Sex workers (the term coined by Carol Leigh, a.k.a. Scarlot Harlot) may include pimps, madams and prostitutes, escorts, strippers, and peep-show workers, professional dominants and submissives, webcam girls, phone sex actors and operators, erotic models and photographers, porn actors and directors (and everyone else involved in making porn movies), erotic writers and editors, adult webmasters, sex therapists/surrogates/instructors, and sex boutique owners. In this chapter, I generally use "she" to refer to the sex worker and "he" to refer to the client, because the majority of the sex industry involves female sex workers and male clients.

Part of the reason why it might be difficult to conceive of sex work as sacred has to do with the lens through which we are viewing it. Traditional feminism (i.e., from the 1950s to the early 1980s) was vehemently antiprostitution and antipornography. Such viewpoints still exist in feminism. Ironically, as argued in *Whores and Other Feminists*, this viewpoint smacks much more of patriarchy than a philosophy that is truly pro-woman. If a woman is doing something like porn modeling or prostitution, the assumption would be that she has either wound up in this line of work because of her own mistakes (like becoming addicted to drugs) or through the manipulation of others (generally men). In this way, the sex worker is treated as a child, someone who doesn't know what she's doing, and who needs rescuing. Going along with the mainstream conception of sexuality as something women only want to share with one male partner, feminists wouldn't believe that a woman can possibly enjoy sex work—if she says she does, she is lying or misguided. Those who argue against sex work are by and large not in the business; the opinions of those who are, are disregarded.[2]

Since the 1980s, there has been a trend in feminism, which starts with the assumption that sane and sober women are in fact intellectually capable of making their own decisions, and which argues that the idea of being able to choose one's own career as a woman should be expanded to include the choice of sex work.

Any job can be done with conscious intent and a mind toward creating positive change in one's self and the world. Sex work, from a Pagan viewpoint, lends itself particularly well to this. As people interested in ancient religion, we can look to the past for inspiration and bring what we value into the future.

MAGDALENE MERETRIX: *Knowing something about the history of sacred whoredom in different cultures and times has left me feeling like a link in a long, connected history of my people. Knowing that what I do today is closely related to what men and women did thousands of years ago gives me a sense of my place in a progression of sacred service through the ages. Naturally, it's not an unbroken progression, and many of my beliefs and practices are not what my ancestors believed or did, but still I feel a kinship to those who have gone before me.*

Every single person I interviewed felt that prostitution should be legalized. (In my experience, this is representative of what most NeoPagans believe.) Many added that they felt prostitutes deserved health care and other job-related benefits.

OBERON ZELL-RAVENHEART: *I have not personally worked in the sex industry, but I've had many friends and lovers who have. I have considered them to be engaged in holy work—a uniquely Pagan attitude, I expect! I think the suppression and outlawing of sacred harlotry is one of the biggest problems of post-Pagan civilization, and the foundation of its gynophobia and misanthropy.*

RAVEN KALDERA: *I think that prostitutes are the living priest/esses of Aphrodite, even if they don't know it. In my book* Urban Primitive, *I advise people to make offerings to the Love Goddess by giving gifts to sex industry workers, without asking anything in return. I think it should be not only legal but sacred, and run out of temples like it used to be in ancient times.*

SHAI SHAHAR: *I look forward to the day when all prostitution is sacred prostitution. . . . I most definitely believe prostitution should be legal. Why should it be illegal to sell something that can be given away for free?*

JEZEBEL DAWN BLESSING: *Hell yes, I think [prostitution] should be legalized; if prostitution were legalized, then these women would have health care, retirement, worker's compensation, and legal protection, not* to mention some modicum of respect from society and from the men who should be grateful for their time.

Modern Sex Workers

Several of the people I interviewed currently identify as sex workers. It's not an easy choice of career. You become automatically marginalized in society, much more so if you have personal contact with clients. You can get arrested for prostitution, whether or not you are actually having sex with your clients. Even if your work is completely legal, our sex-negative culture is inclined to punish you for it.

PHIL BRUCATO: *Sexuality has been considered "vice" for so long that most law enforcement bureaus simply assume that anyone teaching "sacred sensuality/sexuality" is just another hooker. It's all too easy to be busted for what we do—technically, it's illegal in many states and provinces.*

MAGDALENE MERETRIX: *I've spent a bit over seventeen years as a sex worker. I've worked as a photographic model, a dancer behind glass in "peep shows," a dancer on stage in strip bars, a phone sex girl, and I've had one tiny role in a porn movie. I've worked with fetish sexuality as a dominatrix and as a professional submissive. I've worked as a prostitute, picking up a few clients on the street when I was young and just getting started, working for an escort agency, working as an independent, and in a legal brothel in Nevada. Though I currently don't take off my clothes, engage in fetish work, or have sex for money, I am still involved in the sex work community and I still consider myself to be a sex worker—or at least a close cousin—due to the sexual nature of most of my writing.*

SHAI SHAHAR: *About a year after coming to Amsterdam, I was invited to join a small escort agency [which] specialized in providing sexual* services for . . . ladies visiting on diplomatic or business conventions in the Benelux. I did that full-time for more than a year, averaging four to five clients a week . . . but it barely covered the costs of the lifestyle I had chosen, so I took my escorting freelance and decided on a change of venue.

I moved back to Amsterdam and teamed up with "Sherry," an Australian girl . . . (and one of the "bawdiest" women I have ever had the privilege to love). She confessed to me that she felt drawn to prostitution as a calling, but was reluctant to actually work as a hooker. I asked if she minded if other people watched her (us) fuck and she said no. So, we placed an ad in the local papers offering to come and give live sex shows in the home or hotel room.

Three months later, we went pro, and started working for the many peep-show arcades here, fucking in the round, with mirrors on the ceiling and disco music, while patrons jerked off to us in private booths and dropped coins in slots to keep their windows opened. Then we moved on to doing live sex shows (with choreography!) on proper stages at the Moulin Rouge and the Casa Rosso theaters. Then we were invited to shoot a few triple-X videos for a series called Real Dutch Couples.

In the meantime the S/M scene was experiencing a renaissance, and I found myself caught up in the fervor. So I modeled fetish fashion and delved into bondage and submission fantasies, master-slave games, and "dark rooms." I became a professional S/M master and rented my services out to bad girls seeking "discipline." In those dens and dungeons . . . more than anywhere, you'll find an abundance of Pagan symbolism in jewelry, dress, and tattoos: pentagrams, death heads, cups, snakes, and a lot of tribal and Celtic runery. And I must say I had not met so many Wiccans under one roof before. To my delight, they were mostly female.

In 1995, I helped Mariska Majoor, ex-window prostitute and founder of the Prostitution Information Center based in the heart of the city's red light area, to organize the famous "Lady's Day" experiment.

The idea was to rent four windows and see if women would hire the services of the gigolos standing behind them, and we had preselected twenty studly "volunteers" to work in shifts from noon to midnight. There were only three pros among us, the rest being wannabees, and since I was the best known in the red light, I went first.

To make a long story short, news of the (very successful) experiment made headlines around the globe, and so did my picture. And that marked me as the "Real American Gigolo" in Europe. Which means that although I am not an icon in the sex industry, I am an icon of the sex industry. As to how all that has influenced my Pagan beliefs and vice versa . . . well . . . you might have seen me featured on French billboards and in high-gloss mags like GQ, Homme, *and* The Face *a couple Saturnalias back. . . . I'm the guy naked on the couch except for the white socks and the Accu.2 wristwatch (of course) under the caption "The Secs Machine." I look like a cross between Pan and Bacchus. If you can find a more Pagan image, I'd sure like to see it!*

Sacred Prostitution

There are people today, mostly women, who identify as sacred whores/harlots/prostitutes. Granted, there aren't any temples to keep them as priestesses, but they keep the faith by making love with sacred intent, by working in the sex industry, and so on.

LaSara Firefox: *A sacred slut or sacred whore is someone who uses the sexual component of human interaction as a joyful, healing, worshipful form of communication and experience. It means being respectful of our own needs and those of others. Honoring our bodies. Nakedness is optional. Choice, and the conscious exercise of it, rules supreme.*

This vocation tends to be the kind of work that infuses one's entire life; it's not the kind of job you can leave at the office.

Those who feel called to be sacred whores often find themselves providing sexual healing almost by accident.

MAGDALENE MERETRIX: *The modern manifestation of the sacred whore tends to take many forms, but the common denominator I've seen so far is that the whoredom is an integral part of the individual's spirituality. Not the entirety of their spirituality, mind you, but a vital and living part. Some sacred whores view their role as that of a healer, using sex as a physical, psychological, and/or spiritual healing modality. Some sacred whores view their role as that of a priestess, using sex as a sacrament for the deity or deities of their choice. Some view their role as a catalyst, assisting in bringing about whatever changes the client is seeking. Some view their role as a combination of any or all of these choices. I wouldn't be surprised if I've left out another form of modern sacred whoredom as practiced by someone out there.*

Although the colloquial definition for "whore"—at least in its use as insult—is someone who has a large number of sex partners, proponents of sacred sexuality say that it's more a matter of attitude than numbers. Money may or may not be involved.

MAGDALENE MERETRIX: *Know that when I talk about "sacred prostitution" I don't just mean sex for money. To me, the path of the sacred whore can be taken by a monogamous person as well as a multisexual person. It can be taken by a person who has sex without commerce . . . or by a person who accepts money for sex. When I talk about what it means to be a sacred whore, I'm not just talking about time spent with my clients, but time with my personal lovers and time with my chosen partner. To me, the path of the sacred whore is a path of healing and spiritual sexuality that includes yet also transcends the workplace.*

JEZEBEL DAWN BLESSING: *As a priestess of Ishtar, I am called upon now and again to take the role of the sacred prostitute. I have had people literally ask me to be a sacred prostitute for a magical act, a*

180

healing ritual, or as a sacred gift to their partner. [Another way] I might be called upon is when I meet someone and Ishtar whispers in my ear that this person needs my help to blossom sexually; this is the most common example. When this happens, I discuss what I see, or what Ishtar has shown me needs to happen, and we talk about the best way we should approach the healing. I have taken money for sex; I've also received gifts, or just a smile and a heartfelt "thank you." I find this to be very fulfilling and wish that all women could be viewed as sacred prostitutes when they offer the pleasure of their bodies in exchange for monetary compensation.

It is not only the sacred prostitute who's holy in this exchange; the client or worshipper must be granted the same esteem and respect, else the Pagan belief of everyone's inner divinity falls short. Cosi Fabian writes, "It seemed only fair that if I were to claim sacred lineage for my desire, then I must grant the same to men: as they worshipped the Wondrous Vulva, I in turn approached each man as the *fascinum*, the 'sacred phallus,' the 'anointed one,' the *Christos*."[3] This is an important aspect, whether or not every john is spiritually inclined, or whether he himself acknowledges the sacredness of his phallus.

ANNIE SPRINKLE: *To me, every human being is sacred, and special, and unique, and sexy. When I was a prostitute, even if I didn't like the person, when you take the clothes off, and you get naked together, there's some humanity there. I had a "Beauty and the Beast" fantasy, anyway, so it worked for me.* [laughs]

Money

Cyndi Lauper sang "money changes everything," and indeed that's the perspective with regard to sex work. If money changes hands, it doesn't matter how tender, spiritual, or transformational the experience has been—to the majority of people, it's just a hooker and john in an illegal act.

The issue makes me think of the ongoing debate about whether there should be paid NeoPagan clergy. One of the arguments against it is that, in a religion where *everybody* is supposed to be clergy, it would somehow lower the status of those who weren't paid. On the flip side, there's the idea that the presence of money will somehow taint or cheapen whatever work the person is doing.

> DANIEL DEL VECCHIO: *If prostitution means money for sex, then I don't see it as any more sacred than any other form of commerce. What has been called "temple prostitution" was, I believe, the practice of healing sexuality. I assume there was some form of energy exchange involved that was less commercial than say, modern-day sex therapists' fees.*

I think most will agree that money and sex are two areas in which our society is pretty screwed up. It's no big surprise that we can't handle putting them together. But if you accept the entire body as natural, normal, clean, and even sacred, then what would be the difference between going to a massage therapist and going to a whore? Both these people touch you to make you feel good, and you pay them for it. Whether or not money is exchanged does not change the quality or meaning of the service.

Just like pleasure, our culture has a catch-22 with regard to money. We all want more of it and treat wealthy people with some measure of awe, yet we also believe on some level that it is more honorable to live humbly.

> MAGDALENE MERETRIX: *I've had people try to convince me that I'm not a sacred whore if I charge money for sex. There's this whole thread of morality surrounding spirituality and money that shows up in Christianity (simony), some Native American beliefs, and some flavors*

of NeoPaganism, that says that charging money for spiritual goods and/or services inherently takes the spirituality out of them.

Just because what I do as a sacred whore is a spiritual discipline and an attempt at healing doesn't mean I shouldn't be able to earn a living doing it as well. Sharing food is an intimate and sacred thing, yet people readily pay someone to cook their food and serve it to them. Spirituality is a very sacred thing, yet many people pay a tithe or zakat to their church. Talking about one's troubles to an understanding person is a very spiritual and intimate act, yet many people pay a counselor to listen to their worries. What makes the sanctity of sex any more important than the sanctity of my body's work or the sanctity of my mind?

Western culture tries to teach that a spiritual person must be poor and a wealthy person cannot be spiritual. Western culture tries to teach that using money as a barter scorecard is dirty and inherently unethical but an evil we must hold our noses and tolerate. But what is money? If I dance a beautiful dance and receive a percentage of the money my audience paid to watch my dance, isn't that money a symbolic representation of my dance and the audience's appreciation of it?

The fact is that we all need money to survive, including those who are counselors, teachers, clergy, doctors, and those who practice all sorts of careers that we put on the highest echelon of value. The president receives a handsome salary for his work: Would we ever expect him to do it for free? In *Whores and Other Feminists*, Stacy Reed writes, "If a man wanted to degrade a woman, he wouldn't pay her for anything; money is a form of acknowledgement and appreciation."[4]

MAGDALENE MERETRIX: *Margo St. James, the founder of COYOTE* once said, "To be able to fulfill a need of a fellow*

---

*"Call off Your Old Tired Ethics," a prostitute's rights organization.

human being and profit by it, is good business, besides being an act of faith and sometimes charity." Appropriately enough, the word charity *(yet another word for love!) comes from the same Indo-European word root as the word* whore. *From the beginning of recorded history and beyond, certain people have served the sexual needs of others and received financial compensation for it.*

Finally, many sex workers comment that they find the concept of working for minimum wage *much* more degrading than what they're doing now.

CAROL QUEEN: *Prostitution is illegal because Western culture doesn't want women to have this option for financial autonomy and strength. . . . Christian dogmas are codified in our country's laws.*[5]

Sex Work as Healing Magic

There are many ways in which a sex worker can enrich her clients' lives: simply giving or enhancing sexual pleasure, teaching body acceptance, providing affection and nurturing, releasing tension, teaching sexual techniques, bringing them closer to the divine through ritual and even just through good ecstatic sex, healing after a negative experience, promoting self-esteem, just listening, and more.

MAGDALENE MERETRIX: *There are two . . . concepts in Thelema that are represented by the Egyptian godforms Nuit and Hadit. Hadit is the singular point of consciousness—the smallest possible thing that is still a thing. Nuit is the totality of consciousness—the largest possible thing that is still a thing. Many Thelemic beliefs and practices are about "becoming the body of Nuit," which can be loosely translated as "becoming one with the universe." Every time there is a connection of*

184

agape (love) made in the universe, two "points" communicate with one another, and each comes closer to the experience of becoming the body of Nuit. To me, this is a big part of what my sex work is about—by connecting with many people on a sexual and spiritual level, I am putting more of the pieces together of the giant jigsaw puzzle of the body of Nuit. Teaching by example (and sometimes by words), I attempt to help others feel safe and free to open to the universe and create more love in the world, hopefully spreading the meme and bringing the world closer to an experience of complete expansion, a "big bang" of agape.

Over the years, I've had sex with many different people who told me afterward that they felt healed in some way that they couldn't express to me because words wouldn't wrap around it properly. I genuinely enjoy sex, and giving pleasure, and opening myself to another human being, and I think that these things can be healing in and of themselves, whether a person has any other healing skills or talents.

If I were to venture to say what it is that I am healing through my work, I'd say that a good part of it is an attempt to heal the wounds of a society that's afraid of sex. My work is sex-affirmative and hopefully helps to undo some of the damage that some men have sustained from being told repeatedly that their sexual instincts were bad, that it was somehow wrong to feel sexual lust toward women, that they were contributing to the oppression of women by wanting to view pornography or patronize a prostitute. I try, through an attitude of reverence and respect, to impart a sense of acceptance and love.

My acceptance can sometimes help heal the pain and lowered self-esteem that sometimes surround a failed relationship. By combining certain massage techniques designed to give a kinetic sense of wholeness in one's body with sexual techniques, I can sometimes help people feel more at one with their sexual urges and anatomy, more connected with all aspects of themselves. . . . I try to help teach people more about their own bodies and their connection to it by offering new sensations and helping them to explore their reactions to them.

ANNIE SPRINKLE: *I did a masturbation ritual called "The Legend of the Ancient Sacred Prostitute" in my show "Post-Porn Modernist," which toured for five years. I performed a sex magic ritual on stage dozens of times in about fifteen countries, and it was an amazing experience. I learned a hell of a lot about sex from doing that, and about life in general. It was the most difficult and the most rewarding thing I've ever done. On stage, at the end of my show, I would do a ritual, put oil on my body, and then use a vibrator and a dildo. There were beautiful theatrical lights, and intense music, and I would go into ecstasy while the audience all shook rattles. The idea was that I would go into trance and take our prayers and wishes to the divine. I would try to become a channel for ecstasy and energy. I would circulate sometimes very intense energy with the audience. Some days not much would happen, and other days, it was a mind-blowing, transcendental, amazing experience. I had to learn to have no expectations, accept whatever happened or didn't happen. People from the audience would sometimes have spontaneous orgasms; sometimes people cried; sometimes they threw away their crutches! Nothing makes a girl feel more like a real live Goddess than doing a sex magic ritual live on stage.*

The main way in which sex workers can effect positive change is simply through demonstrating a lack of shame. Although there will always be those who condemn them for it, others will be jolted into realizing that they have nothing to be ashamed of, either. In *Whores and Other Feminists*, porn star and sex educator Nina Hartley says, "I do not find it particularly demeaning to make a living with my body, because I don't think sex is intrinsically bad. I don't think vulvas and penises are dirty, and I don't think that lust is horrible or anti-love. Nonconsensuality and self-destructive behavior are the evils."[6]

Speaking of nonconsensuality: Is it ethical to act as a sacred prostitute, to intentionally move energy, heal, transform—when the client just wants a blow job and a fuck? In a way, a sacred whore is a priestess; this means that a client entering her bedroom may have just accidentally slipped into a church of a religion that he doesn't believe in.

MAGDALENE MERETRIX: *I came to the conclusion that I am not being unethical, because I am not forcing something on clients, and I am giving clients those things they came to me for. I am also offering further depth and exploration, but I cannot force a client to open or accept, and so there will always be those clients who show up for a fun time and leave with nothing more than memories of a fun time. I'm perfectly okay with that.*

Someone once asked me, "Even if in my mind I know that when I am with a client that it is a sacred space, if he doesn't know that, does it still have value? Can worship and healing be one-sided? . . . Does it still count as a sacred act?" I replied by putting the question in a different context: "If I feel a sacred calling to feed the hungry, does it still have value if the hungry are only thinking of their empty bellies becoming filled? If they never think of me or my spiritual beliefs, but only of that spoonful of hot soup or mouthful of chewy bread? If they're just grabbing their nutrients . . . is my feeding them still a sacred act?" I believe that my sex work is still a sacred act, even when the client has chosen to open to the sex but remain closed to the spirituality. . . . [And] I believe that a "simple roll in the hay" can be a powerful force for good just by itself.

I am open about my spiritual beliefs in a nonthreatening, nonconfrontational, nonevangelistic way. If clients bother to read the things I've written in articles and on my Web site, they know that I will approach our session from a healing and sacred perspective, and invite them to do the same, while also trying to help them accept the rightness and sacredness of pleasure, if I sense any guilt or shame in them about their body or sexuality. When working in a brothel, though, I often get walk-in clients who have never had a chance to read anything I've written. These clients have enough hints in the books and things they will see in my room to be able to ask about spiritual matters if they are

187

interested, but otherwise I treat the session externally as secular sex while internally maintaining the beliefs and attitudes that leave me open to serving them in any way they might require. I focus on opening my Anahata (heart) chakra; I stay centered as much as possible, approaching the coupling as a meditation, using my partner as a center of focus; I apply modern and ancient sexual techniques and/or teach them to my client if he shows interest during the session.

In addition to sex workers who focus on helping and healing their clients, some notice huge positive transformations in themselves.

LaSara Firefox: *Working in porn, and the sex trade in general, has helped me to work through my sexual wounding more than just about anything else. That, and being involved with a wonderful partner who is willing to work and support as well.*

Shai Shahar: *Sex for me started out as both the ultimate shame and the ultimate escape. My issues with my sexuality, my mother's view of it, and women in general prevented me from attaining what I'd call "spiritual growth" for the longest time. Certainly, it prevented me from feeling (spritually) whole and fulfilled. This, despite having lost my virginity . . . at fifteen, having had numerous girlfriends through college and my young adult life, having married at twenty-eight and fathered a child at thirty.*

After my divorce and subsequent reevaluation of my life at age thirty-five, I delved into the sexual lifestyle in a big way. Instead of being at war with my nature, afraid of my fantasies, and at odds with society's version of "normal," I sought out like-minded individuals in the subculture [of Holland] and threw myself, or should I say "dared" myself, into exploring my sexuality and embracing it as inherently life-sustaining . . . to the point where it became my major source of income. . . . For the better part of a decade, I tasted forbidden fruits and pleasures, and heard the sexual histories of at least a thousand people.

This has certainly helped me to put my own sexual history into perspective, to understand my mother and forgive both of us . . . to amend the relationship with my ex so that there is no anger, no bitterness, and to see women . . . in a fundamentally different light. This has, in turn given me a way to connect with and embrace my feminine side . . . to rely more on intuitive insights than I used to, and to identify with Mother Earth and Mother Goddess . . . to see my wife and daughters as the ties that bind me to eternity . . . and the One.

Sex work helps people strengthen their own boundaries. It's critical that sex workers become good at saying no firmly and politely to clients when they want something that is unacceptable. Also, when someone gets paid for something, it is assigned value, and then, she may think twice before giving it away for free. It makes her body and time that much more precious. Some women may feel that men are entitled to the use of their (the women's) bodies; sex work teaches them otherwise. This is the complete opposite of what anti-sex-work arguments warn will happen. Of course, if someone has emotional issues to begin with, her mileage may vary. Sex work can also broaden the worker's horizons by showing her the sexual side of people, like the elderly and the handicapped, who tend to be desexualized by society. (Now, we just need to get and patronize more elderly and handicapped sex workers!)

Porn: Sacred or Profane?

In feminist circles, it used to be politically incorrect to like porn—God forbid, to actually *produce* the stuff. The party line was that it objectified and demeaned women. Today, there is a growing movement of sex-positive feminists who say, "Hey, if we are free to do what we want with our bodies, that means we are also free to pose naked for a skin mag, and to even jill off to a porn video once in a while." No, not all porn is necessarily good for you. Sure, it can be used addictively. Sure, it can be used by some people as a substitute for real human contact. But you can say all these things about food, and we don't try to outlaw food.

> ANNIE SPRINKLE: *Some people certainly do avoid communicating with their partner, and run off and hide in their computers, have sex online with someone they don't know, and then the marriage suffers—but that's their priority. I think that porn is basically neutral. It's what you bring to it.*

Some believe that the only reason to use porn is as a substitute for real sexual satisfaction. On the other hand, Nina Hartley, who refers to herself as a "humble handmaiden of Aphrodite," says, "Over the past twelve years, I've observed that the more uncomfortable a woman is with the state of her sex life, the more outraged and irritated she is by the existence of porn and the women who are proud to make it."[7] One of the particularly encouraging things about porn from a body-sacred perspective is that there is a market for every possible body type, body part, and body function—it's all potentially sexy.[8]

In chapter 1, you'll recall how there was some question about Venus figures and whether they were Paleolithic porn or Goddess statues—or both. As someone who has read, written, and thought about Pagan spirituality for about fifteen years, and who has been writing porn for adult magazines for almost ten, I have wondered about the connection between the porn model and the Goddess. Magazines geared toward heterosexual men have distilled female bodies into what they perceive as the essential elements: lips, breasts, hips, butt, and vulva. You may say "Hey, objectification!" but what about those Goddess statues we place on our altars? They are mostly composed of the same elements. I have often wondered if the huge success of the porn industry (specifically the one geared toward heterosexual men) is a sign that the men long to connect with the Goddess—and this is the only way they know how. Of course, it's equally possible it's just a side effect of living in such a sexually repressed society. I'm no sociologist.

There's a big problem when you try to make porn politically correct. The things that we believe in are not necessarily the things that get us off. I know many women who say they like porn as long as it isn't degrading—but what if you, as a feminist, are turned on by the thought of being humiliated, and that's exactly what you want to see in your porn?

Of course, it depends on your definition of "degrading."

JEZEBEL DAWN BLESSING: *I don't get turned on by images or media that are degrading, and by degrading I mean "anyone who looks like they are not having a very good time."*

Although political incorrectness can be fun, it's worth noting that, just like all the other media outlets, the content of pornography does have power. It has an effect not just on our libidos, but on our more everyday assumptions and expectations. Probably few pornographers do their work with an eye toward how it may shape their audience.

FRANCESCA GENTILLE: *The men that I know who grew up in clothing-optional environments . . . have much more freedom in their own bodies and much more open appreciation of the diversity of women's bodies. . . . Men who I know . . . who grew up in this hidden, shame-based sexuality, where the first time that they saw a naked woman's body was airbrushed in a magazine, that's what their sexuality is cued off of . . . I think that they have issues . . . I've had men tell me, "Oh, gee, if you*

*lost twenty pounds, you'd really be beautiful." So in that way, I feel
that pornography is very detrimental, because it's a man's initiation into
sexuality with a woman.*

RAVEN KALDERA: *I'm a pornographer. I've published innumerable
erotica, including the infamous* Best Transgender Erotica. *I really
believe that porn is a way to change people's heads, because it gets
concepts in under their radar, through their groins. I think porn can be
amazingly subversive. I constantly write either trans stuff or
spirituality into my erotica. I've had lots of people tell me that their
heads were changed about sacred sex by reading my stuff. We need
more good, raunchy, hardcore Pagan porn. No fluffy stuff.*

One very recent trend, about which I am giddily happy, is
porn geared specifically for a Pagan audience (Pagan Pleasures
International has a series of videos). Religion is normally taboo in
porn; when I got started writing fiction for adult magazines, I was
told that you could never mention anything having to do with
clergy, church, religious worship, or deity (with the exception of
the obligatory "Oh my God!"). Sex and spirit, to the mind of the
average Joe, are completely separate, and we as pornographers
would run the risk of offending someone if we tried to bring the
two together. But all consensual forms of sexuality are acceptable
and celebrated in NeoPaganism, plus they can be a route to communion with the divine. Can you imagine porn that gets you off
and inspires you spiritually?!

SHAI SHAHAR: *I would like to see more "ritual" sex in porn: conscious
sex with a conscious purpose, that portrays intercourse as something
deeper and more sustaining than the mere use of another person's body
to masturbate with or onto. I mean something closer to Marilyn
Chambers'* Behind the Green Door. *Films in which the ideal
initiation ritual is portrayed in all its digital glory. Films in which
"virgins" are sexually sacrificed on the altar. Films that celebrate Pagan*

notions of sexuality and not that of our Judeo-Christian friends in which "Pagan" and "perverse" are used as synonyms.

Many of the folks I interviewed said they preferred erotica over porn. Yet, everyone has their own definitions of the two. My own definition is that while erotica can arouse, it also has some other literary or artistic reason for existing. Porn is written expressly for the purpose of turning the audience on. In my opinion, there's a time and place for both.

DON KRAIG: *I would guess that some 90 percent-plus* [of porn] *is absolute garbage. I mean, how do you honor each other when watching a plotless video that seems to consist of two Brillo pads fighting over a sausage? But if you stick with the top 10 percent, you can find things of literary and social interest, as well as powerfully arousing ideas, concepts, mental images, and visuals.*

FRANCESCA GENTILLE: *I think that there's more than enough raw fucking behavior pornography, the kind of visuals that I call "cue mating behavior"; it's like you can't look at it without almost feeling like, "Wow, I have to go fuck something". . . . What I would want to see is beautiful, visual cueing that would inspire us to love, and to make love, and to touch one another with tears in our eyes.*

MAGDALENE MERETRIX: *Intellectually, I support all porn and erotica, but viscerally I have varied reactions to it. Some of it I find beautiful and emotionally stirring. Some I find sexually arousing. Some I find boring. Some I find disturbing. It's a tough stance to be fiercely in favor of freedom of speech and expression, yet know that there are some forms of expression that are disturbing to me. . . . But I do feel safe in my pro–First Amendment stance in saying that I believe that photographic or film porn/erotica that was nonconsensual in its creation (as opposed to being created consensually yet dealing with nonconsensual themes) should not be legal. Beyond the issue of consensuality, I support all*

193

porn/erotica whether I personally find it fulfilling, yucky, boring, happy, beautiful, ugly, politically correct, or whatever.

PHIL BRUCATO: *Although I've written erotica professionally and have a modest collection of underwater erotic pictures and videotapes, I'm not really into porn. For the most part, I find it distasteful, misogynistic, silly, and poorly made. To me, splayed clits, inflated tits, cum shots, and other shopworn clichés are as erotic as a bag of rocks—perhaps even less so. There have been a few books or films I've found arousing, but they're few and far between. I'm not down on erotic entertainment—quite the opposite! I'd just like to see more of it that's well made, fun, and respectful of the power and play of sexuality and the human beings who share it. Occasionally, I even fantasize about being rich enough to make a Pagan porn film that captures sexual magic in all its savage beauty.*

Certainly, sex work can be damaging to some people, even those who enter it of their own free will. To some, sharing one's body freely makes it seem generic and cheap: less sacred. As a Pagan who believes in the sacredness of earth, air, sun, and water, which are (at least in theory) free to all, I don't share that position. But regardless, those who feel this way should definitely not become sex workers. Ultimately, as independent adults, we should not have to do anything with our bodies that we do not want to do. Sex work, like all careers, is not suited to everyone.

It will likely be a very long time before American culture begins to value sex workers and acknowledge the value and right to exist of sexually explicit media. But as magic workers, we can do our part to help that process along.

MAGDALENE MERETRIX: *Modern society does not always recognize the importance and value of sex workers, unfortunately. I hope to be able to assist in some part to change public opinions—if in no other way, then at the least by the example of living a good and loving life.*

8. SEX MAGIC AND MAGICAL SEX ❧

IN MY FIRST TWO BOOKS, I discussed sex magic: a way to use sexual arousal and release as a means to raise and release energy to achieve a magical goal. Here I widen the frame to also include what I call "magical sex": any type of sexual exchange that has an extraordinary nonphysical effect on the people involved, in which they work to achieve altered states with a goal of mystical enlightenment. Magical sex might be practiced just for the delight and pleasure of it, or for worship of the divine, either in general or as a specific deity. In Paganism and Wicca, the boundaries between magic and worship can get blurry. When Pagans worship, we are not just reciting liturgy; we are often active, moving energy, calling on Gods and Goddesses, evoking and invoking. In this same way, magical sex may become sex magic, as the Gods take things in an unforeseen direction. In general, the Eastern path (Tantra and Taoism) has a focus on magical sex, whereas the Western path (inspired by Aleister Crowley and favored by Wiccans and Pagans) emphasizes sex magic. In this chapter, I touch on both paths, with more material on standard Western sex magic, since that's more prevalent in NeoPaganism. Both these kind of encounters can be anything from highly ritualized to completely spontaneous.

ANNIE SPRINKLE: *A couple of days ago, I did an erotic massage ritual with my girlfriend. We have a huge kitchen, so I put my massage table in there and brought in all my toys, props, oils, scents, bells and whistles, literally* [laughs], *and put them on the dining table so they were handy. I put candles all around and we spent about seven hours making love, having sex, doing massage, etcetera. But first I cast a circle, and I called on spiritual guides. We dedicated our . . . energy to a certain goal, to make it into a little sex magic ritual. I find that casting a circle before sex really contains the energy and makes it more intense. I also like to open the circle at the end, because it's a beautiful closure to the experience.*

DOSSIE EASTON: *Long before I found a Tantra community to study with, I'd been opening up the chakras and raising Kundalini in play, and it was just sort of happening—not that I haven't done that kind of meditation before, but all of a sudden, I'd be playing, and all of a sudden I'd realize that I was strung on Big Snakey.*

PHIL BRUCATO: *From a consciously magical perspective, I use energy-sharing techniques; massage and stimulate my lover's chakra and meridian points; do a lot of eye-gazing and breath-sharing; concentrate on projecting my self beneath my lover's skin to feel what she feels (and helping her feel what I feel); and occasionally exchange sacred endearments ("my Muse, my Goddess") with my beloved. To date, I've never practiced a "formal" or public sexual ritual. Though I'm not closed to the possibility at some point, I'm not sure that's my style.*

WYRDOTTER: *To me, "sex magic" per se seems to give the subject more emphasis than necessary. Some sexual experiences are more spiritual than others. Not every sexual encounter has to be the height of spirituality, but then, not every encounter has to be "just fun." It's a spectrum along which humans may wander as need and mood dictate.*

Here, I explore how a diverse group of people practice both magical sex and sex magic, and give ideas for how to use sexual arousal and release for whatever nefarious purposes you like. Of course, even the most everyday variety of sex, by its nature, heals, relaxes, and opens us up, and that's a form of magical transformation in itself.

JUDY HARROW: *Sex is an act of worship, when properly done.*

The Basic Principles of Sex Magic

In sex magic, the energy raised by sexual arousal and/or release is directed toward a specific goal. The goal can include one or more of the following:

1. To achieve visions
2. As worship
3. To achieve a magical end

Are goals one and two "better," or for a higher purpose, than goal three? That's a matter of interpretation. Personally, I rarely cast any type of spells anymore, because of the difficulty in making the focus specific enough to avoid any unforeseen outcomes. It's not because I think working magic for personal ends is selfish or unethical, but just because I tend to find the mundane world more predictable in terms of cause and effect. So I'd say goals one and two are certainly *safer* than goal three, but hey, I'm not averse to throwing a whammy now and then.

The usual formula through which we use sex for a magical end involves choosing a goal, getting aroused, and at an energy peak (usually orgasm), seeing that goal in your life as a present reality, and then letting it go.

History of Sex Magic

Prehistoric people probably practiced some form of magic related to sexuality and fertility, either to influence the physical world or to invite the blessings of the divine, or both. Riane Eisler says that "the art of the Paleolithic, Neolithic, and Minoan Crete suggests that probably very early in Western culture . . . there is strong evidence that sexual ecstasy was once . . . an important avenue to mystical or ecstatic states."[1] But as usual, with such ancient history, there's a large amount of speculation involved.

The first *recorded* use of magical sex lies in the Indian tradition of Tantra, which, as mentioned in chapter 1, originated around 5000 BCE. Donald Michael Kraig, himself a Tantra practitioner, suggests in his book *Modern Sex Magic: Secrets of Erotic Spirituality* that the origin of *Western* sex magic lies in the sacred sexual practices of the premonotheistic Hebrews. (I will talk much more about this stuff in my next book. Yes, I am a tease.) Bits of it came through into mainstream Judaism by way of the Kabbalah, but most of it was ignored because it did not fit in with the rabbinic laws of the Hasids who made that tradition so influential and famous. There isn't room to go into the entire history of Western sex magic here. Its development was complex and winding, incorporating elements of many paths, including the Freemasons, hypnosis, spiritualism, ceremonial magic (especially through Aleister Crowley), and finally Wicca and NeoPaganism.

One of the main ways in which Crowley influenced Western sex magic was in his divergence from the Tantric inclination toward self-discipline and seminal continence. Believing that sexual release was essential to good health, he saw no reason to skimp on either the sex or the ejaculations.[2] It is probably in large part because of this that the focus in NeoPagan and Wiccan sex magic is on orgasm as the release for the spell, rather than on the use of controlled arousal as a means toward enlightenment.

Barriers to Sex Magic

The largest hurdle to overcome in practicing sex magic is discomfort with our sexuality. If you're full of guilt and shame, this leads to inhibition, and you're apt to get all tangled up in your own energy if you're inhibited. If you feel like you're oversexed, that's just as much of a problem. Either way, something is out of whack.

On introspection, you may discover that the source of the issue is an internalized assumption. Much of our discomfort around libido comes from our ideas about how we think we are supposed to be, as beings of a certain age, gender, marital status, occupation, religion, and even socioeconomic level. If you have successfully isolated the issue from the context, and it's still something you feel needs to be addressed, take the time to connect with yourself and figure out what you really need. It may be that what you need is to take a month or two off from sex. Or you may be happiest and most fulfilled by attending orgies regularly. In either case, you are not necessarily "frigid" or "a sex addict." If everything else in your life is going great, then it ain't broke—don't fix it. Be yourself. Both the lack of connection with one's sexuality and the feeling of being overwhelmed or controlled by it can prove to be stumbling blocks in sex magic and, in my opinion, NeoPagan spirituality in general.

The next hurdle to tackle would be body health, awareness, and relaxation. This is not about conforming to media standards. In sex magic, you are using the body as a tool, and your tool must be in good working order for maximum effectiveness. If you are unfit, your endurance will be lower, and you will have distractions from your work in the form of aches, pains, and those pesky little heart attacks. While you're at it, it couldn't hurt to exercise your PC muscle.*

SHAI SHAHAR: *There is no accounting for "sexual demons" in Tantra, and yet you'd be surprised how many people believe they have them, especially Westerners and those who come from strict Christian backgrounds. I must say, it is difficult if not impossible to bring men or women to a state of sexual nirvana through tantric massage if and while they are locked in their heads, wrestling with their "demons."*

FRANCESCA GENTILLE: *It took me a long time to figure this out, but I became addicted to falling in love. When we fall in love, when we first smell those pheromones or get triggered by this new being, our bodies are flooded with phenylethylalamine, which is like Ecstasy; there's a sense of euphoria, of not having to eat as much, of having extra energy, of competency and well-being, and of the ease of merging with another person. Well, it's not going to last. It's predicated to wear out anywhere from six months to, at a maximum, two years. So at forty-five, I'd had twelve or thirteen two-year relationships. And what it would look like from my perspective is, "You've changed. You're not the man I fell in love with . . . I'm no longer attracted to you, and therefore, I'm going to . . . find somebody new."*

And then I would look for the next person who would spark my phenylethylalamine cascade, and then he would become the be-all, the

---

*This is the muscle that connects the anus and genitals to the sit-bones and legs. By intentionally cutting off the flow of urine when you're peeing, you can get a sense of how to exercise this muscle. Having a strong PC muscle is one of the first things sex therapists recommend for a kick-ass sex life. It also helps you in childbirth and helps keep you from being incontinent. The exercises are called "Kegels," after the man who invented them.

end-all, the perfection, the wonderfulness, we have so much in common. Do you know we like chocolate? And you like sunsets, too? . . . And then pretty soon, the phenylethylalamine starts to wear off, and it's like, "What do you mean, you like chocolate with nuts? No one in his right mind likes it with nuts." . . . And pretty soon, we're arguing about everything, and I'm not realizing it's the drugs wearing off. I couldn't choose who I was going to love; I just had to wait for the next person who triggered me or smelled right. And then, I could be with somebody really wonderful, but once the drugs wore off, the person wasn't going to look wonderful to me, and I had no control over my passion. It was something that someone else had to do to me and for me, and inspire me, and trigger in me.

And at a certain point, I'd had enough two-year relationships to have a statistical sampling, and I said, "Goddamn it . . . if people can learn biofeedback . . . and they can increase their circulation, and they can slow their heart rate . . . then I am going to learn where the control knobs are for my passion, and I am going to be at choice in this. I am going to be at consciousness in this, or die trying." And I developed a whole series of techniques that allow me to be at choice with regards to who I fall in love with, how much, how much passion is in the relationship, and to generate it ongoingly over time. I developed this whole process of consciousness in passion, and I want to write a book and teach about it, because I think it could save a lot of people from a lot of sadness.

Next, sex magic moves a whole heck of a lot of energy. If you're not used to such a thing, it's best to first acquaint yourself with it outside the bedroom. When I talk about energy here, I don't mean scientific energy, although I keep hearing rumors about scientists finding ways to measure this sort. It's been called Kundalini, chi, prana, and orgone. This is the kind of energy that we raise, shape, and move in ritual, and it's the kind of energy that powers magic. Sexual arousal raises this energy; even more so if it's done with conscious intent. I write in 21st Century Wicca about how to get started with energy work.

Finally, as Margo Anand puts it, "Avoid the trap of expecting cosmic ecstasy after five minutes."[3] If you are unfamiliar with anything but the most mundane ways of making love (which of course are still pretty great), it will take practice to learn a different way of doing it. Even when you're experienced with these techniques, impatience and expectations will get you nowhere.

Preparation for Sex Magic

Make yourself comfortable with regard to safer sex/birth control/relationship boundaries, shutting off phones, and so on. Respect the limits of the most conservative person—if your partner prefers to use condoms for oral sex, but you tend to prefer bareback, then slip on the rubber and deal with it. People need to feel safe and secure. These should all be the minimum requirements for any kind of sexual expression, but much more so in sex magic. You may also want to purify the space and cast a circle. Finally, what gets you into a sexy and magical frame of mind? This is a very personal and idiosyncratic thing. Music, scents, certain clothing?

Some use drugs, herbs, and other aphrodisiacs to enhance their sexual experiences, and to bring them to another level. (My previous book, Wicca For Lovers, lists a number of legal aphrodisiacs.) Shamanic paths throughout time have employed such substances. There is, of course, a difference between the use of substances as a tool and/or sacrament, and the use of substances in addiction. As with LSD, it's possible that mind-altering substances can provide a stepping stone to attain new states of consciousness that can then be revisited without the chemical or herbal help. I have never used any illegal substances in sex magic, although in my experience, a little mead (honey wine) is a pleasant addition to any feast—sexual or otherwise.

> SHAI SHAHAR: *We employ natural herbs to help stimulate our libido and thus increase the efficacy of our magic, when appropriate.* [Jen: Which herbs do you use for this, and in what forms?] *Gosh . . . this is one of those Fifth Amendment-type questions, isn't it? I can tell you that one of them is marijuana . . . both to smoke (pure) and to use in baking little chocolate-goddess cookies. But I can only tell you that because I live in Amsterdam where it's legal. We also use ginseng, cat's paw, belladonna, juniper, milk-thistle, guarana, myrrh, thyme, cloves, damiana, and sage. We love making and receiving little mandrake talismans and potions. Under guidance, we've ingested both fresh and powdered psychotropics like "magic mushrooms" and hiawasca. And yes, we've tried both natural and chemical Ecstasy, more than once . . . and usually to very positive effect. Please do not take this as a confession of reckless or rampant drug use and overindulgence. This is not our daily diet. In many ways, we view our taking of such drugs ceremonially, as part of a ritual to be on a par as Catholics drinking wine and chewing a wafer to represent the body of Christ . . . to be in communion with God.*

There is no reason why sex magic must involve a male and female, or a penis and a vagina. Sexual energy can be shared between two (or more) people through any form of contact—or none at all, really, but the contact is easier and more fun.

Although sex magic needs to be at least somewhat planned and structured, beware of loading it down with too much seriousness. Sex is meant to be playful. Sex can be downright hilarious. There is no reason why laughter or teasing should interfere with energy-raising. On the contrary, if you take the process too seriously, you will become waylaid by fears, concerns, rigidity, and all the rest of our neuroses that hamper the process and effect of magic.

Setting a Goal

It's critical that you be as precise as possible in the goal of and focus for your working, without closing off any possibilities, and working for the end rather than the means.

MAGDALENE MERETRIX: *If I can honestly say, "I desire X," "To what end?" "So that Y," "To what end?" and within three or fewer "To what end"s, reach "That I may attain the Great Work as I understand it," then the purpose is acceptable to me. As an incredibly oversimplified example: "I desire boots." "To what end?" "That my feet may stay warm and dry." "To what end?" "That I may stay healthy and comfortable." "To what end?" "That, rather than wasting energy on healing, I can direct it toward the accomplishment of my Will and the Great Work as I understand it."*

I once did a working to find a job that perfectly suited me. I wrote out a full resume and job objectives, and everything in intimate detail. I did a working. I got the job—a job that was absolutely perfect for me in every way I'd mentioned. The universe laughed at me: the only detail I neglected to include was pay rate . . . the job was a volunteer position.

JACQUI OMI: *I'm beyond asking, because I've gotten what I asked for too many times, and it was the wrong thing. One of the things I try to teach anybody who asks me is, if you want a certain person in your life, don't ask. Just say, "Bring more love into my life." If you think you're short of money, say, "I'd like to have more prosperity," but if you're specific, you're always going to be sorry.*

Once you know precisely what you want, remember that magic is an imperfect art and that the universe will always choose the path of least resistance.

RHOMYLLY FORBES: *Before Alex and I got together, I went through a pretty desperate period when I was literally begging the Gods to give me a life partner. Irony—Alex was my best friend at the time! Anyway, I used to offer up orgasm energy to them as prayer, okay, shameless begging, to hear my plea. Really pathetic, to look back on it now, so sad. But they must have heard me, because I finally got over my fear of Alex's mother (can you say mother-in-law from HELL?) and married him anyway!*

You then need to simplify your objective into a symbol or word that you can focus on while in orgasm. You're not going to be able to read a resume or think about anything at all complex. For most people, thinking about anything but their own pleasure at that moment is foreign and difficult enough. You can create a sigil (SIH-jil) by writing the letters of your intent precisely on top of each other and then making the resulting shape your focus. Or you can just draw or visualize a simple symbol that represents your goal. You may come up with a mantra—some word or short phrase—that encompasses what you're working for. You could also or instead create a charm or amulet to be charged or anointed in the spell.

MAGENTA: *I have, with a partner, dedicated the energy of the sex act to achieving a spell, such as a healing. One time, when I was young and inexperienced, as was my partner, we didn't transform the energy we were sending very well. The person who was in the hospital with a broken leg said he could tell when we did the working, because he got a hard-on, and couldn't do anything about it. This convinced me I needed to learn more about what I was doing—but that it worked!*

Arousal and Orgasm

In most Western sex magic traditions, orgasm functions as the pinnacle of the working, the time when you send your energy into the universe to accomplish your goal. But I don't want to imply that if you don't cum, your spell isn't going to work. Orgasm just gives your energy a convenient jumping-off point. If it's possible to work magic without any kind of sexual involvement—and of course it is—then orgasm is obviously unnecessary.

MAGDALENE MERETRIX: *For the sex magic techniques I practice . . . the sex serves a similar function to training wheels when learning to ride a bicycle. . . . Some kids learn to ride a bicycle without training wheels, but most kids learn more quickly when they use the extra wheels— though they then go through a period of dependence on the training wheels . . . so you sneak the extra wheels off when the child isn't paying attention, and he suddenly discovers he can ride without them after all. . . . [Likewise, sometimes] the sex magic energy springs up in the middle of something else and the practitioner discovers s/he can work magic without an orgasm. . . . Still, sex is "fun" and sex magic is "easier" than most other forms. Sometimes, it's relaxing to put the training wheels back on after you don't need them anymore. . . . After years of practice, these . . . steps can be done very quickly . . . and with lots of Kundalini work, I'm able to raise the energy while fully clothed and sitting in public.*

On the other hand, we all love to cum. Besides being a spiritual experience in itself, orgasm can also help to induce an altered state of consciousness—before, during, and after. In *The New Bottoming Book*, Dossie Easton and Janet W. Hardy write, "Every orgasm is a spiritual experience. Think of a moment of perfect wholeness, of yourself in perfect unity, of expanded awareness that transcends the split between mind and body and integrates all the parts of you in ecstatic consciousness. Sound familiar?"[4] To attain this state is basically the purpose of all religions, mystical traditions, and spiritual disciplines that have ever been and ever will be. No wonder we're all such sex-crazed weasels.

MAGDALENE MERETRIX: *In my experience, effective sex magic results in an orgasm that's "swallowed" by the working. The orgasm is normal in every sense except that the pleasure response is sublimated by the focus of Will of the magic. A sex magic orgasm also results in a distinctly different consistency, color, smell, and taste of bodily fluid from a regular orgasm.*

The serene and relaxed postorgasmic state can also be utilized as a time for magical work or communion with the divine.

HONEYBLOSSOM: *I've done the "simple version" of sex magic, where you use the postorgasmic state as a time to visualize your magical goals. I'm not remembering what the results were at the moment, but it definitely feels like a magically powerful time for me.*

ANNIE SPRINKLE: *I think after some people . . . cum, they don't necessarily feel spiritual, but at least there's certainly a sense of relief, and relaxation. Me, I almost always feel spiritual after sex. In any case, I usually feel happier!*

There are various ways to raise the energy, but the bottom line is that the longer you take to raise it, the stronger it will be when you finally release it. Slowing down is important, in good sex, and especially in sex magic. If you or your lover is on SSRIs (a common type of antidepressant), you may notice it takes much longer to cum. This can be quite frustrating, but the benefit is that it makes you less focused on orgasm and more focused on the journey, the process, the here and now. You can help take your time by intentionally extending your awareness from your genitals to include the rest of your body. And emphasize your partner's pleasure, rather than your own.

MAGDALENE MERETRIX: *I developed a technique . . . somewhere in my mid-twenties . . . I don't really have a name for it, but it's a form of sexual meditation. Basically, I masturbate almost to the point of orgasm but stop one stroke before cumming. I "pull" the sexual energy throughout my body, then begin masturbating again. After several cycles of this practice, I'm "charged up" and when I finally have an orgasm, I get visions or ideas. They are divinatory visions, not "fortune telling" but divination in a more Jungian sense—insights into myself or into the true nature of a current situation in my life.*

ANNIE SPRINKLE: *On the first night my girlfriend and I got together, she asked me, "So, what do you like?" and I said, "To take a long time." That's my thing. There's no real name for that orientation, that fetish. I like to get into the really superaltered states, into cosmic realms, to get out of my head totally. I love quickies, but I want to fly, to dive deep, to become totally in sync with my lover, to enter into an over-whelming erotic vibratory trance. I don't just want an orgasm, or three, I want to enter into an orgasmic state, a mystical state. That simply takes time.*

If you're lucky enough not to have any problem cumming, you'll need to force yourself to slow down. If the energy feels too intense or if you're finding yourself more centered in your genitals than you want to be, slow down the movement and stimulation, breathe deeply, and relax. Anand describes "High Sex" as "not, as one may experience in ordinary sex, an alternation between arousal and relaxation, but a simultaneous *resonance* between them."[5]

Relaxation actually helps in a few ways. First of all, it helps men last longer, if they are concerned about cumming too fast. Orgasm requires muscle tension. Second, it may actually help women cum more easily, since it helps alleviate anxiety about whether or not they're going to cum. And finally, you become more aware of your body when you're relaxed, which increases your ability to feel pleasure—and that's always a good thing.

Prolonged states of arousal can be employed to push someone into an altered state of consciousness; this can be used to have visions and for divination. In Tantra, the technique is to hold off orgasm and instead keep yourself in a charged-up state for as long as possible, until trance is induced. This technique can be used not only for divinatory purposes, but also as an end in itself, to enter into a blissed-out state that is more prolonged and fulfilling than the usual ten-second orgasm.

SHAI SHAHAR: *It took me forty-two years before I could experience the wonder and liberation of a total-body orgasm . . . beyond anything mere ejaculation can provide, no matter how intense. It was a journey through the God-spot in the brain into a state of timeless-weightless ecstasy. It was an epiphany. Only then did the words* sacred sex *seem to belong in a sentence . . . that one was not indistinct from or at war with the other. And I realized the value of "not spilling my seed" . . . of how sex energy could be used to create more than babies.*

A beautiful "light" form of sex magic is the simple dedication of orgasms.

SHAI SHAHAR: *Cora and I often . . . dedicate our orgasms to people and projects in the same way some people dedicate prayers . . . and donations. We dedicate our orgasms to people and causes in the way other artists dedicate their novels or their songs . . . the way athletes dedicate their next home run or touchdown to the sick coach or the child cancer patient in Ward C. There may be a great deal of magic in that. I mean, for me, it is undeniable. Dedicating an orgasm to people we love is another way, for us, of sending them a get-well wish or a birthday card.*

In Eastern practice, male ejaculation is said to deplete the male's life essence (*jing* in Chinese), and thus it's useful for men to learn how to have orgasms without ejaculation. A woman, on the other hand, is encouraged to have multiple orgasms, at least in part so that her male partner can absorb the energy she generates. (I don't believe that female ejaculation is considered depleting.) Regardless, on a purely hedonistic level, learning how to hold off ejaculation is good, because it prolongs and intensifies pleasure.

SHAI SHAHAR: *Tantra is not about preventing ejaculation, it is about making it a voluntary decision and well under the control of the man, to give a man power over his ejaculation instead of the way it usually works: that his ejaculation controls him. The traditionalists believe the sacredness of sex is not only to be found in the fluids but the flow . . . and derives from the intent, not the practice.*

Of course we're depleted [from ejaculation]! Else why would the women keep repeating the complaint about how 70 percent of men roll over and go to sleep after having sex . . . (and the rest go home to their wives). This is not a bad thing at all, if you ask me. And proof once again that a well-fucked and properly screwed male of any age tonight will make a really lousy soldier on the battlefield tomorrow morning . . . that is, if he even bothers to show up. You know, according to legend, the famous author Balzac, after having had a sexual climax, once exclaimed, "Oops! There goes another novel!" Had he been Tantric, he could have had his orgasm and sown the seeds for a new masterpeice in his brain instead of in his lover.

On a . . . pragmatic (dogma free) level, the witholding of ejaculation can have its uses on purely personal terms . . . .to promote an intense sense of well-being, to boost the body's immunity system, to hypercharge and clear the mind.

When the orgasm finally overtakes you—and this is the tricky part—you need to focus as much as possible on your symbol, sigil, or mantra.

After orgasm (or whenever you feel done), it's critical that you let the desire go and "stop caring" about it. This allows your will to go out into the world. If you cling to it and think about it, especially if you're worried or obsessing, that will hold it back, or may transform it into exactly what you don't want. If you used a charm or amulet, don't forget to destroy it after it has fulfilled its purpose. Leaving it "in use" is sloppy magic, analogous to neglecting to open/disperse a circle after it has been cast.

> MAGDALENE MERETRIX: *[After orgasm], I drop the desire. I become empty. Numb. Vacant. I stop wanting it. . . . I no longer think, talk, write about the working. It is as if the working does not exist. This "intentional forgetting" is, in many ways, the most important part of the working. The burst of energy . . . is what puts the desire "out there" . . . the forgetting . . . is what keeps it "out there."*

There are other methods of using sexual arousal and release for magical ends. A student of Crowley invented "erotocomatose lucidity" as a method of achieving an altered state of consciousness—this was attained by several people literally wearing out the individual from sexual pleasure and then holding him between arousal and sleep until he entered into a trance state.[6] Hell, even if nothing else happens, I think it still counts as a success, don't you?

Monofocal Sex Magic

To use masturbation as a means of focusing energy toward a goal is arguably the easiest kind of sex magic, because you only have to think about and control your own energy and focus. You don't need to try to coordinate orgasms, or think about making someone else feel good. You already know what feels good to you, so you can go ahead and do it, while getting on with the business of the working.

MAGDALENE MERETRIX: *I tend to prefer masturbatory sex magic to coupled sex magic because I don't have to worry about another person and his or her sexuality distracting me from the working.*

FRANCESCA GENTILLE: *"When . . . I'm self-loving, I would take the energy and breathe it up to my heart, and breathe it up to my third eye, and really do it as a self-blessing and as a self-healing. And then sometimes I would also be sending that energy out, maybe, into the world, or for peace, or for something else. And hold the image, whether it was a beautiful, healed, self-loving me . . . somebody who's whole . . . hold that image in orgasm, or hold peace, or something else, in orgasm.*

SHAI SHAHAR: *I frequently engage in masturbation for other reasons than self-gratification these days. I often employ it as a ritual in which I direct my orgasms to higher goals and the manifestation of my desires in life. I offer my earthly or ghostly "seed" to the Goddess. It works!*

JUDY HARROW: *Masturbation magic, yes. Sex magic, no. I'd really rather be focusing on my partner(s) than on some external purpose, however worthy. Masturbation magic, however, is absolutely a perfect way to raise and direct energy, when you're working alone.*

Sex Magic and Safer Sex

Traditional sex magic makes use of sexual fluids: menstrual blood, pre-cum, saliva, amrita, vaginal fluid, and semen. Mixed, they're considered an elixir, infused with magical power. A Tantric and Crowleyan technique is to ingest this elixir, either straight up or mixed into a drink. This personally grosses me out; I have no desire to ingest menstrual blood, period (pardon the pun). As for the others, I have no problem with swallowing, but I'll take mine direct from the source, please. Now *there's* a graphic image! At any rate, ingesting these fluids is supposed to improve one's physical and spiritual state.[7]

Now, of course, the issue of safer sex comes in. It's very unlikely that you'll catch HIV orally, but you can certainly catch other diseases that way. If you want to play it safe, you can use these fluids to anoint an object (something with ritual, religious, or magical significance) or to put on yourselves or each other, in significant designs and/or in significant places (like chakras or body parts that come into play, such as your legs if you have a marathon coming up or your fingers if you are a writer). Shai Shahar has a lovely skin cream recipe.

SHAI SHAHAR: *In our (personal) sex-magic rituals, we never spill the seed or allow a woman's nectar (amrita) to flow into the "void." When I choose to ejaculate, it is always with purpose. If my semen is not destined for immediate (oral) consumption by my sex partner of the moment, usually Cora, or the gleeful anointing of her body and others, it usually ends up in a small alabaster jar where it will be mixed with oil to be used later as an altar offering or even as a facial or skin cream.* [Jen: Can you share your recipe?] *Well, frankly, we were trying to have it patented, but the Feds never got back to us. No, I'm kidding. Actually, there is no set recipe, just basic ingredients mixed to individual taste . . . ahem. Get a very little olive (or pure vegetable) oil, pure aloe or concentrated aloe vera (jojoba works very well, too), an essential oil if you wish, like spikenard, and jasmine, some rose-hip oil or "rosewater." Add a drop of spirit alcohol and mix with sperm, whipping until smooth and creamy. Use in initiation rituals by priest and priestess . . . also as an ointment on blemishes . . . or as a home-remedy skin/face cream and night mask. Just how much of what to use quite literally depends on how much fresh sperm you have on hand. ;)*

The folks I interviewed disagreed about whether safer-sex barriers could affect the energy flow in sex magic. But they all agreed that, regardless, it would still be prudent to use barriers with someone you don't know very well.

MAGDALENE MERETRIX: *I know that some people believe that safer sex will impede their sex magic because their magic is based on mingling fluids. My sex magic is based on raised energies, so latex barriers don't affect the efficacy at all. If I were to practice magic based on mingling fluids and I were practicing with someone I didn't feel comfortable having unprotected sex with, I'd just mingle the fluids in a dish after sex because I don't believe that fluid mingling has to take place within the body for the magic to work.*

LEON: *I believe there is a greater mixing of magical energies without a condom. However, finding a condom is easier than finding a babysitter.*

MAGENTA: *The main way I've found latex to interfere is in having to stop to put a rubber on. I've heard from guys that the change in sensation is noticeable. Sometimes it's actually helpful for sex magic, as it tends to prolong the erection. I do not think it blocks the energies, though I have heard people say that. I think latex, like most plastic, is magically neutral.*

JUDY HARROW: *To me, the notion that condoms block energy is just completely illogical. Some of us even consider clothing to be some sort of barrier to energy flow. You'll sometimes hear that as the reason for working skyclad. So we raise energy and send it 1,500 miles away, through the brick walls of a hospital building in, say, Chicago, for a healing. But my T-shirt is going to block it? Nonsense!*

Using safer sex precautions is a way of caring for your partner and yourself; it's a kind of positive magic to help protect yourselves, your future lovers, and their lovers.

Jezebel Dawn Blessing: Safer sex is very magical; when I reach for that condom on the nightstand, I'm stating to my partner, "I care about the health of all of the people that we love right now and all of the people that we will love in the future." I usually put the condom onto my partner as a way to connect myself with the act and to prepare myself to accept this person inside of my body. A condom is not a barrier, but an affirmation of our caring for one another.

Polyfocal Sex Magic (or, Yet Another Section on Orgies, Sort of)

There are two kinds of polyfocal sex magic. One is to do a time-coordinated working where folks in different locations masturbate or make love all at the same time for a common purpose. The other kind is where the people involved are all in the same location, and they either all masturbate or in various configurations make love with each other. In both circumstances, as one might imagine, this kind of magic is potentially very powerful and also very difficult to coordinate.

DON KRAIG: *This is not simply a ritual where everybody gets together and says, "I know: let's do a sex magic ritual!" Usually, these are people who have worked together before, both as pairs or small groups. As such, they are familiar with each other's needs and wishes. . . . Most polyfocal sex magic groups I've encountered and/or worked with stay rather small in number and become familiar with each other. Larger ones tend to split up and fall apart.* [Jen: What if you're not attracted to everyone there, even equally?] *It's not about attraction. It's about magic. I've been in groups which have had petite people and large people, people who might be generally considered "attractive" and others*

215

who are generally considered "not attractive." What happens, in my experience, is that the energy itself becomes the focus and power for the ritual, and the body/mind/spirit is heavily aroused not by the people, but by the energy. On a practical level, people tend to start with people they are familiar with and expand from there.

As Kraig mentions in *Modern Sex Magick*, it's important to have someone who is not involved in the sex, whose role it is to direct the energy.

SHAI SHAHAR: *I have participated in "magic circles" of [masturbatory sex magic] several times. . . . The last one, I think, was when we all celebrated the 2002 spring solstice. We broke out the oil and the incense. We made corn offerings and wine offerings to our Goddess icons on the altar. We lit our votive candles, wrote our negatives and fears down on scraps of paper and burned them. We gathered and sat nude, within the circle and pentagram we had marked out on the floor, and annointed each other with oil and myrrh. We then stood and scattered rice to the four corners and threw coins into the air. Then, boy-girl-boy-girl, we sat down again and chanted while holding hands. At the end of the chant we each relaxed into our own quiet meditation and at the sound of the gong and chime we began entering into sexual communion with ourselves. Our deacon and deaconess, for want of a better word to describe their function, were appointed as custodians of the offering. They each held a cup/basin in which to catch the sacred fluids of our ejaculate. As each man came, he praised Goddess and aimed his seed into the cup held by the deacon. Those girls who could and did ejaculate upon climax found the deaconess there between her legs with her basin to catch the "amrita," her holy nectar.*

The amrita of the ladies is mixed in the basin with honeyed beer or mead . . . bloodwine . . . or Bailey's and goat's milk . . . and ladled out into small wooden cups and passed to the men to drink. A prayer is read . . . something along the lines of "We are all of one Mother. . . . We are Sons of the Earth. This is the blood of our Mother . . . the Water of Life." What is left is placed in an offering jar and held by the deaconess who sits beside the altar. The seed (ejaculate) of the men in the cup or chalice is laced with bloodwine, or Bailey's and goat's milk, or sparkling cider, and passed to the women to drink. Their prayer goes something along the lines of, "We are of One Father. . . . We are Daughters of the earth. This is the body of our Father . . . the Staff of Life."

The remnants . . . in the chalice are now brought to the deaconess by the deacon and carefully poured into the offering jar and placed upon the altar. At the end of our ceremony, we will each kiss the jar before getting dressed. The contents of the jar represent the commonality and unity of our physical essence as tribe and coven . . . as well as the sum of our dreams. Sometime within the next three days we will find a large shrub or small tree to plant. After digging the hole, we will take the offering jar, pour its contents into the pit, and break the jar and throw that in as well. Once the plant or shrub has been neatly set, we hold hands, recite a prayer to the Goddess, and go off on our way.

Dark Eros Magic

Dark Eros techniques may include pain (flogging, spanking, piercing, and such), bondage, dominant/submissive power exchange, sensory deprivation, and so on. It can either be used instead of traditional genital sex, or in addition to it. It could be done as a sacrifice, an offering, a spell, or just a way to create an altered state. As far as spellwork, here, it's much less about the orgasm. The folks involved decide when and how to send the energy out. It can happen when stimulation builds to a crescendo, or it can happen at a plateau of intensity, in which case you have a lot more time to hone your focus.

RAVEN KALDERA: *It was from the writings of Aleister Crowley that I*

*first got the idea that you could raise energy by whipping a partner,
and although I generally think that Crowley was an egotistical dipshit,
I do have to thank him for teaching me that inducing pain in someone to
the point where he or she goes into trance is just as good as an orgasm
for raising magical power, and maybe even better—an orgasm only
lasts a minute, but you can float in an endorphin trance for a long time!*

*There's this point that people who do pain play understand. Not
everybody can get to it. I can't. But there's the endorphin point, when
they get beyond that, that's just as good as orgasm, in terms of putting
energy out. You just keep pouring the energy out. And it's up to the top
to figure out how much is too much. But an orgasm lasts for seconds.
This can go on for half an hour.*

Any kind of repetitive action and sound helps those involved
to trance out and raise power, so as you might imagine, flogging,
or even literally drumming on the submissive, is a great way to
use BDSM in sex magic. The dominant throws the energy into
the submissive, who magnifies it and sends it back. It can be a
self-perpetuating cycle that can send both participants quite far
into orbit.

MAGDALENE MERETRIX: *In my experience, the ecstasy attained
through the intense sensations of S/M practices can be used magically
in all the same ways that the intense sensations of orgasm can be used.
In some ways, S/M can be more productive because practitioners who
are skilled in the art can hold an ecstatic trance state for far longer than
most orgasms last. I have experienced divinatory visions similar to what
I described earlier as masturbatory sexual meditation when in an S/M-
induced trance and I have used the intense energies of S/M for sex magic
purposes much as I described using the intense energies of orgasm to
focus Will.*

Of course, you can be creative with the symbolism of the

stimulation, making it apropos to the goal of the spell. Sensory deprivation is great for divination. Being struck with something is good symbolism for bringing something into your life. Doing the striking may help the dominant manifest something for herself as well.

RAVEN KALDERA: *I did a money spell once with a friend. It was totally nonsexual; it was just S/M. She desperately needed some emergency funding, and she was willing to basically trade pain for it. First, she sat down and talked about how bad things would be if she didn't get this, and how much it meant to her, and sort of made a little verbal offering to the Gods, as it were. And then she lay down and I beat her. And one of the things I beat her with was a belly-dancing scarf that I had that's trimmed with gold coins, with all these little serrated-edge gold coins on both ends. And that was basically the money idea. And during that, she had a short mantra, less than ten words, that she could say that would focus on the goal, and I had another mantra of less than ten words that was sort of like a call-and-response, so it was like, "Whack! Call, response." Obviously, this is something that needs to be created individually for the situation.*

Pain play can be extremely purifying, to help you visualize cleansing something out of your system—either as the top, the bottom, or both. It's particularly useful for bringing out and exorcising negative and/or painful emotions.

DOSSIE EASTON: *My bottom and I were in deep grief over a mutual friend and mentor we had lost to AIDS, and we had decided to seek release in ritual S/M. I tied her to a padded table and flogged her to the point of weeping, all the while chanting, "Om Krim Kalyae Namaha," an invocation to Kali, the terrifying Hindu Goddess of death and rebirth. As I struck with the whip in rhythm with the chant, I felt*

*myself go into trance, the words of the chant serving to occupy my
conscious mind, leaving me free to feel the energy flowing through the
whip, my bottom's grief surging beneath me, until I felt in myself Kali
the inexorable, the implacable force of nature which dictates that
everything we love must die. My partner struggled with her grief,
writhing and thrashing, held safe by the bondage, and wept copiously,
chanting "Jaia Ma," an invocation to the Mother Goddess, over and
over, until both of our grief and despair had finally poured out, and we
had reached a sense of exhausted peace with the universe.*[8]

Sex Education as Magic

One of the main tenets of magic is that words have power. A
kind of sex magic is to live every day in a way that corresponds
with our beliefs about sexuality. We need to notice when we are
using sexual phrases as *"curse* words." The term becomes eerily
meaningful in this context. Think of how many of our curses and
expletives have to do with sex and genitalia: that blows, that
sucks, fuck you, cunt, dickhead, asshole, and so on. I had a pro-
fessor in college who suggested that instead of saying "Fuck you,"
it would be much more apropos to say, "May you never be
fucked." But this is something difficult to train out of ourselves.

DANIEL DEL VECCHIO: *One initial and obvious challenge is living
and speaking in a sex-positive manner while living in a sex-negative
culture. I avoid such locutions as "That sucks" (I thoroughly enjoy a
bit of friendly sucking, and note that little babies suck, too), but note
that the body parts that come to mind to call someone when I am angry
(say at another driver), refer to sex . . . in a negative way.*

Just being a sex educator is a powerful kind of magic, which
can have an exponential effect.

LaSARA FIREFOX: *I modeled all the way through my second pregnancy, and had a wonderful time feeling that I was offering a substantial shift in sexual awareness just by exposing my pregnant body in a sexual manner.*

MAGDALENE MERETRIX: *One of my biggest goals in life is to liberate sexuality. The biggest reward for me, whether in one-on-one practice or teaching through writing or speaking, is to learn that someone has learned things from me or felt validated by something I've said, and, as a result, liberated him- or herself more than he or she was before. I see too much shame and guilt and fear surrounding sexuality for too many people, and chipping away at those negative feelings that people have surrounded the precious gift of their sexuality with is its own reward.*

LEON: *I do delight in changing someone's frame of reference, getting him to see things from a different point of view, and presenting him with evidence he hadn't considered.*

Shai Shahar suggests that a Pagan practice of sexuality could even be a tool to end war:

SHAI SHAHAR: *I have noticed that where the sexual taboos are strongest, and where women are regarded as inherently weaker or as "property." . . . where people are taught to be ashamed of sex, that is where most of the violence and corruption is to be found. It is where we find wars and rumors of wars. I have faith that societies adopting a NeoPagan view of sexuality would be more respectful of the females within it . . . and that ultimately these wars and rumors of wars would cease.* [Jen: How do you think a NeoPagan view of sexuality would work to promote peace?] *Those who feel incomplete within themselves become agitated in their behavior . . . and sometimes self-destructive. They tend to overconsume . . . to be short-tempered, short-sighted, and prone to suffer from anxiety. Frequently, they project their insecurities and their rage onto others. It is not uncommon for those*

221

afflicted to "objectify" or dehumanize the individuals they fear. In no time at all we find ourselves at war with them, over symbols of power we use to prop up our sense of self-esteem and importance. And what we have, we dare not share freely with others. Does that sound familiar?

NeoPaganism is a pragmatic and dynamic engagement with Mother Earth on a conscious, spiritual, and sexual level, and a dedication to align oneself to live in reverence and in harmony with her rythyms and cycles. If we can all agree that the moon is the moon and the sun is the sun and that we are all equal under their light, perhaps we can learn to share the earth and utilize her resources in more enlightened ways without wondering whose God has the bigger dick, as George Carlin so succinctly put it.

JEZEBEL DAWN BLESSING: *Human sexuality is an acknowledgment of our unique gift of pleasure, the very thing that makes life worth living to the fullest. In order to completely embrace the human experience, which is the goal of the NeoPagan movement, we need to understand sex and sexuality as part of the fullness of life. This is also why I feel the issue of sexual rights and complete sex education for all members of the human race (regardless of age, sexual orientation, or marital status) is paramount in the NeoPagan religion.*

Glossary ❧

NOTE: I'm aware of the heterosexism involved in some of these terms, but for brevity's sake, I'm giving the traditional definitions. Adjust rituals and terminology as you feel so inclined.

Amrita: A woman's sexual fluids, especially ejaculate.

Amulet/talisman: A small, easily worn item, often a pendant, that is charged with a spell. It can be worn to ward off energies or draw them to the wearer.*

Anoint: To rub or dab with oil. This can be done to people or objects.

Athame: A double-edged dagger used in Wiccan and Pagan ritual to symbolize the element of air, and the male/active/yang principle.

BDSM: Pronounced "bee-dee-ess-EM," it stands for three pairs of complimentary opposites: bondage and discipline; dominance and submission, sadism and masochism.

Beltane: One of the eight seasonal holidays of NeoPaganism, traditionally falling on May 1.

Bottom: A man or woman who enjoys consensually receiving physical sensation (often pain) from a top as part of a BDSM scene.

---

*Rabinovich and Lewis, *Encyclopedia of Modern Witchcraft and Neo-Paganism*, 6.

Chakra: According to the Tantric tradition, there are seven major energy centers in the body. The sex chakra is at the perineum (the space between the genitals and the anus). It is red and has to do with sex drive and survival. The lower belly chakra, just below the navel, is the body's natural center. It is orange and has to do with strength and vitality. The solar plexus chakra is in the hollow just below the ribcage. It corresponds to personal power and self-assurance, and its color is yellow. The heart chakra is in the center of the chest, is green, and corresponds with empathy and compassion. The throat chakra has to do with communication and being at ease with oneself. Its color is violet. The third eye, in the middle of the forehead, between the eyebrows, has to do with intuition and intellect, and it is indigo. The crown chakra, a brilliant white, is slightly above the top of your head. It is where your energy connects with that of the divine.

Chalice: A cup used in Wiccan and Pagan ritual to symbolize the feminine/receiving/yin principle.

Circle: 1. A temporary sphere of magical energy designed to protect the people and contain the energies within it. 2. A Pagan ritual.

Condom compact: An agreement to use condoms with all partners outside a primary relationship or fluid-bonded group.

Coven: A close-knit working group of three to thirteen Witches or Wiccans.

Crone: An aspect of the Triple Goddess, or a woman past menopause.

Dark Eros: Defined by Cerillian, Dark Eros is "light S/M techniques combined with a Pagan/spiritual belief system. It utilizes BDSM techniques such as bondage, flogging, and role play within the context of a ritual to enable participants to intensify the intention behind the work. This can manifest itself by using the body and mind's natural reactions from scene work (endorphins, adrenaline, fear, trust, discomfort, etc.) to center, build, and release the work at hand."*

Degree: A word to describe a Wiccan initiate's level of experience in that tradition. Usually, there are three degrees, with third-degree people being qualified to start their own covens.

Divination: Using various props or techniques to promote clair-voyance ("clear seeing"), with the goal of obtaining knowledge not otherwise accessible.

Dominant: A man or woman who enjoys consensually dominating others as part of a BDSM scene, or (more rarely) as an intrinsic part of her relationship with a submissive.

Domme: A woman who enjoys consensually dominating others as part of a BDSM scene, or (more rarely) full time in partnership with a submissive.

Drawing down the moon: A Wiccan ritual in which the priest invokes the Goddess into the priestess; she may manifest through speech, movement, and/or energetically. Although tra-

---

*Cerillian says that he came up with the term on his own independently in the early 1990s, but has since heard it used elsewhere in other contexts. "I was asked to portray the god Eros in a ritual. During the course of the ritual, Eros actually showed up and decided to manifest through me (uninvited, and really freaked me out by the way...those Gods sure do have a sense of humor, don't they?). He spoke, spontaneously, of the distinction between good, evil, and darkness. Suddenly I knew that darkness isn't evil if venturing through darkness is done out of love. That like attracts like, and if there is darkness within you, sometimes venturing further into the darkness will allow that darkness to stay behind once you reenter the light. This epiphany was the foundation of the work that I now do."

ditionally the Goddess is invoked into a woman, there's no reason why she can't be invoked into a man, and vice versa.

Drawing down the sun: See above, but with genders reversed.

Duofocal sex magic: Sex magic done with two people working in partnership.

Duotheistic: A belief system with two deities—in most of Wicca and NeoPaganism, this is a God and Goddess, the Lord and Lady.

Endorphins: Neurotransmitters released into the body in response to pain; a natural opiate.

Energy: The as-yet-not-understood force that powers life and our magic. Energy is a neutral means that can be put to positive or harmful ends.

Elements: Earth, air, fire, water, and spirit/center—used in ritual, meditation, and spellwork to symbolize various aspects of existence.

FTM: Female-to-male transsexual.

Fakir Musafar: A "modern primitive" who practices body modification and ritual pain as part of his spiritual practice.

Fluid-bonded: A couple or group who do not use barriers with each other in sex.

Frottage: The act of rubbing against another person for sexual stimulation.

Great Rite in token: A Wiccan ceremony of the hieros gamos, in which the energies of God and Goddess are brought together through magical tools. Originally, in the ceremonial magic society the Ordo Templi Orientis, the man held the athame (blade) and the woman the chalice; Gerald Gardner reversed these.

Great Rite in truth: A Wiccan ceremony of the hieros gamos, in which a priest and priestess, having drawn down the sun and moon, allow the God and Goddess to make love to each other using their physical bodies. Although some covens choose to enact the Great Rite in truth in front of the coven, Doreen Valiente stated that it was done in private after circle in Gardner's coven.*

Handfasting: A NeoPagan wedding ceremony.

Hieros gamos: "Great marriage," a sacred sexual union.

High Priest/ess: The male and female leaders of a coven, respectively.

Horned God: A Wiccan deity inspired by ancient polytheistic Gods such as Pan, Herne, and Cernunnos; he has horns or antlers and sometimes hooves as well, but otherwise a man's body.

Initiation: 1. A ceremony marking a rite of passage into a coven or tradition. 2. A transformative experience that guides the initiate into a new stage of life.

Intersexed: A natural variation in which an individual is born with ambiguous genitalia.

Kundalini: Sexual/life energy as described by the Tantric tradition; it is symbolized by a snake that lies coiled at the base of the spine and that rises up the body when awakened.

Magic: The use of will to effect change, usually manifesting on the physical plane.

Magical sex: Sexual pleasure experienced in a sacred context, with the goal of personal transformation, union with the divine, divination, and healing.

Monofocal sex magic: Sex magic worked with only one participant, through self-pleasuring.

---

*Hutton, *Triumph of the Moon*, 236.

Monotheism: Worship of only one deity, either with or without the acknowledgment of other deities' existence.

MTF: Male-to-female transsexual.

NeoPaganism: A modern religious movement that draws inspiration from a variety of sources, including mythology, literature, ceremonial magic, and improvisation. Generally, it involves reverence for and celebration of nature, positive magic, and a commitment to personal growth.

Phallus: An erect penis.

Play party: A gathering in which participants engage in sexual and/or BDSM-related activity with each other.

Polyamory: Ethical and consensual nonmonogamy.

Polytheism: Belief in more than one deity, either as separate entities or as aspects of one entity.

Priest/ess: In Wicca, an initiate into a coven or tradition. In Neo-Paganism overall, it varies, but can be anyone who leads a ritual or in some way communes directly with the divine.

Radical Faeries: A gay men's Pagan-inspired group who are playful, irreverent, genderfuckers, and eclectically spiritual.

Sacred space: An area defined by ritual and energy barriers as consecrated to magical work and/or the Gods. This is usually temporary, but can be permanent.

Safer sex: The more recent derivation of "safe sex," which acknowledges that with regard to preventing the transmission of STDs, it's not a matter of 100 percent safe versus unsafe, but rather that there are degrees of risk. Safer sex refers to the use of latex and other types of barriers, as well as alternative sexual practices, to make disease transmission less likely.

Safeword: A prenegotiated word spoken or action taken by a submissive that tells the dominant that something is wrong and that an activity must be stopped, at least temporarily.

Scene: A BDSM experience, usually involving some kind of power exchange between two or more people for a limited period of time.

Serial monogamy: Having more than one partner, but not simultaneously.

Sex magic: The use of sexual arousal and release as a method for sending one's energy toward a goal.

Shaman: In indigenous religions, the tribal member who "walks between worlds" and has special abilities for healing, magic, and divination. Among NeoPagans, may be defined according to personal belief.

Shamanism: A spiritual tradition that tends to be primal, body-centered, dramatic, and concerned with intimate communion with deities, elementals, or spirits.

Sigil: A shape, either drawn and/or visualized, that was created to symbolize a magical goal.

Skyclad: Nude, for purposes of ritual.

Solitary: A Wiccan who does not belong to a coven.

Spell: A symbolic action that enables an individual to focus her will in order to effect change, usually with the intention of manifesting that change on the physical plane.

Submissive: A man or woman who enjoys consensually being dominated as part of a BDSM scene, or (more rarely) as an intrinsic part of her relationship with a dominant.

Tantra: An ancient magical/religious system from India that (among many other things) utilizes techniques for the raising, control, and direction of sexual energy.

Thealogy: The study of Goddess.

Theology: The study of God.

Top: A man or woman who enjoys consensually applying physical sensation (often pain) to a bottom (the person, not the body part, although that's pretty common too) as part of a BDSM scene.

Transgender: A person who has changed genders or exists in between.

Transsexual: A person who lives full time as a gender other than his or her original one.

Transvestite: A person who cross-dresses for fun and arousal.

Vanilla: A term used by people who practice BDSM to describe people who do not, or to describe a sexual encounter that does not involve BDSM.

Wicca: A religious sect of NeoPaganism that is structured, magic-oriented, and initiatory.

Wiccan: Someone, male or female, who practices Wicca.

Witch: Someone, male or female, who practices what he or she identifies as Witchcraft.

Witchcraft: Definitions abound, but most include some working of magic and a particular connection to nature.

Yin-yang: In Taoism, the dynamic relationship between the female/receptive/dark principle and the male/active/light principle, in which each contains a seed of the other.

Notes ❧

INTRODUCTION

1 V. Vale and John Sulak, eds., *Modern Pagans: An Investigation of Contemporary Pagan Practices*, 176.

2 Ibid., 172.

3 Margo Anand, *The Art of Sexual Ecstasy: The Path of Sacred Sexuality for Western Lovers*, 51.

4 Ibid., 32.

5 Georg Feuerstein, *Sacred Sexuality: Living the Vision of the Erotic Spirit*, 16.

6 Dossie Easton and Catherine A. Liszt, *The Ethical Slut: A Guide to Infinite Sexual Possibilities*, 31.

7 Riane Eisler, *Sacred Pleasure: Sex, Myth, and the Politics of the Body—New Paths to Power and Love*, 268.

8 Feuerstein, *Sacred Sexuality*, 199.

9 Anand, *Art of Sexual Ecstasy*, 54.

10 Easton and Liszt, *Ethical Slut*, 96.

11 Ibid., 20.

12 Carol Truscott, "S/M: Some Questions and a Few Answers," in *Leatherfolk: Radical Sex, People, Politics, and Practice*, edited by Mark Thompson, 27.

13 Eisler, *Sacred Pleasure*, 283.

14 Anand, *Art of Sexual Ecstasy*, 34.

15 Ibid., 301.

1. A VERY BRIEF HISTORY OF PAGAN SEXUALITY

1 Eisler, *Sacred Pleasure*, 204.

2 Vale and Sulak, *Modern Pagans*, 150.

231

3 Feuerstein, citing British historian J.G.H. Clark, *Sacred Sexuality*, 45.

4 Eisler, citing Alexander Marshack, *Sacred Pleasure*, 59.

5 Feuerstein, *Sacred Sexuality*, 47.

6 Ronald Hutton, *The Triumph of the Moon: A History of Modern Pagan Witchcraft*, 32.

7 Eisler, *Sacred Pleasure*, 59.

8 Feuerstein, *Sacred Sexuality*, 53.

9 Eisler, *Sacred Pleasure*, 127.

10 Ibid., 64.

11 Ibid., 89.

12 Feuerstein, *Sacred Sexuality*, 62–63.

13 Eisler, *Sacred Pleasure*, 97.

14 Ibid., 8.

15 Cosi Fabian, "The Holy Whore," in *Whores and Other Feminists*, edited by Jill Nagle, 47.

16 Rufus C. Camphausen, *The Encyclopedia of Sacred Sexuality*, 39.

17 Fabian, "The Holy Whore," 48.

18 Priscilla Alexander, citing Gerda Lerner, "Feminism, Sex Workers, and Human Rights," in *Whores and Other Feminists*, 86.

19 Eisler, *Sacred Pleasure*, 8.

20 Feuerstein, *Sacred Sexuality*, 71.

21 Leela Dance Theater (n.d.) <www.nrithya.com/leela/repertoire/ddasi.html> accessed Dec. 25, 2003. According to *Hinduism Today* (Aug. 1993) <www.hinduismtoday.com> accessed Dec. 25, 2003, the Indian government officially abolished the custom in 1947, but it still goes on—in a tragic mutation of its former self. Thousands of young women are forced into this role every year.

22 Lawrence Sutin, *Do What Thou Wilt: A Life of Aleister Crowley*, 92.

23 Camphausen, *Encyclopedia of Sacred Sexuality*, 205.

24 Feuerstein, *Sacred Sexuality*, 65–66.

25 Eisler, *Sacred Pleasure*, 109.

26 Feuerstein, *Sacred Sexuality*, 66–67.

27 Eisler, *Sacred Pleasure*, 148.

28 Barbara G. Walker, *The Woman's Encyclopedia of Myths and Secrets*, 167.

29 Vale and Sulak, *Modern Pagans*, 34.

30 Eisler, *Sacred Pleasure*, 23.

31 Ibid., 203.

32 Ibid.

33 Ibid., 205.

34 Hutton, *Triumph of the Moon*, 182–186.

35 Ibid., 28.

2. SEX GODS AND SYMBOLS

1 In February 2003, Dr. Anthony Perks theorized that, viewed from above, Stonehenge is meant to represent a vulva. The Vagina Monoliths <vaginamonolithstonehenge.homestead.com/index.html> accessed Dec. 25, 2003.

2 Eisler, *Sacred Pleasure*, 16.

3 Feuerstein, *Sacred Sexuality*, 60.

4 Camphausen, *Encyclopedia of Sacred Sexuality*, 12; and About.com: Ancient History <http://ancienthistory.about.com/cs/grecoroman mythl/p/Aphrodite.htm> accessed Dec. 25, 2003.

5 Camphausen, *Encyclopedia of Sacred Sexuality*, 57; Raven Kaldera, *Hermaphrodeities: The Transgender Spirituality Workbook*, 69–70; Christopher Penczak, *Gay Witchcraft: Empowering the Tribe*, 41; and Greek Mythology. com (n.d.) <www.greekmythology.com/> accessed July 1, 2003.

6 Hutton, *Triumph of the Moon*, 44.

7 Ibid., 46.

8 Camphausen, *Encyclopedia of Sacred Sexuality*, 3.

9 About.com, "Kali: "The Dark Mother" (n.d.) <hinduism.about.com/library/weekly/aa051202a.htm> accessed Dec. 26, 2003.

10 The Lilith Shrine (Nov. 1997) <www.lilitu.com/lilith/> accessed Dec. 26, 2003; and Patai, *The Hebrew Goddess*, 221–225

11 *Ile Oshun Funke* (n.d.) <www.geocities.com/enchantedforest/meadow/ 3388/new_page_19.htm> accessed July 2, 2003.

12 *Camphausen*, Encyclopedia of Sacred Sexuality, 211.

13 About.com, "By the Powers of Lord Shiva!" (2003 <http:// hinduism.about.com/library/weekly/aa022001a.htm> accessed Dec. 26, 2003.

14 *Camphausen*, Encyclopedia of Sacred Sexuality, 205.

15 *Walker*, Woman's Encyclopedia, 929.

16 *Dossie Easton and Janet W. Hardy*, The New Bottoming Book, 80.

3. PAGAN RELATIONSHIPS

1 Easton and Lizst, *Ethical Slut*, 69.

2 Ibid., 12.

4. SEXUALITY IN THE PAGAN COMMUNITY

1 Pagan Portal (n.d.) <www.paganportal.com/paganportal/editorial. asp?curpage=3> accessed June 28, 2003.

2 Hutton, *Triumph of the Moon*, 408.

3 Easton and Liszt, *Ethical Slut*, 252.

4 Vale and Sulak, *Modern Pagans*, 173.

5 Proteus Coven, "Sex and Paganism," by Kellen (July 2000) <www.draknet.com/proteus/kellen.htm> accessed Dec. 26, 2003.

6 Eisler, *Sacred Pleasure*, 324.

5. GENDER AND QUEER PAGANISM

1 Eisler, *Sacred Pleasure*, 269.

2 Penczak, *Gay Witchcraft*, 11.

3 Ibid., 17.

4 Ibid., 43.

5 Eisler, *Sacred Pleasure*, 82.

6 Penczak, *Gay Witchcraft*, 27.

7 Easton and Liszt, *Ethical Slut*, 98.

8 Bruce McFarland, "Masturbation throughout History," on Jackin' World (n.d.) <www.jackinworld.com/library/articles/history.html> accessed Dec. 26, 2003.

9 Magdalene Meretrix, as quoted in *The Bisexual Resource Guide*, 4th ed., edited by Robyn Ochs. (n.p.)

10 Vale and Sulak, *Modern Pagans*, 155.

11 Camphausen, *Encyclopedia of Sacred Sexuality*, 38.

6. BDSM AND DARK EROS

1 Peer Group, "What Is BDSM?" (2002) <www.bdsm-peergroup. com/resources_what_is_bdsm.htm> accessed Dec. 26, 2003.

2 Susan Wright and Charles Moser, "What Is S/M?" (Mar. 2000) District of Columbia Sexual Minority Advocates <www.dcsma.org/ MedKit-2.doc> accessed Dec. 26, 2003.

3 Carol Truscott, "S/M: Some Questions and a Few Answers," in *Leatherfolk*, 29.

4 Eisler, *Sacred Pleasure*, 219.

5 Ibid., 245.

6 Ibid., 206, 240–241.

7 Ibid., 109.

8 Scott Tucker, "The Hanged Man," in *Leatherfolk*, 8.

9 Hutton, *Triumph of the Moon*, 235.

10 Stuart Norman, "I Am the Leatherfaerie Shaman," in *Leatherfolk*, 280.

11 Easton and Hardy, *New Bottoming Book*, 31.

12 Ibid., 23.

13 Pat Califia, "The Limits of the S/M Relationship, or Mr. Benson Doesn't Live Here Anymore," *Leatherfolk*, 224.

14 Dossie Easton and Janet W. Hardy, *The New Topping Book*, 12.

15 Easton and Hardy, *New Bottoming Book*, 14.

16 Easton and Hardy, *New Topping Book*, 204.

17 Easton and Hardy, *New Bottoming Book*, 167.

7. SEX WORK

1 Jill Nagle, introduction to *Whores and Other Feminists*, 2.

2 Ibid.

3 Fabian, "The Holy Whore," 51–52.

4 Stacy Reed, "All Stripped Off," in *Whores and Other Feminists*, 185–186.

5 Vale and Sulak, *Modern Pagans*, 161.

6 Nina Hartley, "In the Flesh: A Porn Star's Journey," in *Whores and Other Feminists*, 62.

7 Ibid., 60.

8 For example, see David ustin, "Why Is Period Porn So Rare? An Explanatory Mess" (Aug. 1998) <www4.ncsu.edu/~n51ls801/period.html> accessed Dec. 26, 2003.

8. SEX MAGIC AND MAGICAL SEX

1 Eisler, *Sacred Pleasure*, 145.

2 Sutin, *Do What Thou Wilt*, 93.

3 Anand, *Art of Sexual Ecstasy*, 295.

4 Easton and Hardy, *New Bottoming Book*, 154.

5 Anand, *Art of Sexual Ecstasy*, 29. Emphasis in original.

6 Camphausen, *Encyclopedia of Sacred Sexuality*, 68.

7 Sutin, *Do What Thou Wilt*, 243–244.

8 Easton and Hardy, *New Topping Book*, 195.

Bibliography 🌿

BOOKS

Anand, Margo. *The Art of Sexual Ecstasy: The Path of Sacred Sexuality for Western Lovers.* New York: Jeremy P. Tarcher/Putnam, 1989.

Camphausen, Rufus C. *The Encyclopedia of Sacred Sexuality.* Rochester, Vt.: Inner Traditions, 1999.

Dening, Sarah. *The Mythology of Sex: An Illustrated Exploration of Sexual Customs and Practices from Ancient Times to the Present.* New York: Macmillan, 1996.

Easton, Dossie, and Janet W. Hardy. *The New Bottoming Book.* Oakland, Cal.: Greenery, 2001.

————. *The New Topping Book.* Oakland, Calif.: Greenery, 2003.

Easton, Dossie, and Catherine A. Liszt. *The Ethical Slut: A Guide to Infinite Sexual Possibilities.* Oakland, Calif.: Greenery, 1998.

Eisler, Riane. *Sacred Pleasure: Sex, Myth, and the Politics of the Body.* San Francisco: HarperCollins, 1995.

Feuerstein, Georg. *Sacred Sexuality: Living the Vision of the Erotic Spirit.* New York: Jeremy P. Tarcher/Perigee, 1993.

Hutton, Ronald. *The Triumph of the Moon: A History of Modern Pagan Witchcraft.* Oxford: Oxford University Press, 2000.

Kaldera, Raven. *Hermaphrodeities: The Transgender Spirituality Workbook.* Philadelphia: Xlibris, 2001.

Kraig, Donald Michael. *Modern Sex Magick: Secrets of Erotic Spirituality.* St. Paul, Minn.: Llewellyn, 1998.

Nagle, Jill, ed. *Whores and Other Feminists.* New York: Routledge, 1997.

Ochs, Robyn. *The Bisexual Resource Guide.* 4th ed. Boston: Bisexual Resources Center, 2001.

Patai, Raphael. *The Hebrew Goddess.* 1967. Reprint, Detroit, Mich.: Wayne State University Press, 1990.

Penczak, Christopher. *Gay Witchcraft: Empowering the Tribe*. Boston: Red Wheel/Weiser, 2003.

Qualls-Corbett, Nancy. *The Sacred Prostitute: Eternal Aspect of the Feminine*. Toronto: Inner City, 1988.

Rabinovich, Shelley, and James Lewis, eds. *The Encyclopedia of Modern Witchcraft and NeoPaganism*. New York: Citadel, 2002.

Shuttle, Penelope, and Peter Redgrove. *The Wise Wound: The Myths, Realities, and Meanings of Menstruation*. 1978. Reprint, New York: Grove, 1986.

Sprinkle, Annie. *Annie Sprinkle, Post-Porn Modernist: My 25 Years as a Media Whore*. San Francisco: Cleis, 1998.

Sutin, Lawurence. *Do What Thou Wilt: A Life of Aleister Crowley*. New York: St. Martin's, 2002.

Thompson, Mark, ed. *Leatherfolk: Radical Sex, People, Politics, and Practice*. Boston: Alyson, 1991.

Vale V., and John Sulak, eds. *Modern Pagans: An Investigation of Contemporary Pagan Practices*. San Francisco: Re/search, 2001.

Walker, Barbara G. *The Woman's Encyclopedia of Myths and Secrets*. San Francisco: Harper and Row, 1983.

WEBSITES

Grand Opening! (www.grandopening.com) Sex toys, books, videos, and safer-sex supplies. Pagan-owned.

Wackyjac (www.wackyjac.com) Sexy, Witchy undies and T-shirts. Pagan-owned.

Love without Limits (www.lovewithoutlimits.com/index.html) Polyamory.

Pagan Pleasures International (www.paganpleasures.com) Pagan porn!

RE/Search Publications (www.researchpubs.com)

The Sex Academy (www.thesexacademy.com)

Spiritual BDSM (www.spiritualbdsm.com)

Wasteland (www.wasteland.com) A Pagan-owned BDSM Web site.

Index

239

About the Author

Jennifer Hunter, 32, from Somerville, Massachusetts, is a self-employed freelance writer and editor who lives with her young daughter Ilana and their cat Ember. She has a B.A. in English, and has written two previous books, *21st Century Wicca* (1997) and *Wicca for Lovers* (2001). Some of her passions include spending time with her chosen family, sexual and spiritual exploration, food, music, reading, organizing things, and sleeping. Her Live Journal username is "anotherjen" and her personal Web site is at www.jenniferhunter.com.